The Feel-Ba...

Edinburgh Studies in Film and Intermediality
Series editors: Martine Beugnet and Kriss Ravetto
Founding editor: John Orr

A series of scholarly research intended to challenge and expand on the various approaches to film studies, bringing together film theory and film aesthetics with the emerging intermedial aspects of the field. The volumes combine critical theoretical interventions with a consideration of specific contexts, aesthetic qualities, and a strong sense of the medium's ability to appropriate current technological developments in its practice and form as well as in its distribution.

Advisory board
Duncan Petrie (University of Auckland)
John Caughie (University of Glasgow)
Dina Iordanova (University of St Andrews)
Elizabeth Ezra (University of Stirling)
Gina Marchetti (University of Hong Kong)
Jolyon Mitchell (University of Edinburgh)
Judith Mayne (The Ohio State University)
Dominique Bluher (Harvard University)

Titles in the series include:

Visit the Edinburgh Studies in Film website at www.euppublishing.com/series/ESIF

The Feel-Bad Film

Nikolaj Lübecker

EDINBURGH
University Press

Edinburgh University Press Ltd
The Tun – Holyrood Road
12(2f) Jackson's Entry
Edinburgh EH8 8PJ
www.euppublishing.com

Typeset in Garamond MT Pro by
Servis Filmsetting Ltd, Stockport, Cheshire,
and printed and bound in Great Britain by
CPI Group (UK) Ltd, Croydon CR0 4YY

A CIP record for this book is available from the British Library

ISBN 978 0 7486 9797 7 (hardback)
ISBN 978 0 7486 9798 4 (webready PDF)
ISBN 978 0 7486 9799 1 (paperback)
ISBN 978 0 7486 9800 4 (epub)

Contents

List of Illustrations

Acknowledgements

The topic and title might not suggest it, but this book has been a pleasure to write. Not least I have enjoyed discussing the ideas with students, colleagues and other friends, first at the University of Aberdeen, then at the University of Oxford. One particularly dark winter evening after a screening of Michael Haneke's *The Seventh Continent* (or was it Ulrich Seidl's *Animal Love?*), I overheard one Aberdeen student say to another: 'Every week I come here, and I think it can't possibly get any worse than last week; then he comes up with this!' Apologies – and thank you for all the discussions that followed.

Many of the analyses were first presented at conferences and workshops in Europe and the US. A number of these events were particularly important for the project: thank you to Tanya Horeck and Tina Kendall for organising the excellent conference on The New Extremism at Anglia Ruskin University; this was my first opportunity to present on material that had not yet crystallised into the present project, and a chance to meet colleagues who worked on similar issues. Many thanks also to Martine Beugnet and Kriss Ravetto for the fantastic workshop on *Figures of the Visceral* at the University of Edinburgh. Closer to completion, I would like to thank Jørgen Bruhn, Anne Gjelsvik and Eirik Frisvold Hanssen who invited me to present at the 2013 conference of The Association of Adaptation Studies, thereby pushing me to consider the relation between transgressive traditions across the twentieth and twenty-first centuries.

Sections of this book have been published in article form: an earlier version of the *Dogville* analysis appeared in *The New Extremism in Cinema: From France to Europe* (eds Horeck and Kendall), *Twentynine Palms* was the subject of an article published in *Studies in French Cinema* (vol. 11: 3), and I engaged in greater detail with Claire Denis's *I Can't Sleep* and with Didi-Huberman's book on Brecht in two articles published in *Paragraph* (30: 2 and 36: 3). I would also like to thank William Brown, Patrick Hayes, Tina Kendall, Angelos Koutsourakis and Simon Ward for delivering feedback on various aspects of this project, and Stephen Ross for helping me to sound more English than I would otherwise have done.

I am grateful to the San Cataldo Foundation for a residential grant that allowed me to work on the manuscript while enjoying the most amazing view of the Amalfi coast (although I should have been writing instead from a basement in the red light district in Bombay (see section 1.1)); and to St John's College, Oxford for giving me the opportunity to travel to the relevant conferences and for generally being such an exceptional place to work. It has been a pleasure to work with Gillian Leslie and her extremely supportive team at Edinburgh University Press: Richard Strachan, Rebecca Mackenzie, James Dale and not least the outstanding copy-editor Anna Oxbury; and I would particularly like to thank the series editors Kriss Ravetto and Martine Beugnet (again) for their excellent critical observations and encouragements.

Finally, I am grateful to my sister Marie d'Origny Lübecker who manipulated and redesigned Lars von Trier's morphing dog on the cover of the book. She taught me that the font used for the title was designed by Eric Gill, the grand old man of British design. He is known not only for his type fonts and many statues – including *Fucking*, a 1911 statue which Tate Britain displays under the more family-friendly title *Ecstasy* – but also for a series of very troubling sexual relations to his sister (lifelong incest), daughters and dog. Any resemblance to fictional characters discussed in this book is purely coincidental.

To my feel-good team: Julie, Beate and Moritz

Introduction

How Does it Make You Feel?

In the first part of Alain Resnais's *Muriel, or the Time of Return* (1963) the female protagonist, Hélène (Delphine Seyrig), prepares for the arrival of her former lover, Alphonse (Jean-Pierre Kérien), whom she hasn't seen since their painful break-up during the Second World War. She leads a busy life as an antiquarian, selling items directly from her apartment. She has an adult stepson, Bernard (Jean-Baptiste Thiérrée), who recently returned from the war in Algeria and now spends much of his time in the same apartment. Although Hélène invited him, Alphonse's visit does not seem particularly convenient – she is stressed by work, Bernard is slightly hostile to the idea of a visit, and there is clearly no space for Alphonse. Before Alphonse's arrival, Resnais communicates this lack of space with a cluttered set and a jagged montage. We begin with a commercial transaction between Hélène and a customer: a montage of body parts and objects, filmed in extreme close-ups, in quick editing rhythm. This opening gives the impression of a cubist composition that has only half the space it requires. Hans-Werner Henze's atonal soundtrack and Hélène's constant moving about further help to produce a nearly assaultive effect on the spectator. It is not surprising that on its release, critics (both positive and sceptical) agreed that it was a deeply unpleasant and disconcerting film (see Wilson 2006: 88).

Alphonse arrives, accompanied by his niece, thereby further exacerbating the already acute space problem. This extra presence is obviously intrusive, but it does distract slightly from Alphonse's disappointing character. He has lied to Hélène in the past, and he will continue to lie throughout the film. Not only has he decided to bring an adult niece to this meeting with his former lover, but this 'niece' also turns out to be his mistress. At first, he refuses to take off his oversized winter coat, remaining in an armchair with a drink that he has poured himself. Watching these opening scenes is suffocating – the discomfort of the characters transfers to the spectators who find themselves unable to relax, pay attention and 'be with' the characters.

In the early scenes of Todd Haynes's *[Safe]* (1995) we follow the mundane life of Carol White (Julianne Moore) in her very big house, in the kind of affluent Californian suburbia we know from so many American films and television productions. Carol walks around looking like a Barbie doll that has been placed in the 3D version of an interior-decorating magazine (there is no essential difference between Carol and the Barbie doll that played Karen Carpenter in Haynes's *Superstar* (1987)). The maid has turned on – and up – a Spanish-speaking radio station without finding the proper frequency. In her piercing voice Carol calls for the maid, but Fulvia (Martha Velez) is vacuuming and cannot hear her. The telephone rings, Carol answers and talks to her mother (who else?), the hoovering continues and the radio begins to play George Benson's 'Turn your love around'. This is all too noisy. It is an assault on Carol – who will soon fall ill, as if she is allergic to life in the modern world. She will suffer from a mysterious illness that drives her into isolation in the Californian desert, away from the smog of Los Angeles, the sound pollution and all the invisible viruses that she believes assault her. But it also an assault on the sensorial apparatus of the spectator. We might be frustrated with the neurotic Barbie-like housewife in her big house (we are meant to be), but more immediately this opening creates a very strong desire for the noises to stop.

These two scenes from films by Resnais and Haynes are micro-examples of what I call the feel-bad experience. In each case the director establishes a universe that will be explored throughout the film, introducing us to the central characters and the key themes in the films. The disharmonious, frustrating experience of these early scenes is therefore diegetically motivated. But the films are also characterised by a very direct disturbance of the spectator. These scenes therefore sit somewhere between establishing a fictional universe and deliberately wanting to get on the nerves of the spectator. They generate a very strong desire in the spectator – *take off the coat, turn off the radio* – while also making clear that the satisfaction of these desires would simply reveal other sources of discomfort. In both films this disturbance will feed into much larger structures of spectatorial manipulation; they will continue in the unpleasant register and become proper feel-bad films. The narrative and cinematographic choices will produce a strong spectatorial desire, which the films will continue to frustrate. This is the defining characteristic of what I term the feel-bad experience: the film produces a spectatorial desire, but then blocks its satisfaction; *it creates, and then deadlocks, our desire for catharsis.*

In the *Poetics* Aristotle writes that 'the end is everything' (Aristotle 1965: 40). When deciding whether a film is feel-bad or not, the ending is indeed important. Many Hollywood dramas will go far into negative emotions, but most will make sure that such emotions are diffused at the end of the film; occasionally they will stay with the unpleasant emotions, but the films will then at least contain them within a fully closed-off narrative. It is precisely this form of satisfaction and narrative containment that the feel-bad film does not deliver. In *Muriel* we will never really understand what happened in Algeria, in *[Safe]* we will never know with certainty why Carol fell ill.

The feel-bad experience exists in different versions and at different intensities. As these two micro-examples indicate, it is not a new mode of spectatorial address, but one which a series of more recent films have taken to unprecedented heights. As Asbjørn Grønstad writes in his study of a corpus of films that partly overlaps with the one I will be addressing in this book, the specificity is that 'these films appear to be about the spectator' (Grønstad 2012: 2). They are aiming for the body of the spectator (see also, Palmer 2011: 57–93). *Muriel* is disturbing, but in a way that we might expect from an art film, and we will not be overly surprised that there is no release at the end. In this sense David Bordwell was right to consider the art film as a genre and the 'open ending' as one of its constitutive traits (Bordwell 1999). Most of the films considered here work in a more confrontational way; they aim more directly for the spectator. In order to do so, they often play with popular genres such as the body genres that Carol Clover (1987) and Linda Williams (1991) have identified (horror, porn and melodrama). This is how they draw us in, appealing to us at a more immediate bodily level than the classic art film. But the feel-bad films are not horror, porn or melodrama, because they do not have the cathartic (and thrilling) dimension we generally find in the body genres; instead they frequently offer a form of generic subversion that places them between the art film and popular cinema. When drawing on – and amputating – the body genres, they thereby maximise the possibility of bodily displeasure (and the potential for annoying spectators who prefer a clear distinction between high and low status genres). In the most exhausting of these films – in the purest examples of feel-bad – the intensification of the feel-bad climate is so radical that the spectators begin to worry where things are going. They begin to wonder about the 'intentions' of the film, about the nature of the spectatorial contract. But the destabilisation of the spectatorial contract is precisely the point, for this is how the films raise political and ethical questions.[1]

WHY, HOW, AND WHY NOW?

This book asks *why* a director would opt for the feel-bad approach. More specifically: what do these directors think they can achieve by establishing a disturbing or an outright antagonistic relation to the spectator that they would not be able to communicate in any other way? This will be the central question in the book, and my answer will involve the analysis of a series of recent

European and American films by directors such as Lars von Trier, Brian de Palma, Claire Denis, Gus Van Sant, Lucile Hadzihalilovic, Michael Haneke, Stan Brakhage, Bruno Dumont and Harmony Korine.[2] In order to answer this first question, I will need to pose a second: *how* do the various films produce the feel-bad experience? Hitchcock is said to have dreamt about the day when the nervous system of the spectators could be wired up to a cinema organ; this would allow him to sit in the corner of the movie theatre and play directly at the spectators' emotions – no need for screen and sound. But until this organ has been invented directors have to rely on various formal and narrative devices to manipulate the emotions of the spectator. There are many different ways to press the keys of 'discomfort', 'unease', 'anxiety', 'stomach-churning', 'frustration', and so on. I shall look at a number of strategies and distinguish between 'assaultive films', 'desperation films', 'suspension films' and the 'feel-bad farce'. However, I have no ambition to exhaust the entire scale of feel-bad keys. For instance, I will not look at abjection films such as György Pálfi's *Taxidermia* (2006), nor will I explicitly engage with the rapidly growing field of 'cringe comedy'. Rather than aiming for a comprehensive study of feel-bad modes, I am interested in the political and ethical potential and problems of the feel-bad genre as such. With this comes a third series of questions: Why have there been so many feel-bad films in recent years? What do they communicate about the contemporary cultural situation? In order to answer such questions, I will examine how the contemporary films can be placed in artistic and intellectual history.

The questions above direct the argument of the book through its three chapters. Chapter 1, 'Assault', studies a set of very confrontational, antagonistic films. My first example will be Lars von Trier's *Dogville* (2003). Von Trier is one of the contemporary directors who has worked most consistently with unpleasant emotions. With *Dogville* he made a film that delivers a series of particularly clear answers to the *why* and *how* questions. For our purposes, *Dogville* is therefore a pedagogical example that clearly sets out what the feel-bad genre can do. Next, the opening chapter will move on to a short discussion of several other manipulative and confrontational films – the canonical case of Michael Haneke's *Funny Games* (1997) and the lesser known *Daisy Diamond* (2007) by the Danish director Simon Staho. These brief analyses show that the antagonistic relation between director and spectator can be found in a series of contemporary films, and also suggest that the various directors establish this relation in different ways, with different results. Finally, a third section in Chapter 1 will analyse Brian de Palma's visceral outcry against the Iraq War: *Redacted* (2007). This film is far from the irony and coolness of von Trier and Haneke, and is also more directly political. What de Palma shares with von Trier, Staho, Haneke and other feel-bad directors is the belief that it is necessary to go through the body of the spectator to reach her intellect. However, my prime motivation for including the film is that *Redacted* allows me to introduce the question of whether feel-bad films can go too far in their assault on the spectators: are there ways of producing feel-bad emotions that the directors should rather avoid? This important question about the limits of feel-bad is often neglected in the academic study of provocative films – most critics are more inclined to explain, rather than challenge, the value of provocation.

This is an opportune moment to emphasise that the title term is meant to be descriptive and analytic, not normative. The main purpose of this book is to offer an analysis of the relation between these films and their spectators – and, much more generally, between art and society. In that process the characteristics of a genre will emerge, and as is the case with all genres, some of the films belonging to the genre are excellent, others less so. It is therefore neither a compliment nor an insult to describe a film as feel-bad. The term simply refers to a particular form of cinematic experience that relies on the production of a strong cathartic desire that is then deadlocked. This being said, I will still argue that the best feel-bad films can raise a series of crucial genre-specific questions. In other words, the genre as such has a unique potential. The widespread tendency to eliminate from the cinematic field the experiences that are *not* pleasurable (a tendency much stronger in film than in literature) feeds into my motivation for analysing the potential of these frustrating, disturbing and occasionally very depressing filmic experiences. I believe it would be a serious problem if we were to limit ourselves to (the analysis of) the kinds of experiences that only 'pleasurable' films provide, and in what follows I shall try to explain why.

Chapter 2, 'Unease', will look at another mode of feel-bad film; it will focus on a series of films that give a very different response to the *how* question. These films are still unpleasant, worrying and perhaps even manipulative; they are still about the spectator, but they are less direct in their mode of confrontation. Instead, they tend to combine a menacing atmosphere with a substantial degree of indeterminacy – my two opening examples, *Muriel* and *[Safe]*, would fit in here. The primary examples in this chapter, however, will be Gus Van Sant's well-known *Elephant* (2003) about American high school killings (largely inspired by the tragedy at Columbine High), and Lucile Hadzihalilovic's adaptation of a late nineteenth-century novella by Frank Wedekind, *Innocence* (2004). Secondary examples include Claire Denis's *I Can't Sleep* (1994), Michael Haneke's *Hidden* (2005) and a short avant-garde film by Stan Brakhage: *Kindering* (1987). Because these films flirt with the indeterminate, the traumatic and/or the uncanny, and because they make it difficult for the spectator to relate to events on the screen, our responses are likely to be more diverse than was the case for the assaultive films discussed in the first part (debates about inclusion and exclusion are, of course, common to all genres). However, like many critics I believe the chosen films operate by establishing an environment of anxiety. I shall argue that a form of affective 'disturbance via indeterminacy' allows the films to bring about what Judith Butler calls an 'unframing', inviting us to rethink our ways of being (a spectator) beyond the security of a clearly defined spectatorial position. Finally, I conclude these first two chapters with the short analysis of Ruben Östlund's *Play* (2011), a film that combines elements of assault with unease.

The last chapter – 'Transgression, Transgression' – adopts a slightly different approach. The first two chapters were centred on the *how* question; they presented experiences of manipulation, unease and suspension, thereby leading to a distinction between different forms of feel-bad films. The last chapter also presents different feel-bad modes (the desperation film and the feel-bad farce), but now the discussion will be structured around the question of how to situate the feel-bad films in intellectual history. I shall be focusing on the notion of transgression, which will be discussed through a detailed engagement with films by Bruno Dumont (*Twentynine Palms*, 2003) and Harmony Korine (*Trash Humpers*, 2009) – and with shorter references to Urszula Antoniak's *Code Blue* (2011), Marina de Van's *In My Skin* (2002), Claire Denis's *Les Salauds* (*Bastards*) (2013), Catherine Breillat's *À ma sœur* (*Fat Girl*) (2001), Werner Herzog's *Even Dwarfs Started Small* (1970) and Lars von Trier's *The Idiots* (1998). Many of the films I describe as 'feel-bad films' have been compared with – and make reference to – works from the historical avant-garde of the interwar period or the neo-avant-garde of the 1960s–1970s (dadaism, surrealism, Viennese Actionism, etc.). Indeed, two of the most common ways of approaching these films are through either Georges Bataille, surrealism and the notions of excess, expenditure, transgression and the formless, or through Julia Kristeva and her theorisation of the abject. As we shall see, these comparisons between the contemporary films and the earlier avant-gardes have often produced a dichotomy: some critics argue that the contemporary films simply repeat – and thereby undermine – the transgressions of the earlier avant-gardes, while other critics contend that the films revitalise the avant-garde by reopening the path from transgression to emancipation. Underlying this dichotomy lies the agreement that transgression *should* lead to emancipation. In a polemical contribution to this debate about recent art cinema, politics and the status of the avant-garde, I will propose that the specificity of many of the contemporary films is to extend and explore the distance between transgression and emancipation. In some cases this distance is experienced as tragic, in other cases it is explored in a mode that is also farcical, but in both cases this distance to emancipation is a source of unpleasure for the spectator. As such the contemporary films do not seem to promote an emancipatory project, but rather manifest a more ambiguous *desire* for such a project. This move from a 'project' to a 'desire for a project' seems to me an important dimension of the contemporary cultural situation.

Before I begin to explain and corroborate such broad claims, I will spend the last part of this introduction outlining my argument's theoretical framework, which is political as well as ethical. Doing so also allows me to introduce the theme of *education* which will follow us through the coming chapters until being addressed more explicitly in the conclusion.

HUMANIST SPECTATORSHIP

Every book is the result of its circumstances. How these play into a given project will largely escape the author, but in some cases they can be difficult to ignore. Since I came to the UK in 2005, academics have been put under increasing pressure to justify their work and the resources allocated (obviously this is not only a UK phenomenon). I doubt there has ever been a good academic in the humanities who did not think about the social significance of the work she was doing, but the way in which the debate is currently being framed tends to produce a specific set of answers – and a very limited conception of the aesthetic field. For obvious reasons (such as the natural inclination to answer in the language of the questions being asked), attempts at arguing for the importance of the humanities often lead to well-meaning statements about the intrinsically humanistic and democratic nature of the artistic experience (see for example Martha Nussbaum's *Not for Profit: Why Democracy Needs The Humanities* (2010)). These sensible arguments do not necessarily exclude an engagement with something like the feel-bad films, but it is nevertheless fair to say that a transgressive, avant-gardist and seemingly nihilist film art that insists on pushing the spectators into the more problematic regions of human subjectivity will not be the first place that scholars go when arguing why funding sources for the humanities must not continue to be cut.

But let me begin a bit further from the contemporary political situation and give two well-known examples of what can be called a humanistic description of the ideal relations between an artist, an artwork and her public. The first is taken from the second essay in Jean-Paul Sartre's *What is Literature?* (first published in 1947), an essay titled 'Why Write?' Here Sartre is interested in the ethics and politics of the experience of art. As the essay title indicates, the art in question is literature, but we are invited to expand Sartre's description to other arts as well. Indeed, in this particular essay Sartre refers indiscriminately to novelists (Stendhal and Dostoyevsky) and painters (Vermeer, Cézanne and Van Gogh).

In a famous passage of the essay, Sartre argues that the best art and literature can be understood as collaborative; author and reader (or specta-tor) realise the work together, and, in that process, they become conscious of – and develop – their own freedom. Sartre's optimism is expressed in a number of paragraphs where he ecstatically celebrates literature as an 'exer-cise in generosity', a 'pact of generosity', a 'dialectical going-and-coming', a 'symmetrical and inverse appeal' and, most curiously, a kind of 'spinning top' hurling reader and writer together in blissful harmony. In this process, reader and writer engage in a perfect collaboration, together creating both the liter-ary work and themselves. A typical passage (which Sartre repeats almost line by line, only four paragraphs further into the essay) sums up the argument:

> Thus, the author writes in order to address himself to the freedom of readers, and he requires it in order to make his work exist. But he does not stop there; he also requires that they return this confidence which he has given them, that they recognize his creative freedom, and they in turn solicit it by a sym-metrical and inverse appeal. Here there appears the other dialectical paradox of reading; the more we experience our freedom, the more we recognize that of the other; the more he demands of us, the more we demand of him. (Sartre 1993: 38)

As Suzanne Guerlac (1997) points out in her reading of the essay, Sartre delivers a very formalist argument about the ethics and politics of reading. He writes nothing about which topics literature should engage, nor is the essay very specific about the writing style that he prefers – only in the very last pages of the essay does he address the question of politics directly (via a discussion of the French fascist writer Pierre Drieu la Rochelle).

Nevertheless, as Guerlac also notes it is clear that the essay is underpinned by a fully developed ethical and political understanding of the role of art and literature. The quoted passage, and the essay as a whole, is modelled on a particular reading of Hegel's analysis of the Master–Slave relation, the so-called 'dialectic of recognition'. It is thus no coincidence that the verb 'recognize' appears twice in the quotation above: it must be understood in this specifically Hegelian sense of a harmonious sublation (*Aufhebung*) of the opposition between the consciousness of the reader and that of the author. The artistic exchange therefore has both an ethical and a political dimension. Ethically, the artwork allows the realisation of the ideal of mutual recognition; it thereby helps both writer and reader to become fully self-conscious, self-aware. This mediation between consciousnesses is so perfect that the artwork – the spinning top – seems to evaporate from Sartre's text, allowing what resembles a direct, almost telepathic communication between author and reader. Politically, Sartre associates this pact of generosity and mutual recognition with democracy and free citizens. On the one hand, it is essential that readers and writers are free, otherwise they would not be able to participate in an exchange of freedom; on the other, the artistic experience is also held out as an ideal form of intersubjectivity, an ideal on which social relations can be modelled, and an ideal that will help to create such relations. In short: art becomes both a *model* and a *motor* for the intersubjective relations that should characterise society. However, what Sartre more specifically means when he suggests that the work of art can be a model for socio-political relations – that is, the specific nature of the democratic politics he has in mind – only becomes clear if we step outside the boundaries of this specific essay and look, for instance, at the last essay in the volume. There we see that Sartre's understanding of a true democratic exchange and the ideal of 'mutual recognition' is Marxist: in 1947, the political name for mutual recognition is 'the classless society'. For our purposes, however, the key point is that Sartre's essay provides us with an exemplary theory about how the artistic experience stimulates a humanist ethics and a progressive, democratic politics. In this theory, art seems inherently ethical; it offers a model for democratic relations. Art is about communication, understanding, empathy, recognition, respect, reciprocity, democracy, co-creation and the understanding of oneself and the other.

Sartre's outline of the ideal exchange between writer and reader (which I will complicate in my conclusion) might seem naïve, and it is perhaps not surprising that Denis Hollier described it as 'bordering on the comic' in its humanistic belief in a full understanding between reader and writer (Hollier 1986: 95).[3] But this comedy appeals to many readers. And the very close relation between art, *Bildung* and democracy is especially attractive when politicians put us under pressure to explain why the humanities are worth spending money on. Furthermore, as my second example will now demonstrate, it is a model that can be been updated and altered.

In his very influential collection, *Relational Aesthetics*, Nicolas Bourriaud wrote the following about the generation of artists that came to prominence in the 1990s:

> What nowadays forms the foundation of artistic experience is *the joint presence of beholders in front of the work*, be this work effective or symbolic. The first question we should ask ourselves when looking at a work of art is:
> – Does it give me a chance to exist in front of it, or, on the contrary, does it deny me as a subject, refusing to consider the Other in its structure? Does the space–time factor suggested or described by this work, together with the laws governing it, tally with my aspirations in real life? Does it criticise what is

deemed to be criticisable? Could I live in a space–time structure corresponding to it in reality?

These questions do not refer to any exaggeratedly anthropomorphic vision of
art, but to a vision that is quite simply *human* . . . What strikes us in the work
of this generation of artists is, first and foremost, the *democratic* concern that
informs it. (Bourriaud 2002: 57, emphases in the original)

In this quotation Bourriaud begins with the community of spectators
gathered in front of the work, and then asks how that community is being
constituted by the artwork: do we want to live in the space the work creates?
When it comes to the contemporary art practices that Bourriaud addresses,
the answer is clearly 'yes'. Bourriaud's theorisation differs from Sartre's in
so far as the producer of the work (the artist, the writer, the director) has no
apparent role in the passage. But Bourriaud compensates for this shortage of
intersubjectivity by producing something that must be called an anthropomorphic vision of art – although perhaps not an 'exaggeratedly anthropomorphic' one. This allows him to insist on what he calls the 'simply *human*' vision
of contemporary art.

Having considered the question of the space that contemporary art practices invite their spectators to join, Bourriaud then makes a move from the
interactions with art to interactions within society. Like Sartre he sees the
'experience of art' as a model for social relations more generally – and, again
like Sartre, this leads him to emphasise how inherently '*democratic*' the artistic
activity is. In the Sartre passage, the word 'democratic' could be translated
into the Marxist ideal of a classless society. In Bourriaud's text 'democratic'
again calls for further clarification and development – and the writer does
give this explanation in other passages in his book. Here it becomes clear that
Bourriaud's 'democracy' takes place at a more micro-political level where the
art practices help to institute a network of relations that undermine the reification of subjectivity, producing instead an open and mobile society (which
Bourriaud is theorising on the basis of Félix Guattari's writings). However,
two important elements remain unchanged from Sartre to Bourriaud: the
emphasis on art as a motor for the development of humanist and democratic
ways of being together, and the desire to move very quickly from the experience of art to social relations (art as a model).

Anti-Humanist Spectatorship?

The films studied in this book all communicate in a very different way. It is
tempting to say that the various feel-bad approaches offer a methodical –
almost a point-by-point – violation of Sartre's ideas about the collaboration
and generous exchange between free subjects. Many of the films manipulate

the spectator, and some of them pull the spectator into the more treacherous waters of what I am tempted to call Baudelarian spectatorship ('hypocrite spectator – my double – my brother'). These films withhold crucial information (von Trier), they shock the spectator (Dumont), they shock *and* bore her (Korine), and they work by seducing her, only to then further disturb her (Hadzihalilovic). Writing about feel-bad films, it is therefore very difficult to employ the vocabulary we encounter in Sartre's and Bourriaud's texts. Watching Haneke's *Funny Games* hardly feels like a collaborative exercise allowing the mutual realisation of our freedom, and few spectators are likely to think of Bruno Dumont's *Twentynine Palms* as a 'pact of generosity'. Furthermore, feel-bad films go against Bourriaud's relational ideal by not offering a space that we would wish to live in. Indeed, the dominant spatial sensation for spectators watching these films is claustrophobia: *get me out of here!* Like Bourriaud's artists, these films might criticise 'what is deemed to be criticisable', but they do so in a manner that seems to leave little space for the spectator; they therefore do not strike us with their humanity. In the light of this, it is perhaps not surprising that many of these directors have been criticised for being cynical, amoral, nihilistic, politically dubious and anti-humanistic. The value of showing such films in an educational setting might not be immediately clear.

But is it true that this particular filmic corpus opposes the ideals we associate with humanism and the ideal of mutual recognition? Or does it simply mean, as Asbjørn Grønstad (2012), William Brown (2013) and other critics have suggested, that we must work a bit harder to understand their relation to the *Bildungstradition*? Does it perhaps mean that the way in which we interpret the *Bildungstradition* needs to be more nuanced?

As these questions suggest, this book is also interested in the relationship between the feel-bad films and 'education', *Bildung*. It is worth emphasising that this is not an agenda artificially imposed on the filmic corpus; on the contrary, many of these films thematise education. *Dogville* is about a well-meaning teacher (Tom) who tries to educate the citizens of Dogville, and it is also about a father–daughter relationship in which both try to educate each other; *Elephant* is partly about the state of the American high school; *Innocence* is set in a boarding school where it shows us 'the bodily education of young girls' (to use the subtitle of the Wedekind novella on which the film is based).[4] More importantly, films such as *Dogville* (again), *Funny Games* and *Redacted* are all 'didactic' – perhaps even 'aggressively didactic'. In this sense they tie back to pre-romantic conceptions of the moral role of art and literature. Finally, some of the theoretical texts that stimulate the analyses I will present – in particular Jacques Rancière's *The Emancipated Spectator* (2009; published in French in 2008) and in a less explicit way Claire Bishop's *Artificial Hells* (2012) – also analyse the relation between education and the arts. The theme of education will therefore follow us discreetly through most of the chapters, until the conclusion where I shall return to the topic more explicitly: why should we teach feel-bad films?

To anticipate the answer to this question, one of the key arguments in this book will be that the inclination to consider the artistic experience as a more or less direct model for social relations – whether along the lines of Sartre or Bourriaud – must not be the only way to think the relation between art and society; in fact, this idea of 'art as model' can have unfortunate consequences. If we require the relation between a film and its spectator to be similar to relations of intersubjectivity more generally, we rob ourselves of the possibility of experiencing and negotiating a relation to that which is ethically problematic, we deprive ourselves of a possibility to think the human psyche in all its complexities. That possibility, however, is one that art has always been keen to take advantage of, and I believe it can be detrimental to the process of enlightenment if we eliminate or reduce it. Over the next three chapters, I will therefore continuously argue that we should allow for different ethical standards inside and outside the movie theatre.

This book is therefore concerned with a form of spectatorship that lies at the limits of a traditional understanding of Hegel's ideals of intersubjectivity (in my conclusion, I shall briefly touch upon alternative ways of theorising the Hegelian dialectic). At this very general level, the arguments presented relate to many other books and articles that have been published over these last decades in the field of film studies, but a more narrow research context is constituted by publications emphasising the role of the senses, the body, the phenomenological experience of film, as well as those suggesting a move from emotions to affectivity. Within this field it has become customary to distinguish between an erotic and a more violent challenge to the spectator. As a representative of the first tradition, we might think of Laura U. Marks's acclaimed *The Skin of the Film* (2000). In this text Marks uses the central distinction between optic and haptic visuality to move away from Hegelian and psychoanalytically inflected theories of spectatorship (Marks 2000: 192–3). With the haptic she seeks to probe the potential of what lies beyond the well-defined subject–object relations, beyond a dialectic account of spectatorship that is now understood to perpetuate, ad infinitum, the master–slave relations it set out to overcome. For an example of the second tendency we can go back to Steven Shaviro's *The Cinematic Body* (1993). Like Marks, Shaviro is interested in the potential of sensation – more specifically, he is interested in the 'primordial forms of raw sensation: affect, excitation, stimulation and repression, pleasure and pain, shock and habit' (Shaviro 1993: 27). But as this quote suggests, his early theory of spectatorship largely focuses on the violence associated with the opening of the subject.[5] On the whole, the cinematic experiences that take centre stage in my text come closer to Shaviro's violent encounters than they do to Marks's erotic encounters; therefore any temptation to think the aesthetic experience as a more or less direct model for social relations is reduced, and the argument for allowing different ethical standards inside and outside the movie theatre will come across more clearly. However, rather than exploring a distinction between eroticism and violence, I would like to emphasise that what is at stake in *all* these debates is the question of film's capacity to destabilise subjectivities, to overcome distances, to open up bodies. The present book belongs to this tradition.

One last comment is required before we begin to look at *how* and *why* the feel-bad films stimulate and frustrate our desire for *catharsis*. This Greek keyword is one of the most slippery and complex terms in film studies and aesthetic theory. It is so slippery, in fact, that Stephen Halliwell has called for a moratorium on discussions of what Aristotle meant in those few passages in his *Poetics* and his *Politics* where the notion appears (Halliwell 2002: 206). Halliwell might therefore be relieved that such discussions fall outside the constraints of the present study. When I propose that the feel-bad film puts a deadlock on catharsis, the term should rather be understood along Brechtian or Hollywoodian lines. Both in the early work of Brecht and in many popular (Tierno 2002) and academic (Bordwell 2006) discussions of Hollywood cinema, Aristotelian catharsis is associated with mimesis, narrative closure and the emotional satisfaction of the spectator. Obviously, Brecht and Hollywood have strongly opposed views on how to evaluate this catharsis. In the Dream Factory, this particularly satisfying form of closure and release is generally perceived as a positive ideal (that will generate positive numbers in the accounts). For early Brecht, on the other hand, Aristotelian catharsis was associated with a pacification of the spectator; it was seen as instrumental for turning what he called 'dramatic theatre' into a form of opium for the public. In a well-known text presenting his opera *Mahogany*, Brecht therefore warned that in the dramatic theatre, 'the spectator . . . gets thrown into the melting pot too and becomes a passive (suffering) part of the total work of art. Witchcraft of this sort must of course be fought against' (Brecht 1978: 38).

But this question of catharsis cannot be settled with a quick reference to Hollywood and Brecht. Some of the directors discussed in this book talk and write about catharsis in a very different way. Most significantly, Michael Haneke wrote an early text about 'Film als Katharsis' in which he advocated for a cathartic cinema (Haneke 1992). Anyone even vaguely familiar with the name of Haneke will know that this was not a call for more Hollywood endings. Haneke used the term to promote an idea of cinema as a place where society can engage with and negotiate its relation to that which is socially problematic. For Haneke cathartic cinema is about raising questions and creating debates rather than delivering closure and satisfaction. With arguments recalling those of Brecht, he therefore opposes mainstream American cinema and instead considers (feel-bad) films such as his own debut *The Seventh Continent* (the title 'Film als Katharsis' refers to) as an example of what will ultimately be a form of cathartic cinema. Along similar lines, but in a less social register, Werner Herzog describes *Even Dwarfs Started Small* (a film we shall consider in the last chapter) as a cathartic film *for him*. It was nightmarish – but having made it, he never felt the desire to make another film like this (however happy he was with the result). Again, this is obviously not the catharsis we associate with Hollywood, nor the one against which Brecht warns.

These remarks are meant to reduce the possibility of misunderstanding my definition of the feel-bad film: I use the term to refer to the emotional state of the spectator *when the lights go on* (rather than what might happen through subsequent debates and discussions). But these remarks also allow me to introduce an important question by playing the two different understandings of the word catharsis against each other: does the deadlock on spectatorial catharsis always feed into a larger – a social – catharsis? Is it always the case that these provocative films aim to, or simply 'will', stimulate productive ethico-political discussions? This is a question I will address in the conclusion, once I have offered my views about *why* and *how* the feel-bad films frustrate the spectator's desire.

NOTES

1. A word of clarification on what I call 'narrative containment' above: I do not mean to deny that more classically constructed narratives can produce intense feel-bad emotions *and* leave the spectator in ethically complex situations. Many well-known films do this – for instance Sam Peckinpah's *Straw Dogs* (1971), John Boorman's *Deliverance* (1972), and Bob Fosse's *Star 80* (1983). However, the feel-bad films chosen here differ from such titles by offering an alternative relation between plot construction and spectatorial manipulation. As will soon become clear, the frustration generated by most of the films I discuss partly originates in their disrespect for the conventions of storytelling. This is why many of the films have been accused of being incoherent, boring, mystifying or otherwise lacking in narrative.

2. This is not to suggest that feel-bad cinema is an exclusively Western phenomenon; many Asian directors, for instance, go very far with the manipulation of negative emotions. However, I have to leave a further internationalisation of the feel-bad idea to colleagues who are more competent than I am in non-Western cinematic traditions.

3. Sartre is not as straightforward as this resumé suggests, and I shall try to do him justice in my conclusion. Already now it is relevant to mention that – contrary to what is sometimes said – the idea of taking the experience of art as a model for ethical relations in society did not lead Sartre towards a narrow didactic conception of art and literature. In the immediate postwar period, he defends Louis-Ferdinand Céline, celebrates Stéphane Mallarmé, begins an extensive study of Jean Genet, and writes enthusiastically about William Faulkner.

4. Yorgos Lanthimos's *Dogtooth* (2009) is another feel-bad film about education. Not unrelated, Grønstad notes that a very high number of the 'unwatchable' films he is studying present narratives about teachers (Grønstad 2012: 31).

5. The relation between these two very influential theories of spectatorship is complex, and both have been met with criticism. For instance, Marks argues that rather than leaving behind the dialectic of master and slave, Shaviro simply turns it on its head: 'Shaviro's assaultive and masochistic model of spectatorship maintains a radical alterity between self and film, merely switching the poles of who does what to whom' (Marks 2000: 151). On the other hand, the more gentle and erotic encounter that Marks advocates (the 'mutual embodiment' as she writes with reference to Vivian Sobchack (Marks 2000: 193)) helped bring about a haptic turn, that has been criticised for '[being] in danger of celebrating a big-tent, inclusive feel-good theory of sensory empowerment' (Elsaesser and Hagener 2010: 127–8). I am not convinced that what we might call Shaviro's 'Hegelianism without reserve' can simply be described as a form of reverse Hegelianism, nor do I believe that the criticism delivered by Thomas Elsaesser and Malte Hagener (a criticism which they leave unaddressed) can be aimed at Marks's writings.

CHAPTER 1

Assault

1.1 THE INNER BASTARD: VON TRIER'S *DOGVILLE*

This chapter focuses on a series of films that establish a very antagonistic relation to the spectator. They do so in view of putting across a political and/or ethical message, and it will be argued that the directors all work from the hypothesis that the best – the most efficient – way to communicate their specific message is to go through the body of the spectator to her intellect. Not surprisingly, the films discussed in this first part have therefore generated a great amount of controversy. My opening example of this confrontational approach is Lars von Trier's *Dogville* (2003). The film might be less graphic than *The Idiots* (1998), *Antichrist* (2009) and *Nymphomaniac* (2013), yet its reception demonstrated that, once again, the director had managed to get under the skin of his viewers. The Cannes jury, for instance, condemned the film with a term that summed up many others' feelings about it: 'anti-humanism!' I shall discuss this label in some detail, but first it is important to consider *how* von Trier creates the feel-bad experience.

For some viewers *Dogville* is a film about Grace (Nicole Kidman). We are in 1932, and she is the beautiful stranger who, under mysterious circumstances, comes to the small town of Dogville at the foot of the Rocky Mountains. The idealist, self-proclaimed author and thinker of the town, Tom (Paul Bettany), is charmed by her beauty and he convinces the citizens of Dogville that by welcoming her they can demonstrate their commitment to the virtues of hospitality and community. Grace makes herself accepted by helping the community, but when both gangsters and police appear to be searching for her the townspeople decide that it is only fair for them to ask 'more' of her (the film repeatedly manipulates this economic vocabulary – which the presence of Grace, as her name clearly indicates, upsets). She goes from being a helper and errand girl to a hardworking servant and, eventually, a sexual slave mercilessly exploited by the male citizens of the town. When Grace refuses Tom, the only man who has not turned rapist, he sends for the gangsters, thereby giving her over to what we expect to be her certain death.

But then (after two hours and thirty minutes), a very late peripeteia: the

Figure 1   *Revenge* (Dogville)

gangster boss (James Caan) turns out to be her loving father. The two had argued about his ruthless business methods and to prove her father wrong the idealistic Grace set out to find the good in human nature. Now that she has failed miserably, her father urges her to judge the citizens of Dogville by her own standards: if she had acted like them, he argues, she would never forgive herself, and she should therefore not forgive them either. Grace initially protests, but then acquiesces, finally putting this principle of equality (I will judge them by the standards I would have judged myself) to work with a cruelty that astounds even her father: every citizen is killed, the town is burnt down, and Grace and the gangsters leave.

This screenplay has allowed its viewers to engage in very varied discussions of a mainly ethical and political nature. *Dogville* has been regarded as a reflection on the logic of exchange and the elements that escape and challenge the (capitalist) economic sphere – grace, gifts and hospitality (Chiesa 2007, Nobus 2007, Moore 2011). The film has been seen as a confrontation between New Testament ethics ('turn the other cheek') and Old Testament ethics ('an eye for an eye'; Fibiger 2003 and Grodal 2009). Encouraged by von Trier's own statements (and an end credit sequence composed of documentary photos of American poverty), American critics such as Roger Ebert and Todd McCarthy considered the film an attack on American society: the film was said to depict a USA in which exploitation and xenophobia are particularly prevalent (for a nuanced discussion see Bainbridge 2007: 142–8). But at the same time, von Trier has also been accused of running errands for George W. Bush by transforming complex political problems into ethical problems of a Manichean character (Rancière 2004). I shall return to some of these ethical and political discussions, but in order to do so, I will first sketch out a second approach to the film that should not, I emphasise, be seen as opposed to the first.

For a second group of viewers (to which I belong), this is less a film about Dogville and Grace than a manipulative 'machine' (Horsley 2005: 18) designed to bring out some strong, antisocial drives in the spectator. In other words, this is not primarily a film about Grace, but about the spectator. I believe *Dogville* focuses on the spectator to an extent that is unusual for a European art film. The fact that von Trier withholds the true identity of Grace until the very end, for instance, is remarkable, and will no doubt seem dishonest to many viewers (this kind of last-minute revelation is also found in *The Idiots* and *Manderlay* (2005)). Adela Abella and Nathalie Zilkha offered one of the earliest variations of this reading in a review of the film in *The International Journal of Psychoanalysis* (2004).

As these authors explain, von Trier first presents Grace as a victim of the sadism of the citizens of Dogville. The very special *mise-en-scène* (discussed below) and a high number of bird's-eye shots 'creat[e] an illusion of transparency and clarity' (Abella and Zilkha 2004: 1521) that lures the spectators into believing they occupy an almost transcendental position in relation to the events. A sophisticated reader such as Caroline Bainbridge seems to fall for this illusion when she suggests that the film 'positions the spectator as god-like' and 'we are aligned with von Trier as director' (Bainbridge 2004: 156). But this is a trap: we *think* we are at a safe distance, and this is likely to make us condemn the citizens of Dogville without questioning our own position. With the final reversal of all power structures we understand that Grace is not a simple victim. She had a choice: she could have sent for her gangster father. Maybe her pride prevented her from doing this, but maybe she has also been inviting these humiliations, drawing them out of the citizens of Dogville?[1] Suddenly we suspect that we have been identifying with a perverse subject. However, this suspicion, continue Abella and Zilkha, comes too late to relieve us of our identification with Grace. After having sided with Grace throughout two hours and thirty minutes of humiliations and degradations we are likely to maintain the identification, deny the perversion, and instead feel relief at the apocalypse:

> owing to the unbearable nature of what we have had to endure while watching the film, we are caught up like Grace in participating emotionally in the final vengeance, experiencing – consciously, unconsciously, openly or covertly – a feeling of relief at the violent destruction of the village which allows us to evade the necessity of thinking. We collude in Grace's perverse destructivity. 'The beast' is lurking in us, too. Lars von Trier has awakened it. (Abella and Zilkha 2004: 1525)

I shall not enter into a detailed discussion of Abella and Zilkha's reading, but I want to emphasise my agreement with their conclusion: the film is manipulating the spectator, and the aim of these manipulations is to bring out 'the beast' in us. There are several good reasons to argue that this film is concerned primarily (although not exclusively) with the position of the spectator, let me mention just two. The first has to do with the dog encountered immediately before the closing credits.

It is widely acknowledged that one of the most original elements in *Dogville* is its *mise-en-scène*. The film was shot in a vast hangar formerly used for the construction of locomotives; there is no natural lighting, and only very few props; houses are chalk lines drawn on the ground, and actors open non-existing doors – that creak. One way of describing the effect of this *mise-en-scène* is to say that throughout the film von Trier expects his spectators to do the imagining. It is therefore significant that in the very last shots of the film, the dog in the town, Moses, suddenly materialises from his chalk lines outside the house of Vera (Patricia Clarkson) and Chuck (Stellan Skarsgård). We see a Rottweiler that rises from the ground and barks in the direction of a camera that descends towards him, before, finally, the screen fades to black. It might be said, then, that the camera movement brings the spectator down to a fusion with the dog.

In so far as this sudden materialisation of the dog breaks with the aesthetic of the preceding two hours and forty minutes, it is worth considering in detail. The spectators have already seen the way in which 'Dogville bares its teeth' (the title of one of the film's nine chapters) and we have just witnessed Grace's horrific yet enthralling revenge. More than that: we helped to produce the image-track for the long-awaited revenge. When this revenge was finally performed with a sublime combination of mathematical logic and unrestricted violence – Grace personally liquidating Tom in a scene that brings to mind the photo of General Nguyen Ngoc Loan's execution of a Viet Cong prisoner in the streets of Saigon (see Figure 1) – it was difficult for the spectator not to feel a rush of excitement. Von Trier capitalises on this. With the appearance of the dog he now takes over and confronts us with the roots of our own imaginary: 'the beast within us has materialised' (Abella and Zilkha 2004: 1525). In this confrontational manner – which is as close as he gets to breaking the fourth wall – von Trier throws the Rottweiler at the spectator: this is what you are!

It is relevant to add a specifically Danish–German interpretation of this shot. In the Danish language there exists the expression 'den indre svinehund', in German 'der innere Schweinehund' – literally 'the inner swine dog' or, more idiomatically, 'the inner bastard'. In Denmark this expression became part of everyday language in the late 1980s, when it was introduced into debates about immigration and the country's extensive xenophobia. For instance, it is often said that the very influential Danish nationalist party (The

Danish People's Party), which von Trier has actively campaigned against, 'appeals to our inner bastard'. In a 2005 interview with the magazine of The Danish State Railway, we find an example of von Trier using this expression:

> The tone that dominates the debate on immigration is awfully misanthropic. . . . this is how the Nazis began – at that point it was the Jews, and today it is the Muslims. There are some easy votes to be had because the inner bastard is lurking just beneath the surface in a part of the Danish population. (Von Trier in Schultz 2005: 56)

This comparison between the 'inner bastard' and psychological drives that can be exploited for xenophobic purposes points back to the most famous use of the expression. In 1932 (the year in which Grace comes to Dogville), the German socialist politician Kurt Schumacher debated with Joseph Goebbels in the Reichstag in Berlin. Schumacher – who was soon to be sent to different concentration camps before becoming the leader of the SPD after the war – created a minor scandal by stating that 'the entire national socialist propaganda is a constant appeal to the inner bastard in man' (Iversen 1987: 89). It is this use of the expression that has found its way into the Danish language, and it is this 'inner bastard' – which, psychoanalytically, goes by the name of Thanatos – that 'bares its teeth' in Dogville, in Grace, and finally in us.

It is worth paying attention to the way in which the Francis Bacon-like dog appears: it is the film's only morphed image. Vivian Sobchack explains that 'in its reversibility of form and apparent ease of shape-shifting, the morph reminds us of the malleable and liquid nature of identity that is at the heart of our phenomenal being' (Sobchack 2000: xii). The identitarian liquidity that Sobchack writes about can be a chance, but also a risk. In this particular case, the malleability of the morph demonstrates how quickly affect can be recuperated in the form of an aggressive Rottweiler, the scene thereby delivering a metaphor for the process of becoming a racist.

Let me turn to the second argument for considering *Dogville* a film that explicitly negotiates its relation with the spectator: self-reflexivity. Von Trier's attempt to use Grace to demonstrate a specific socio-psychological point is mirrored by the film itself, as Tom uses Grace to construct an argument. When Grace arrives in the town, Tom is giving lectures in the mission house on the topic of hospitality. His approach to lecturing is 'evidence'-based; he works with examples. In this regard, the arrival of Grace seems like a gift from above, and it allows Tom (whose second name is Edison) to pronounce his favourite line: 'Let me illustrate!' Considering the link just mentioned between Tom and von Trier (they both use Grace for demonstrative purposes, making an argument about hospitality), it is not surprising that Tom's name signals his ties to cinema. Thomas Edison was the major driving force behind the Kinetoscope and the Kinetograph, and as such he was instrumental to the invention of cinema. This obviously does not mean that Tom simply *is* von Trier: for most of the film, Tom seeks to use Grace to demonstrate the generosity of the citizens of Dogville (and to conceal his own emotional and sexual interest in Grace behind a superficies of intellectualism), whereas von Trier uses her to finally bring out the antisocial drives in the spectator. Nevertheless, the close link between Tom and von Trier makes it difficult to ignore the sometimes very meta-filmic – and self-ironic[2] – dimension of the dialogue. An example is found at the end of the film: the gangsters have arrived, Tom is beginning to understand that their arrival is a threat to him, and he now addresses Grace:

> Although using people is not very charming, I think you have to agree that this specific illustration has surpassed all expectations. It said so much about being human! It's been painful, but I think you'll also have to agree it's been edifying – wouldn't you say?

Here the dialogue clearly works at several levels: at one level, the pathetic Tom is making a desperate attempt at trying to save his life by emphasising the didactic value of Grace's sufferings; at another level von Trier is mocking himself by taking up a position alongside that of Tom, whose remarks – delivered in a Brechtian acting style (as if in quotation marks) – clearly should be heard as a directorial appeal to the spectator also. And it could even be said that the verb 'edifying' (with its links to Tom, to Edison, and to cinema) mediates this encounter between the diegetic and the extradiegetic dimensions of the film.

With such passages, von Trier enhances the self-reflexive and ironic dimension of the film. However, just as with the images of Moses, these moments of self-reflexivity are not moments at which the film folds upon itself, but rather ones at which it speaks directly to the spectators, thereby implicating us in the film. In the example above Grace does not answer the question, and this obviously makes the address to the spectators stand out even more strongly. Von Trier is making assumptions about our viewing experience, and he is challenging the position that we occupy. I believe these confrontations with the spectator rely on a combination of Brechtian and surrealist aesthetics.

Playing with Brecht and the surrealists

Numerous critics have argued that *Dogville* is a Brechtian film. The reasons for this are obvious, and I shall therefore mention them only briefly. Firstly, it should be noted that von Trier himself has explained that the film borrows a part of its plot from Brecht's and Weil's song 'Pirate Jenny' from *The Threepenny Opera*. Von Trier originally wanted Nina Simone's version of this song (about Jenny's revenge and the killing of an entire town) to accompany the photomontage at the end of the film, but the idea was discarded because he felt it would have been too obvious. This is not von Trier's only reference to Brecht:

> I was also inspired to a degree by Bertolt Brecht and his kind of very simple, pared-down theatre. My theory is that you forget very quickly that there are no houses or whatever. This makes you invent the town for yourself but more importantly, it makes you zoom in on the people. (Von Trier in Bainbridge 2007: 145)

In the light of this remark, it is hardly surprising that the chalk lines and lack of props are generally considered to be *Verfremdungseffekte* (a point to which I will return). Furthermore, the narrator (John Hurt) offers an ironic framing of the melodramatic story, and thereby imbeds an element of distance within the film. Due to the very written nature of his text (reinforced by literary techniques such as the division of the film into a prologue and nine chapters), the narrator also gives *Dogville* an epic character that (at least initially) prevents the spectator from 'throwing herself into the action like a stone into the river' – as Brecht writes of the kind of drama he seeks to avoid. Add to this the *Lehrstück* dimension that I have already mentioned (the fact that von Trier so clearly and self-consciously presents this film as a didactic engagement with 'the problem of Dogville'), and it seems obvious why Brecht is the most common intertext in studies of *Dogville*.

Moving on from these more technical aspects of Brecht's aesthetic and looking to the ideological motivation that underpins the dramaturgy, we encounter the well-known fact (briefly touched upon in my introduction) that Brecht's ideas are motivated by a materialist philosophy and a strongly anti-cathartic, anti-Aristotelian stance. The reason Brecht does not encourage his public to throw themselves into the 'plot-river' is that he seeks intellectual engagement rather than (just) character identification and emotional absorption: he wants us to search for political solutions to the dialectical conflicts that his plays engage.

We may, though, begin to wonder about the limits of von Trier's Brechtianism. Is von Trier's film not an example of the emotional manipulation about which Brecht is generally so sceptical? What is the status of catharsis in *Dogville*? If we say that the film manipulates the spectator to a point at which a beast is unleashed (via what is, until ten minutes before the end of the film, an exercise in concealment and mystification), then it is obvious that von Trier's film is far from being a case of orthodox Brechtianism. In order to understand how the *Dogville* 'machine' works, it is therefore helpful to introduce a very different conceptualisation of the cathartic experience.[3]

Contemporaneous with Brecht (in the early and mid-thirties; when Grace comes to Dogville), we encounter a very different theorisation of catharsis, Greek tragedy and Dionysian activities at the margins of the surrealist movement in Paris. Just like Brecht, authors such as Antonin Artaud and Georges Bataille were interested in creating a politically progressive aesthetic along (unorthodox) Marxist lines. In Artaud's case (as in Brecht's) this attempt was tied to a subversion of the naturalist drama. Crucially, however, these authors of surrealist sensibility did not share Brecht's critique of the cathartic. Inspired by Nietzsche, they rethought the desire for catharsis as a ground for the production of revolutionary subjectivity. For Artaud and Bataille the emotional and physical immersion of the spectator was a precondition for the production of a new form of subjectivity; only by taking a step beyond the intellectual address and appealing to the body of the spectator would it be possible to liberate the public:

> Infused with the idea that the masses think with their senses first and foremost and that it is ridiculous to appeal primarily to our understanding as we do in everyday psychological theatre, the Theatre of Cruelty proposes to resort to mass theatre, thereby rediscovering a little of the poetry in the ferment of great, agitated crowds hurled against one another, sensations only too rare nowadays, when masses of holiday crowds throng the streets. (Artaud [1938] 1970: 65)

Inspired by rituals from ancient Greece and from non-Western cultures, these surrealists attempted to provoke and overwhelm the spectator (or reader) in the hope that he or she would emerge revitalised from the ritualistic experience. In Artaud's famous theorisations of the 'Theatre of Cruelty' and Georges Bataille's writings at the time of *Contre-Attaque* (1935–6) and *Acéphale* (1936–9), we thus find a strong belief in a correlation between immersion, transgression and emancipation.

A similar correlation can be found in many of von Trier's films.[4] Therefore it is unsurprising that in *The Five Obstructions* (2003) fellow Danish filmmaker Jørgen Leth makes a strong case for summarising von Trier's methodology as a form of romantic avant-garde thinking. For this film Leth has agreed to play a sado-masochistic game with von Trier: to reshoot his own black and white short film *The Perfect Human* (1967) – a film von Trier testifies to being 'obsessed with' – according to various sets of rules that von Trier devises. In the most famous of these 'obstructions', von Trier orders Leth to reshoot the dinner scene from the earlier film. In the original, this is a meal with silverware, salmon and a bottle of Chablis; our protagonist is wearing a black tie, and he is alone in a white, seemingly borderless 'room' in a *mise-en-scène* that clearly anticipates the staging we find in *Dogville* and *Manderlay*. Von Trier sets the following rules for the remake: Leth must reshoot this scene in the most horrendous neighbourhood he knows (Leth chooses the red light district in Bombay); Leth must play the role of the man himself; and finally, even if the scene is to be shot in this horror place, it must not show the poverty, it should only be there indirectly. Lying in his hotel room, Leth analyses the challenge. He believes that von Trier wants to see how the social horror reflects back on him (Leth). Can it be measured on me? Will I become a screen? More generally, Leth knows that von Trier's ambition is to put the perfect human in such conditions that suddenly the 'façade' will crack, and something else – something truthful – will reveal itself.

Leth does not sympathise with von Trier's project. He does not believe that the social horror will be visible on him; at least there is no physical law that guarantees this. He does not share either von Trier's fascination for a breaking point. Unlike many avant-garde artists, he does not think that the breaking point is the moment that reveals the truth about a character.[5] It is von Trier's faith in the link between breakdown (transgression) and truth that Leth describes as 'romantic'.

Leth is right. This is *the Lars von Trier moment*. Perhaps not the only moment, but certainly one of the most important and recurrent moments in von Trier's films: the moment where an extreme situation and the ensuing breakdown is supposed to reveal the truth about the character. The moment where we go behind the social façade, the conventions, and find a supposedly more authentic expression of human subjectivity. In the 'Dogma 95 Manifesto' this is said in a very direct way as von Trier and Vinterberg write: 'my supreme goal is to force the truth out of my characters and settings.' But the logic can be found in most of von Trier's films and projects. An obvious example is the series of marathon interviews that von Trier conceptualised for Danish television in the mid-1990s. Here a well-known Danish journalist and his camera crew moved into the house of the interviewee. The journalist and the 'victim' then spent twenty-four hours together, cameras rolling, neither of them allowed to sleep or leave the house. Everything was edited down to a one-hour interview and von Trier put a clock in the corner of the screen, allowing spectators to see where in the twenty-four-hour cycle we were. The aim, once again, was to get beyond the social performance and reach a breaking point where suddenly something authentic and exciting might happen. The interviewee would reveal sides of himself or herself that weren't previously known to the public. (It is relevant, in this context, to add that the last of these six interviews featured Pia Kjærsgaard, at that time the leader of the aforementioned Danish People's Party. This interview did not reveal any surprising dimensions of Pia Kjærsgaard's personality, nor did it dent the rise of the Danish People's Party. It did, however, find its place in the long and ongoing series of confrontations between Lars von Trier and the Danish extreme right.)

Returning to Brecht, it is well known that his aesthetic developed considerably over the years. In *A Short Organum for the Theatre* ([1948] 1960), for instance, he expresses regret at some of his earlier remarks about setting aside the emotional appeal of the theatre. At the same time, Bataille's theorisations (more than Artaud's) also developed towards a gradual disappearance of both the anti-rationalist stance and the dubious celebration of the agitated masses found in some of the earlier texts. Nevertheless, even if Brecht and surrealism are less irreconcilable than one would think (I shall return to this point), it is undeniable that the Epic Theatre represents a very different aesthetic position from that of the Theatre of Cruelty (Artaud) and the Literature of Evil (Bataille). The specificity of *Dogville* is to hold these frameworks together and, indeed, derive tension from the conflictual relation between the two. Needless to say, in combining the epic and the surrealist, von Trier deviates from both of these sets of theorisation.[6]

We saw above the way in which von Trier talks about Brecht's pared-down aesthetic, stressing that it allows spectators to focus on the intersubjective relations in the film (something which could be understood along the lines of a Brechtian prioritisation of the sociological). However, we also saw that he remarks that this pared-down aesthetic 'makes you invent the town for yourself' (Bainbridge 2007: 145). Another von Trier quotation goes further in this direction: in the extra material on the *Manderlay* DVD (a film that uses a similar *mise-en-scène*), he describes the way in which children play, explaining that they can create a world from things that are absent, and that these fantasy universes become more exhilarating than any toy universe could possibly have been. Von Trier thus suggests that the pared-down aesthetic can be used to make the cinematic experience as absorbing as possible. This does not mean that von Trier's minimalist set isn't alienating – it is. However, it is also, and at the same time, engaging. This complex balance between distanciation and immersion, between Brecht and Artaud, is immediately experienced in the viewing process. As a self-reflexive student of mine remarked in relation to a scene in *Manderlay*: 'when the gangsters and slaves find water in the ground, I thought it was completely artificial to see them celebrate the water that wasn't there . . . but obviously this meant that other scenes hadn't seemed artificial.'

That *Dogville* very consciously plays this game of distanciation and emotional involvement can be seen in one of its most powerful scenes. When Chuck rapes Grace on the floor of his and Vera's house, the first part of the scene, which leads up to the rape, is filmed primarily as a series of close-ups and with a very mobile handheld camera (like so many other scenes in the film). The intimacy is unbearable, and it is heightened by the whispering voices that draw attention to the oppressive nature of small-town life. The second part of the scene, the actual rape, is dominated by long shots: Chuck and Grace are in the background – but the rape remains clearly visible if we look through the townspeople in the foreground who are unaware of what is happening. A number of zooms link the foreground and the background, thereby communicating the complicity of all the citizens of *Dogville* (see also Laine 2006). The scene thus pushes the spectator from an unbearable intimacy into a number of more 'structural shots' in a way that invites intellectual engagement while remaining excruciating in its emotional charge. It is a clear example of von Trier manipulating his spectator into an ethical relation to the events enacted on screen.

Transgressions and their deadlock

At this point, a clarification is required. On the one hand, I have argued that von Trier often shares the avant-gardist belief in the correlation between immersion, transgression and emancipation (a point I shall develop in Chapter 3). He brings Grace and the spectator to a breaking point in order to reveal a 'truth' that we would not otherwise confront. On the other, I have analysed how *Dogville*'s moment of transgression coincides with the revelation of the beast in all of us. It would thus seem that while at times von Trier advocates the potential of the transgressive experience, at others he warns against such a transgression. Is this a tension that runs through his body of work? Should we, for instance, say that Karen's 'spassing' in the final scene of *The Idiots* is liberating and authentic, whereas Grace's transgressions (in both *Dogville* and *Manderlay*) are simply destructive?

The short answer is 'yes': the final scene in *The Idiots* is largely meant to inspire optimism with regard to transgression, while Grace – both in *Dogville* and in *Manderlay* – performs some much more problematic transgressive acts. At the same time, this answer is also too short. It reduces the complexity of *The Idiots*, in which certain transgressive experiences are far from being idealised, and more importantly it overlooks the point I have been trying to make here above: although *Dogville* warns against transgression, it also testifies to a very strong belief in submitting the spectator to a transgressive experience. At the diegetic level, *Dogville* offers a critique of Grace's final revenge. The materialisation of the inner bastard suggests that this is not a film where justice is finally done, and the conversation that precedes the gruesome revenge is therefore no different from the justifications of hideous crimes that we find (for instance) in Le comte de Bressac's rationalisations in the Marquis de Sade's *Justine*. The fact that these explanations (at least to a certain extent) seduce our intellect only demonstrates that we want to be convinced, that our inner bastard is seeking an outlet. At another – spectatorial – level, though, *Dogville* testifies to a strong belief in the transgressive experience: it is precisely by putting the spectator through Grace's cathartic experience that von Trier seeks to make his point about the dangers associated with transgression. This demonstrates the importance of maintaining a distinction between artistic and actual transgression (a distinction that many critics of so-called extreme cinema have difficulty observing, a distinction to which this book will return on a number of occasions). Whereas the spectator's transgression is imaginary, Grace's is 'real' – by inviting us to forget this distinction, von Trier puts to work Artaud's idea that 'in our present degenerative state, metaphysics must be made to enter the mind through the body' (Artaud 1970: 77). Already in 1984, von Trier expressed himself along these lines when he promoted the idea of a more direct address to the emotions and the unconscious:

> Today film is dying, it is being rarefied to the extent where it is no longer recognisable. The values lovingly brought forth in the 1930s and 40s have disappeared through intellectualisation. The foundational elements must be rediscovered, film must again appeal directly to the emotions and the unconscious. (Lars von Trier in Braad Thomsen 2011: 125)[7]

In *Dogville*, he is now suggesting that we must 'live' these drives in order to familiarise ourselves with them (– and, in the process, he also demonstrates that the drives can be used for intense artistic experiences).

The combination of 'inviting the spectator to lose herself' and getting her to think about what such a self-loss might mean puts a 'deadlock' on the catharsis. Using Brecht's vocabulary, we might say that von Trier invites us to throw ourselves into the action 'like a stone into the river', but that the river turns out to be so shallow that we soon find ourselves bumping against the bed, thereby regaining awareness of ourselves (a process helped by the morphing dog barking into our faces). The manipulative director seems to tease the spectator in accordance with a formula that could be summed up like this: 'So you want catharsis? So you want catharsis? Here you have it! . . . Was that really what you wanted?' This experience originates in a singular confrontation between the Brechtian aesthetic and the surrealist invitation to immersion whereby these two aesthetics arrest each other: on the one hand, we are not given the distance that Brecht recommends; on the other, we are deprived of the cathartic release that Artaud and Bataille aim for. This is the source of the 'feel-bad' experience; this is how von Trier puts a deadlock on catharsis.

Figure 2   ... *Was that really what you wanted?* (Dogville)

Given von Trier's tendency to work within a psychoanalytic framework (from *The Element of Crime* (1984) and *Epidemic* (1987) to *Antichrist* (2009) and *Nymphomaniac* (2013)), it is logical to offer a psychoanalytic supplement to this analysis of the feel-bad experience. In 'The Fiction Film and its Spectator: A Metapsychological Study', Christian Metz theorises what he calls 'filmic unpleasure' (Metz 1982: 110). According to Metz, this unpleasure arises whenever the spectator's phantasm (which to some extent is generated by the viewing experience) remains unsatisfied by the film. It is true that Metz theorises on the basis of 'narrative' film and he emphasises that the 'impression of reality' (1982: 119) plays a key role in the creation of unpleasure. Nevertheless, his theorisations remain pertinent to a formalist work like *Dogville*, since he explains that unpleasure can come from either of two sources. Firstly, it can originate in the 'id', as typically occurs when a film does not nourish our phantasm sufficiently, creating frustration in the spectator, who becomes bored or annoyed. Secondly, it can come from the 'superego', as happens when the satisfaction of the id is so overwhelming that the superego feels compelled to move in and protect the ego. For instance, the superego might step in and discard certain cinematic experiences (and genres) as being in bad taste.

If we relate these ideas to *Dogville* it can be argued that the first unpleasure in von Trier's film comes from the id. As Jake Horsley points out in a stimulating analysis (with which I often disagree[8]), von Trier deliberately uses the length of the film to frustrate the spectator. The repetition of the humiliations, the fact that almost every man and woman takes advantage of Grace (she even gets tied up as a dog) means that long before we reach the ending, we've had more than enough. The desire for an ending is therefore overwhelming, a constant in von Trier's work. His films are often too long; the viewer feels as though she is being subjected to a marathon interview (in

Björkman's portrait film *Tranceformer* (1997) von Trier himself notes that the films he really admires – whether by Tarkovsky, Widerberg or Bergman – are all too long). However, as Horsley goes on to explain, while this is exasperating, it is also absolutely necessary, because 'Trier needs us to need his apocalyptic ending' (Horsley 2005: 16). To reformulate this in a vocabulary closer to that of Metz: von Trier creates unpleasure by deliberately starving our id.

A second unpleasure is then produced, as we finally get the phantasm that our id has been craving. In fact, we get more than we had hoped for. If the ending of *Dogville* overwhelms it is also because this film came close after the 'Gold Heart' films. In 2003, von Trier's spectators had got used to a plot revolving around a good, pure female protagonist who would live through a long series of traumatising humiliations. In *Breaking the Waves* (1996) and *Dancer in the Dark* (2000), the stories ended with what was basically self-sacrifice – in *The Idiots* the situation was more ambiguous, but, like Bess and Selma, Karen nevertheless remained a golden heart. Grace, on the other hand, does not. For a long time we think she will, but in the very last scenes her revenge is immoderate. After more than nine hours of golden hearts, we get what we no longer dared to hope for. But at this point, the film also turns 'bad taste' by transforming itself into a Charles Bronson/Clint Eastwood-esque vigilante film. Therefore the superego steps in to censor. And as already mentioned, von Trier adds to the punishment by relieving us of our image-making duties, taking control and mockingly showing us our inner bastard (our id) as it morphs from the ground. Rephrasing *Dogville*'s feel-bad experience in these psychoanalytic terms, it thus becomes clear that the film's ending can be read along the lines of the famous Freudian maxim: 'where id was, there ego shall be.' In other terms: *Dogville* turns the cinematic experience into a visceral practice that pushes the spectator towards ethical reflection.

Feel-bad humanism

By now it should be evident that I do not agree with the Cannes jury's assessment of *Dogville* as a film that displays a lack of humanism. To further clarify, let me conclude this analysis with a comparison to a five-minute radio talk that Julia Kristeva delivered on the France Culture channel in 2001. Two weeks after 9/11, she presented under the title 'How Can One Be a Terrorist?' ('Comment peut-on être terroriste?', in Kristeva 2003).

Kristeva did not seek an answer to the title question, which was not even hers. It was raised by numerous commentators desperately struggling to come to terms with the terror attacks. Kristeva's own concern was different: how can we be so surprised? History has shown, again and again, that under the wrong circumstances, man is capable of many such destructive acts. She wonders how we got to the point where these destructive drives became not only shocking (because they are), but also inconceivable and unthinkable for us. Without denying the importance of sociological and political analysis, she uses this generalised bewilderment to lament the small influence psychoanalysis has had on contemporary political culture: thinking about the death drive (and more generally, about the human psyche in all its complexities) is something our culture seems to neglect.

To frame her point, Kristeva goes back to the Enlightenment, not to reject its tradition but to cite it as the origin for the modern sciences of the mind. The Enlightenment, in fact, had a much more nuanced and composite view of human subjectivity than the one with which it is often associated today, Kristeva notes. She also draws religion into the text. Again, she does so not simply to reject religious traditions (although she does criticise how fundamentalists deny the polysemic nature of religious texts), but to remind us that these traditions had a vocabulary and an iconography for thinking about the destructive dimensions of human subjectivity. Having gone through a widespread process of secularisation, have we perhaps also lost some of our ability to think evil? It is essential that art has the freedom to explore these destructive drives in the human psyche.

Dogville can be understood in this context: it is a film inviting us to think the destructive drives in human subjectivity, not at a remove, but rather – if the spectatorial manipulation works – from the inside. Among other things, it prompts us to consider how our desire for catharsis can be exploited for anti-democratic purposes. Like Kristeva's small text, von Trier's film also negotiates its relation to the Enlightenment and to religion. Tom conceives of himself as a man of the Enlightenment. He is interested in educating the townspeople, and therefore brings them together in the mission house, to illustrate and illuminate. However, the form of rationality he represents yields only a very limited form of self-knowledge, and he ends up sending for the gangsters because of an inability to deal with his own sexual frustrations. *Dogville*, however, is not a critique of the Enlightenment or of humanism, but rather a reminder of the dangers of a too-narrow conception of human subjectivity. (This warning against the dangers of a limited conception of humanism is repeated in *Manderlay* where Grace's attempts to liberate and educate end in tragedy and tyranny.) In any discussion of the film, it is thus important to insist on the crucial differences between the following three positions: (1) denying the presence of the inner bastard, (2) confronting the spectator with her inner bastard, and (3) making films that allow (the unreflexive) spectator to satisfy the inner bastard. This might very well be the difference between what we could call a naïve (and therefore dangerous) humanism, a self-conscious humanism (which takes into account the destructive dimensions of the human psyche), and simple anti-humanism.

Essential for my argument is the ability to acknowledge the difference between ethics in the artistic sphere and ethics in the extra-artistic sphere. As the case of *Dogville* demonstrates, it may not always be unethical to put the spectator through what in everyday life would have been an unethical experience. Obviously, this should not be taken to mean that in the (home) movie theatres all is allowed, but, like Claire Bishop in *Artificial Hells*, I believe that sometimes art is best considered an 'experimental activity' (Bishop 2012: 284) that has ethical norms that are different from the ones we would hope to find outside the movie theatre. It is not an experience that is detached from social and political concerns, but it is an experience whose relation to these spheres cannot be taken as one-to-one. The asymmetry of the relation is rich in potential because it allows art 'to communicate . . . the paradoxes that are repressed in everyday discourse, and to elicit perverse, disturbing and pleasurable experiences that enlarge our capacity to imagine the world and our relations anew' (Bishop 2012: 284). Wanting to reduce, or even abolish, the asymmetry will not only lead to a policing of the artistic sphere, but also to a reduction of the ethical potential of art.

The importance – and difficulty – of distinguishing between ethics inside and outside the movie theatre can be illustrated if we turn to von Trier's infamous press conference in Cannes 2011. After the world premiere of *Melancholia* (2011), von Trier himself seemed to forget this distinction and therefore came across as being far from the position I have associated with self-conscious humanism. Asked about his German family background, von Trier tangled himself up in the following infamous statement:

> The only thing I can tell you is that I thought I was a Jew for a long time and was very happy being a Jew, then later on came [Danish and Jewish director] Susanne Bier, and suddenly I wasn't so happy about being a Jew. That was a joke. Sorry. But it turned out that I was not a Jew. If I'd been a Jew, then I would be a second-wave Jew, there is kind of a hierarchy in the Jewish population . . . but anyway, I really wanted to be a Jew and then I found out that I was really a Nazi because my family was German, Hartmann. And that also gave me some pleasure. So, I . . . what can I say? I understand Hitler. I think he did some wrong things, absolutely, but I can see him sitting in his bunker. I'm saying that I think I understand the man. He is not what we could call a good guy, but yeah, I understand much about him and I sympathize with him . . . But come on! I'm not for the Second World War. And I'm not against Jews. No, not even Susanne Bier. I am very much for them. No, not too much because Israel is a pain in the ass . . . but still . . . How can I get out of this sentence? As for the art, I'm for Speer. Albert Speer I liked. He was

also maybe [not] one of God's best children, but he has a talent that it was kind of possible for him to use during . . . Okay, I am a Nazi. (Video clip on YouTube[9])

Rather than taking von Trier's capitulation at the end of these ramblings at face value, the remarks can be read as the director – unsuccessfully – trying to carve out a position in accord with the one I have found in *Dogville*. He is acknowledging the existence within himself of an inner bastard. But instead of sticking to the principle of using film to explore and trying to understand these destructive drives ('I think I understand the man'), he then introduces the more ambiguous idea of sympathy ('I sympathize with him [Hitler]') that was bound to produce the response we know. It can be said that von Trier's performance in Cannes fails to acknowledge the differences that exist between filmic provocations and the provocations allowed in a social setting such as a press conference. This failure is not entirely surprising: there is a performative aspect to a press conference, and von Trier has never been shy of performing for the press; nevertheless, on this occasion he clearly overestimated the freedom he had at his disposal (I will argue later that this also happens for Claire Denis in an interview about *Les Salauds* (2013)). In this manner the press conference shows the pull of provocation, it suggests how difficult it is for the provocative director to maintain a clear distinction between ethics inside and outside the cinema. Later that same day von Trier tried to put things right by issuing a statement explaining: 'If I have hurt someone this morning by the words I said at the press conference, I sincerely apologize. I am not antisemitic or racially prejudiced in any way, nor am I a nazi.' In this statement he also explained that in the press conference he had 'let himself be egged on by a provocation', but obviously, at that point it was all too late, and von Trier's self-imposed ban from journalists was the only sensible response.

1.2   ETHICS VIA THE BODY:
FUNNY GAMES, DAISY DIAMOND AND JACQUES RANCIÈRE

The analysis of *Dogville* aimed to deliver a fairly detailed account of the spectatorial manipulation that the *mise-en-scène* facilitates. I believe the film's key 'trick' is to create a very strong desire for catharsis in the spectator, and then to foreclose the satisfaction of this desire (effectively by 'satisfying' it in a way that is immediately mocked by the film). Thereby, we are made to consider this desire for catharsis; von Trier is creating a semi-ironic form of moralising that goes via the body to the intellect. Reduced to this account (and the catharsis formula I noted above: 'So you want catharsis? So you want catharsis? Here you have it! . . . Was that really what you wanted?') von Trier's film is not an isolated case in the contemporary cinematic landscape. As a route towards the broader question of spectatorial address, I would like to briefly mention a couple of comparable titles, in order to corroborate the claim that the manipulative feel-bad approach is not a phenomenon specific to von Trier; and eventually, to suggest that the manipulation can be done in different ways leading to different results.

One of the best-known and most studied examples of a didactic feel-bad film is Michael Haneke's *Funny Games* (1997). This film anticipates von Trier's by confronting the spectator with her 'inner bastard'. As most readers will know this is the 'story' of two sociopaths terrorising a wealthy family who have just arrived at their large summerhouse in the Austrian countryside. The film ends when the sociopaths have killed the three family members, and then move on to the family next door. The ambition of Haneke, as presented in numerous interviews, was to make an anti-violence film: a film that criticises a culture in which violence has become spectacle. To reformulate in terms that bring us closer to *Dogville* (without thereby suggesting that the films are 'similar'): Haneke is critical of the confusion between violence and pleasure. He wants to warn us against enjoying the destructive drives of the human psyche. He seeks to 'bring out the violence in the violence', and thereby make a film that decouples violence and pleasure.

As with *Dogville*, critics have often stressed the meta-filmic and Brechtian dimensions of *Funny Games*. At the same time, however, it is obvious that Haneke constructs an emotional terror machine that aims at the specta-tor's body before (and, at least as much as) her intellect. Even the so-called Brechtian moments of distanciation – for instance, when Haneke breaks the fourth wall by having the main character address the camera – might best be understood as instances of emotional manipulation. Whereas Brecht's tech-niques were intended to provide the theatregoer with a space (a critical dis-tance) in which to think for herself, Haneke's protagonist aggressively asserts his dominance by locking the spectator into a sado-masochistic relation. Like *Dogville*, *Funny Games* can therefore be considered an exercise in manipulation that works not only with Brechtian techniques, but also along the aforemen-tioned Artaudian lines: 'In our present degenerative state, metaphysics [or here "ethics"] must be made to enter the mind through the body.' This is the process that Haneke famously described as 'trying to rape the viewer into independence' (Haneke in Wray 2007).

Much has been written about Haneke's film, how he controls the spectator, and how successful he is in raping the spectator into consciousness. In this context, it suffices briefly to refer to Catherine Wheatley's excellent analysis in *Michael Haneke's Cinema* (2009). Wheatley argues that *Funny Games* (1997),

The Piano Teacher (2001) and *Hidden* (2005) all combine three overlapping frameworks: a '"benign" first-generation modernism', an '"aggressive" second-generation modernism', and a 'system of generic convention (including the use of stars) that allows for a minimal emotional engagement' (Wheatley 2009: 153). If we should try to specify these three categories, we could say that in *Funny Games*, Haneke's use of the long take forces the spectator to consider the actions depicted in a manner that could be associated with the first-generation modernism such as Italian neo-realism.[10] For instance, the murder of the son is followed by a ten-minute almost static shot of the devastated father, which gives us time to consider the magnitude of the tragedy.[11] The '"aggressive" second-generation modernism' could refer, for instance, to the aforementioned 'Brechtian techniques' (such as the address to the camera) that recall aspects of Godard's work from mid-sixties onwards. And finally – stepping out of the European Art Film – the play with generic conventions can, as Wheatley writes, be associated with the name of Kubrick whose *The Shining* (1980) is invoked from the opening bird's-eye shots of a car driving through the forests. The use of international stars – and the appeal of these stars – is more relevant for the remake, *Funny Games US*, than it is for the original.[12] But the main point of teasing out these three traditions is that the combination of (for instance) long takes, self-reflexivity and emotional investment will result in a film that brings out our desires, and gives us a chance to critically reflect upon the nature of these desires.

Even if I come to *Dogville* and *Funny Games* with a different set of references (Brecht and Artaud), I share with Wheatley the fundamental idea of an encounter between non-cathartic and more pro-cathartic traditions. To some extent *Dogville* could be analysed as a clash between the European Art Film and Hollywood; furthermore, there is little doubt that the casting of Nicole Kidman (and other famous actors such as Gena Rowlands, Ben Gazzara, John Hurt and James Caan in more peripheral roles) facilitates spectatorial investment. I also share with Wheatley the belief that this results in a tension – felt at the level of the spectator's body – that aims to engage the spectator in ethical reflections. Like von Trier, Haneke installs what I call a deadlock on catharsis. For *Dogville*, I have provided a catharsis formula; and such a formula can also be given for *Funny Games*. If we take into account the (in)famous rewind sequence,[13] Haneke's manipulative approach can be summed up with this sadistic formula: 'So you want catharsis? So you want catharsis? Here you have it! . . . No, I was just kidding: you are NOT going to get it!' Like von Trier, Haneke aims to frustrate, and make us confront our inner bastard.

A third and lesser-known example of a confrontational feel-bad film is the Danish director Simon Staho's *Daisy Diamond* (2007). Like von Trier and Haneke, Staho seeks to go via the body of the spectator, transforming the viewing experience into a physical ordeal. This time the aim of the exercise is not to bring out a destructive drive in the spectator, but rather to test our capacity for empathy. In its diegesis *Daisy Diamond* plays with fiction and reality, repeatedly 'deceiving' the spectator. Ultimately, this provokes the spectator to doubt the reality of what is being shown, thereby pushing us towards a cynicism that resembles the human relations the film criticises.

The plot revolves around a young, Swedish woman who lives alone with her baby in a housing estate on the outskirts of Copenhagen. Anna (Noomi Rapace) is desperately trying to make a name for herself as an actress, but her colicky daughter makes it difficult for her to fulfil these ambitions – Daisy, as the daughter is called, interrupts the auditions and her constant crying prevents Anna from learning the scripts she has been given. Everyone Anna encounters in the theatre and film industry takes advantage of her – not least sexually. The film begins on a low, and then continues downward until Anna has drowned her baby, become a porn actress, then a street prostitute, and finally – perhaps – dies.

Daisy Diamond is certainly a grim social film, but it is also a particularly exhausting play with fiction and reality, with the spectator's empathy. From the very first scene, we are thrown into what appears to be an abusive relation between a young male drug addict and his girlfriend; less than five minutes into the film we have a first rape scene. We then hear a baby screaming, and it turns out that the scene we have been watching was an audition, and that Anna's baby has just made it impossible for her to get the role. This play between auditions and diegetic reality is repeated so often that the spectator begins to hesitate about whether the events on screen are fictional or not. The spectatorial confusion is heightened by two more elements: throughout the film, scenes from Ingmar Bergman's *Persona* (1966) permeate Anna's world. She quotes long passages, watches the film on her television and has auditions that involve the original text; Staho films all these monologue-driven scenes in Bergman-inspired close-ups. The intertexual play with *Persona* is, as should be clear, more than just a gratuitous reference: *Persona* is also a film about madness, acting, sexuality and the mother–child relation. Not surprisingly it is therefore first of all nurse Alma's (Bibi Andersson) famous monologue on 'motherhood' that weaves its way into *Daisy Diamond*. The fact that Noomi Rapace speaks Swedish in an otherwise all-Danish cast further strengthens the reference to Bergman, helping to make of Anna the scrambling point between what the film presents as reality and what it presents as fantasies and rehearsals. Secondly, after she has killed her baby there are a number of scenes in which Anna hallucinates conversations with Daisy, negotiating questions of guilt and motherhood. Again, these scenes work to undermine a clear distinction between fiction and diegetic reality.

Figure 3   *Drowning Daisy?* (Daisy Diamond)

The result is a film full of extreme emotions (motherly, violent and sexual) that gradually threaten to detach themselves from the images. This culminates in the final scene when Anna sinks into the bathtub, seemingly ceasing to breathe. We are now caught between two radically different interpretations, and that undecidability very effectively puts a deadlock on catharsis: it is possible that Anna is playing dead for a camera-crew that is in the process of transforming her terrible life story into a successful feature film, that would finally give her the recognition she has been craving (but a recognition that comes at a price so high, that the spectator will not feel relieved); it is also possible that the story about the feature film is one last fantasy that Anna invented for herself before she slipped into the bathtub and took her own life.

In our context it is particularly interesting to note how the film uses intertextuality and self-reflexivity to create an extremely visceral form of filmmaking. As already mentioned in relation to *Dogville* and *Funny Games*, the form of self-reflexivity that the contemporary feel-bad film deploys does not move the film into a more detached and intellectual region. Most clearly, when the protagonist in *Funny Games* addresses the spectator directly, explaining that the horrors cannot end yet, because we are not at feature-film length, the effect is aggression, rather than traditional self-reflexivity and distanciation. Although, not quite as aggressive (and more obviously ironic), *Dogville*'s moments of more or less direct address to the spectator (such as the morphing dog) also further the antagonistic relation to the spectator rather than making the film fold upon itself. In *Daisy Diamond* this aggressive self-reflexivity is taken to an extreme. Staho exhausts his spectators by constantly soliciting strong emotional empathy. Sometimes the events turn out to be fictional, sometimes they are real, and in the end it is difficult to determine which are which. The result is a sado-masochistic play and a spectatorial Catch-22: crying wolf again and again, it is almost as if the director taunts us to give up on empathy (for how long will *you* keep on caring?) while at the same time satirising a society that is precisely lacking in empathy towards the young protagonist (when will you be just like them?).

Other contemporary European (and non-European) art films can also be described as assaultive, and many of these have attracted considerable popular and critical interest. Consider the films of Gaspar Noé. His first feature-length film, *I Stand Alone* (1998), contains many of the elements described above. For instance, we find a scene at the same time reminiscent of the 'rewind' sequence in *Funny Games*, and anticipating the confusion of diegetic reality and imagination we encounter in *Daisy Diamond*. In this scene Noé first shows a horrific incestuous rape, and then reveals that the scene was imagined, taking us back to the point before this phantasm/nightmare happened. Furthermore, the scene is introduced by another of these aggressive forms of direct address to the spectator that we have encountered several times now: the screen goes almost black – apart from a countdown warning us that we have thirty seconds to leave the cinema if we do not wish to see the horrors to come. One can also think of the beautiful, romantic and utterly pseudo-cathartic (and therefore non-cathartic) images at the end of the same director's *Irreversible* (2002). Because Noé tells this story in reverse chronological order, the spectator knows that the beautiful images of the pregnant Alex (Monica Bellucci) constitute the beginning of a horrific story of rape, extreme violence and murder. Therefore the beauty of these last images feeds the feel-bad experience, catching the spectator between the desire for these images to be the end of the story, and the knowledge that they are in fact the beginning.

In the third section, I shall return to a number of other confrontational films (that go through the body of the spectator to reach her intellect) in an attempt to further place this approach in intellectual history. For the moment, I would like to emphasise that these films all share an ethical ambiguity that results from what we might call their attempt to engage in a form of 'resistance by mimesis': the directors do exactly what they warn us against.[14] They work with aggression, coercion, manipulation and a 'lack of empathy'; they pull us into master–slave relations, and frustrate our desire for catharsis – but they do all this in an attempt to replace the master–slave relations with warmer, healthier, more empathetic and human relations. This paradoxical logic, having to do with the mode of address, merits further consideration.

Playing the master

Their mode of address is one of the most common objections to these assaultive films. Even if *Dogville* can be presented as a film that strives to make us aware that there are aspects of the human psyche that we must treat with caution, even if *Funny Games* can be seen as a film that warns against the tendency in our culture to entertain by combining violence and pleasure, and even if *Daisy Diamond* offers a critique of the cynical theatre and film indus- tries, and Staho ultimately insists on the importance of empathy, these sen- sible messages are delivered in such an aggressive and manipulative way that many spectators have felt the directors undermine the ideas they are trying to put forth. Many therefore continue to consider *Dogville*, *Funny Games* and *Daisy Diamond* as anti-humanist and cynical films. This question of the mode address is key to any discussion of feel-bad spectatorship; I shall approach it via Jacques Rancière's essay on *The Emancipated Spectator*.

In this essay, Rancière engages with the theorisations of Brecht and Artaud. He writes about the widespread tendency to oppose the two, but he also suggests that the opposition is so clear-cut that it necessarily rests upon a common foundation: the two drama-theorists both aim to produce an 'active spectator'. In order to activate us, they reduce the distance between stage and public, between actor and spectator. Artaud experiments with abolishing the scene, putting actors among the spectators, recommending that plays take place in a giant barn rather than in a theatre with a stage (a bit like in *Dogville*). Brecht famously invents techniques to break the fourth wall, he includes song and dance routines, uses film projections, and is inspired by the ways in which the public participates at boxing matches. Rancière does not deny that Artaud's spectator is emotionally, affectively active (Rancière talks about a 'vital participation'; Rancière 2009: 5), and that Brecht's spectator is generally a more intellectual being (a 'scientific investigator or experimenter'; Rancière 2009: 4), but the fundamental point is that both Artaud and Brecht agree to consider the traditional spectator as 'passive', and therefore bad, bourgeois and politically reactionary.

Obviously, these matters present themselves differently in cinema where ideas of participation, direct engagement and the creation of a living com- munity of spectators and performers are necessarily 'weaker'. However, there is little doubt that many contemporary film directors, not least the ones I am looking at here, and many contemporary film theorists (whether these are phenomenologically inclined and talk about hapticity and embodiment, or cognitively inclined and talk about mirror neurons and simulation theory) share the ambition of reducing the distance between film and spectator; they want to promote an active spectator. Indeed, one common way to present the field of spectatorship studies is to say that the contemporary theories share the resistance towards the Althusser- and Lacan-inspired theories of the 1970s which were said to rely on the idea of a passive spectator (for an overview, see Geil 2013). My reading of *Dogville* as a film that pulls Brecht and Artaud together, a film that is about the spectator (at least as much as it is about Grace), also fits this paradigm of the active spectator.

Rancière, however, is critical of this ambition to overcome the distance between actors and spectator. He does not believe in the dichotomies that structure many of these writings on theatre, film and participatory art.[15] Prime among these dichotomies are the ones that associate 'knowledge' with 'being active', and 'vision' with 'being passive'. Why, asks Rancière with very good sense, should it be true that a spectator who sits in her chair and *simply looks* is passive? Why should that form of distance be bad? Why does it need to be disturbed? Indeed, 'distance is not an evil to be abolished, but the normal condition of any communication' (Rancière 2009: 10). Why not have instead a spectator that operates like a reader in her armchair, or an interested museumgoer standing in front of a painting? This so-called 'passive spectator' is in fact very actively involved in finding her own way through the material presented, relating it to experiences that are proper to her. Obviously, Rancière's point is not that the spectator should be 'passive', but rather that the vocabulary of activity and passivity is misleading. Such dichotomies only serve to uphold certain power relations; they maintain the conventional allocation of places that the aesthetic experience can in fact work to disrupt.[16] Here we therefore begin to see that the more direct mode of address, prioritised by many contemporary film and theatre theoreticians, can be associated with interference, indoctrination and stultification rather than dialogue and freedom.

At this point, it is necessary to mention – as Rancière does – the context for the essay. The text responds to an invitation from the Internationale Sommer Akademie in Frankfurt. The Swedish performer Morten Spångberg had asked Rancière to think about the relation between contemporary theatre practices and an argument Rancière had delivered many years earlier in *The Ignorant Schoolmaster* (1987). In this book, Rancière presented the pedagogical thinking of the early nineteenth-century French university teacher Joseph Jacotot. Having been forced to leave the university in Dijon during the turbulent years at the beginning of the nineteenth century, ending up in the (at that time) Dutch-speaking university in Leuven (Belgium), Jacotot suddenly found himself in the situation of teaching French language to Dutch law students. Jacotot did not speak a word of Dutch, the students did not speak a word of French, but on the basis of a line-by-line reading of a bilingual edition of Fénélon's *Les Aventures de Télémaque* (1699), Jacotot nevertheless managed to teach the students French over a period of only two semesters. After this encouraging experience he expanded the experiment and successfully taught students a range of topics (mathematics, law, music) that he did not know himself, thereby developing a method that came to be known as 'universal pedagogy'. Two of the core principles in this method are emphasised by Rancière. First, there is the working assumption, the axiom, that intelligences are equal. Students can learn by themselves and by observing their peers; the role of the teacher is to make sure that they realise this, and then do their best. In fact, they learn more when the teacher is not a specialist trying to communicate her knowledge to the student, but instead limits herself to keeping the students to the task. Second, a book (or some other object such as a musical score) is required. It is important that students have something to work with, that they can compare, relate and contrast on the basis of the material they have been given, and also: something that can screen them from the professor.

The enemy of this form of pedagogical thinking (for Jacotot and Rancière) is the traditional 'explicative order', which Rancière also calls a 'method of stultification'. This is the method presupposing that a student needs a master (a teacher) who can explain what the student does not know. This form of pedagogy therefore begins by putting students in the position of not knowing. It is a system that works by explaining explanations ('I will tell you what is in the book that I asked you to read'), a system that can be expanded endlessly (the seminar leader will explain what the lecturer explained about what the book explained . . .), thereby constantly extending the distance between student and text, the very distance it set out to abolish. It is a system of power in which students do not learn to believe in their own intelligence and its emancipatory capabilities, where teachers possess all the knowledge, and students aspire – at best – to be like their teachers.

It is these ideas that Rancière largely accepts to import into his analysis of the theatrical situation. This explains his resistance to the ambitions of Artaud, Brecht and others who wish to communicate directly with the spectators.[17] For Rancière, direct address is not an ideal; the existence of a product (book, painting, film, a play up there on the stage) that mediates between the artist and reader – and also *protects* the reader from the artist – is key. It is via this object (which the spectator may receive in ways unexpected to the author) that the spectator has the possibility of setting herself free. The direct address, by contrast, is potentially dictatorial, overwhelming and frustrating. When someone *wants to* produce an active spectator, the response of the spectator is anticipated, and her field of response reduced. Ultimately, it is thus a question of politics and emancipation: the risk of theories such as Brecht's, Artaud's and – not least – their epigones is to consolidate the hierarchies of power they wish to oppose. Rancière therefore argues that the spectator who looks, thinks, relates and translates has more freedom than the active spectator that Brecht and Artaud want to set free. In other texts this leads him towards the cinema of Pedro Costa and Abbas Kiarostami, it leads him to see Straub and Huillet not simply as the cinematic inheritors of Brecht, but also as the directors who allowed cinema to move beyond the 'Brechtian paradigm' (Rancière 2008: 8).

It can be said that Rancière's response to the Internationale Sommer Akademie has a provocative edge. The invitation to the workshop (an invitation Rancière quotes) talked about theatre as a unique place because it allows the public to understand itself as a collective. This text relied upon well-known ideas about the theatre being particularly communitarian because of the co-presence of actors and public – their direct exposure to each other. To this Rancière responds with a stimulating polemic against a naïve celebration of theatre as presence and community, and, more generally, a welcome critique of the sometimes very ecstatic theorisations of the political potential of participatory and relational art (see also Bishop 2012).[18]

If we now link back to the assaultive films, it is obvious that the aesthetic encounters I described with the very sadistic catharsis formulae given above are radically different from the ideal that Rancière associates with emancipation. Indeed, these films offer precisely the form of aesthetic encounter that Rancière dislikes. This is the form of pedagogical stultification that starts from the position 'you – spectator – are not as sensible as you think you are! I will show you that I know more about you, than you do about yourself.' This is the director as puppeteer, perhaps even as a scornful master – a director who begins by installing the very hierarchies and oppositions that Rancière is seeking to remove. As von Trier says: 'What is important to me with a film is that you use an impeccable technique to tell people a story that they don't want to be told' (in Lumholdt 2003: 10). There is little doubt that it is precisely by playing the role of master that von Trier and Haneke alienate so many spectators.

In *The Five Obstructions* we could watch – from a safe distance – how this relation between von Trier (the puppeteer) and Leth (the test person) is played out. Here von Trier explicitly tells Leth 'I know you better than you know yourself', and then he takes on the role of master. But even if von Trier undoubtedly believes there is an element of truth in this claim, such hyperbolic statements also invite us to nuance the idea of von Trier as master. Indeed, an alternative, and in my opinion more accurate, reading of von Trier's work is to say that he performs the role of the master *as a role*. As a provocation. In so doing, he does not exactly undermine the moralising, headmaster-like position, but he plays it theatrically, and thereby introduces an element of self-irony (and ultimately, freedom) that a scornful master would not allow. In other words, we might say that von Trier pushes the master–slave relation to the point where it becomes theatrical, and thereby unstable. He moves away from the position of being the one who knows, and towards the position of being the one who plays at knowing. Another, perhaps simpler, way to formulate this is the one von Trier uses in *Tranceformer* (1997) when he states that 'a provocation has the purpose of making people think. If you make a provocation, you give people credit for having their own opinion about what happens.' The manipulations in *Dogville* therefore not only allow the spectator to engage with the 'inner bastard' in a more intimate way than otherwise possible; by so aggressively and ironically playing the master, the spectator might also think that the director saves the film from facile moralising, and opens up a self-ironising breach that allows the spectator to use her freedom.[19]

With *Funny Games* Haneke also runs the risk of alienating spectators, probably even more so than von Trier. He begins by assuming that we want violence and pleasure in a tantalising combination, and then tells us that we should not want it. But again, it can be argued that the moralising is undercut by a (self-)ironic stance. It is a paradoxical film and Haneke is obviously aware of this: 'I will create an experience so violent that it will put you off violence.' He hopes that spectators will walk out of his film, and has recently gone so far as to claim that only psychopaths would watch it to its end. It is therefore appropriate to modify the sentence that opened this paragraph: Haneke does not run the risk of alienating his spectators by adopting an aggressive mode of address, in fact he is aiming to alienate his viewers, hoping that this 'alienation' will stimulate reflections and debate. This being said, I believe Haneke is less inclined than von Trier to put the role of master into play.[20] And one may even feel that in the many interviews that tend to be included on Haneke's various DVD releases, he is too willing to hold on to the role of the explicatory master. With *Funny Games*, he does (to some extent) expose himself to the form of criticism that could extend from Rancière's text, which is that he locks spectators into a predetermined position of subservience.

But even if we think that Haneke occupies the position of master, we may still think that the feel-bad experience – when played out *in the cinema* over a running time of 108 minutes – can be justified. This is not a situation in which we have Haneke as a teacher; it is about being exposed to *Funny Games* in a movie theatre, and perhaps even about being prompted to think about the asymmetrical relations between art and pedagogy. Although Rancière has a very good point when he polemicises against certain dogmas about the emancipatory virtues of active spectatorship, this does not mean that the direct – and manipulative – address that we find in these films should necessarily be associated with stultification and reactionary politics. The shrewdness or aggressiveness with which these directors address the spectators (very often *playing with* the Hegelian master–slave dialectic) can stimulate wildly disparate responses in the spectators. So even if the films lie far from Rancière's ideal of moving beyond the active/passive dichotomy, some of these feel-bad films can be seen as ambiguous carnivalisations of master–slave relations, parodies of stultification.

As mentioned, it is logical to consider Rancière's response to the Sommer Akademie as polemical. However, I would rather argue that he is too generous. He effectively gives in to modelling his analysis of spectatorial relations on the pedagogical relation that he described in the fascinating story of *The Ignorant Schoolmaster*. But I do not think that the egalitarian relation between Jacotot and his students (in which there is no master – the presence of the text diffusing the authority of the master) should be used as a template for the aesthetic situation to the extent that *The Emancipated Spectator* suggests. Instead, my argument has been that when it takes place in the movie theatre the violation of the dialectic of recognition, and even the aggressive stultification, can pave the way for a number of experiences that possess an ethical potential. It is one thing to be told that under extreme circumstances we may all act unethically, it is another thing to *feel* – just for a moment (until the dog materialises) – the overwhelming satisfaction of seeing Grace destroy the town of *Dogville*. If von Trier needs to manipulate grossly and pull his spectator into a sado-masochistic relation to do so, then he should be accorded this freedom. However, this does not mean that in the movie theatre anything goes. In the last part of this chapter, I would like to consider a film that I find problematic, even if it is both effective and driven by a political agenda that I agree with: Brian de Palma's *Redacted*.

1.3   GOING TOO FAR? DE PALMA'S *REDACTED*

In his classic book about Alain Resnais, James Monaco begins the chapter on *Hiroshima mon amour* (1959) by highlighting his ambiguous sentiments towards Duras's and Resnais's film. Monaco has a number of reservations about the film, but he has come to the conclusion that the reasons why he does not like it are also the reasons why the film is successful on its own terms. He therefore writes: '*Hiroshima* is a closed system, impervious to judgment. It feeds on its faults. You may not like it, but it doesn't matter in the least' (Monaco 1979: 37). Brian de Palma's *Redacted* is very different from *Hiroshima mon amour*. But to some extent, the peculiar logic Monaco finds in *Hiroshima* also functions in *Redacted*: this is a film that thrives on its own deficiencies. The many elements that one might (justifiably) criticise serve to make this film a most unpleasant viewing experience; unpleasure is clearly what de Palma wants to produce. Whether this also makes de Palma's film 'impervious to judgment' is another matter (to which I shall soon return).

Redacted is based on the true story of a war crime that took place in March 2006 in Iraq. A group of five American soldiers raped a 14-year-old Iraqi girl before killing her and members of her family. Subsequently one of the soldiers who had been involved in the 'mission', but not in the act of rape, went to the authorities, the story made it to the press and eventually a scandal ensued. It is a film that has often been described as a companion piece to the earlier de Palma film *Casualties of War* (1989); and clearly, de Palma is aiming to emphasise that we have learnt nothing since 1969: *Casualties of War* was based on (a magazine article relating) a war crime that took place twenty years earlier, during the Vietnam War. A group of five American soldiers kidnapped a young Vietnamese girl, raped and killed her. Subsequently one of the soldiers who had been involved in the 'mission', but not in the act of rape, went to the authorities, the story made it to the press and eventually a scandal ensued.

Despite the obvious plot similarities, *Casualties of War* and *Redacted* are two very different films. The differences are worth mentioning because they can help us understand what separates the feel-bad film (*Redacted*) from the more conventional – but also emotionally exhausting – psychological drama of the Hollywood war film (*Casualties of War*).

Hollywood and feel-bad

Casualties of War offers a framed narrative, setting the events firmly in the past. Our hero, Eriksson (Michael J. Fox), is falling asleep on the bus, and his war memories come back to him. We see Eriksson in Vietnam, we see how his life was saved by his charismatic superior, sergeant Tony Meserve (Sean Penn), and how he later had to stand up to this very same superior when Meserve kidnapped and organised the collective rape of a young Vietnamese girl (Thuy Thu Le). We also see that eventually the crime is revealed and the soldiers punished. At the end of the film, Eriksson wakes up, gets off the bus, and has a short suggestive exchange with a beautiful Asian girl, who has also just stepped off the bus.

Throughout the film, we are provided with a focal point in the all-American boy Eriksson – Fox still relatively fresh out of the immense success of *Back to the Future* (1985) – who loses his innocence. Schematically, the film communicates two things. First, that war is an appalling mess in which young men and women (but the focus is firmly on the men) are having their lives destroyed and their moral values corrupted. Next, that some of us have a particularly strong inner moral compass. These heroic individuals (like Eriksson) can face up to a perverse military hierarchy, and eventually – here with the help of a priest – pave the way for justice being done. In this way, the critique of the military system is tempered by the same system's capacity to – ultimately – deliver the justice the courageous individual had been fighting for. All this is presented in the form of a cause–effect narrative, complete with the possibility of redemption for Eriksson as the beautiful girl he meets at the end of the film tells him that his bad dream is over. When she walks out out of the frame, Eriksson seems to realise that 'yes, it just might be over', and that the promises the girl embodies – beauty, love, life – may soon come true. The screen fades to black, and titles appear.

But this is not quite the end. After the title of the film, the names of the director, the main actors, the assistant director and the second assistant director, just before the second unit director – that is, at a point when many viewers will have left the cinema – a text appears on screen. It tells us that even if the film is based on a non-fiction text, it does not completely follow the real-life events. One of the squad members was *not* convicted; after a retrial his original confession was dismissed on constitutional grounds and he was acquitted. In other words, the film slightly alters the events to provide the spectator with a more complete closure than the one its poor sister – reality – had been able to give.

If *Casualties of War* is a film with Hollywood stars, a causal narrative, closure and a redemptive ending, then *Redacted* is not. It is a low-budget film with a traumatising ending, largely featuring first-time actors. Most importantly the film does not have a linear plot, but presents itself as a form of puzzle composed by images from various sources. There is footage from the war zone shot by one of the protagonists on his small DV camera; he is making a video-diary, which he plans to use for his admissions portfolio to the film school at the University of Southern California. Other images are from surveillance cameras and from the Internet – some of them in a YouTube format, some in a Skype format, and others from Islamist websites. We also have images that pass themselves off as television reportages from a French television station, and others from an Arab station. All these different forms of footage are associated with a specific point of view – on a couple of occasions it can be difficult to determine the source, but nowhere do we get a 'neutral', 'third-person' angle. In total, there are about fifteen different sources.

In a dossier that the *Cahiers du cinéma* devoted to the film (celebrating *Redacted* as the best film of 2007), de Palma stated: 'It's all out there! It only takes a click of the mouse to access these images! I have invented nothing' (de Palma in Burdeau 2008: 16). As such the film presents itself as a kind of *montage* in the more art historical sense of this term. De Palma is pulling material from different sources, combining, making constellations, and establishing his (and our) relation to the war via the confrontation between these various images. *Cahiers du cinéma* took up the challenge, went online and established an archive of source material in an attempt to demonstrate de Palma's point about how much he had been – to use his distinction – collecting rather than inventing.

In this sense de Palma's film could be said to operate along the lines of some of the artists recently analysed by the French art historian Georges Didi-Huberman. Didi-Huberman has, for instance, looked at the photomontages that Bertolt Brecht produced during the Second World War. While in exile, Brecht attempted to understand the desperate political situation by cutting and pasting various images, photographs from newspapers and magazines, then putting them together in his diary, in a work called the *Kriegsfibel* (*The War Primer*) ([1955] 2008) and in a number of unpublished picture albums. In this manner, Brecht sought to analyse the political situation, not in the linear way that prose writing thinks, but in the more embodied and proteiform way that a montage of images allows (writes Didi-Huberman in *Quand les images prennent position* [When images take a stand], 2009). To think in montages, Didi-Huberman therefore suggests, allows us 'to disarticulate our usual perception of the relations between things or situations' (Didi-Huberman 2009: 69). The montage aims to produce a new relation to reality, it pulls in the body of the spectator (we are the ones (re)establishing the relations) and thereby offers what Didi-Huberman describes as a sensorial and political re-*education* of the spectator. This pedagogical dimension of Brecht's montage project is underlined by the title of his volume: a *Fibel* is an introductory manual, and the word can refer more specifically to the sort of manual that children use to learn the alphabet. Alphabet books of the Fibel kind very often show letters acted out by bodies (Didi-Huberman's book contains beautiful examples of this). The *Kriegsfibel* thus pulls the adult towards the idea of enactive learning. In this sense Brecht's work with images is also the images' work with Brecht – and with the spectator of his montages.

Didi-Huberman mentions a number of filmmakers who operate in comparable ways. In *Quand les images prennent position* his two examples are Harun Farocki's *Bilder der Welt und Inschrift des Krieges* (1989) and Jean-Luc Godard's *Histoire(s) du cinéma* (1988–98) (more recently he has also written about Pasolini). In these films the directors are thinking their way through very complex questions about the place of film in relation to history and politics by combining archival images. These names also provide Didi-Huberman with the basis for a distinction between two different forms of montage thinking: the first comes close to the ideals of Rancière as the director seems to leave the scene, allowing the material to speak for itself in sometimes contradictory ways (this is Farocki); the second is a montage thinking where the directorial presence is much more clearly felt (this is Godard). Even if de Palma claims that the images are all there and that it is enough to combine them, he falls into the second category. As we shall shortly see, his presence is very strongly felt.

My point is not to present *Redacted* as an avant-garde work, or to say that de Palma's film is comparable to that of Godard. It is rather that the film's shocking nature partly comes from the way in which it works with this logic of the montage, combining elements, in a jagged way, and not bringing them together within a smoother narrative structure. It would be misleading to suggest that the narrative is resolutely non-linear, but we do jump from source to source, sometimes in accordance with a form of dialectic montage where scenes contradict each other, sometimes simply moving between unrelated moments. *Redacted* is a film about the war in Iraq, but it is also a film that formally embodies the war, playing discourses out against each other. It combines scenes of confession (video diary), news reportages, 'raw' footage of rape, and various rants on the internet . . . and it pulls the spectators into this violent confrontation between different image-sources without ever giving us time to settle. There is clearly a desire to work with the war of images, to intensify the conflicts, to make us feel shattered by being in the role of the witness, just like the film's protagonist.

As a consequence, watching *Redacted* becomes an extremely unpleasant experience. Whereas some montages invite us to playfully combine material that does not seem obviously linked, the experience of watching *Redacted* is one of being almost physically torn between images. There is no doubt that de Palma aims for this outcome. We may therefore argue that the reason *Redacted* feels so unpleasant is that the montages work to challenge the spectator's subjectivity by pushing us between opposing image sources that all lay claim to a truth about the war.

Epistemological feel-bad

The analysis given so far is very much in line with the one offered by de Palma himself (and supported by the *Cahiers du cinéma*). As I now move to a second part of my argument, I would like to emphasise that this first argument – which insisted on the unpleasant experience of being worked through by the montage of already existing images – is indeed central to the experience of watching *Redacted*.

However, this is *not* a found-footage film, nor does de Palma claim it is. The soldiers who committed the crime shown in the film were still on trial when *Redacted* was being made, and a lot of the source material (although often available on the Internet) could not be used for copyright reasons and for fear of legal action. Unlike Brecht, Farocki and Godard, this is therefore *not* a film that combines already existing images; it is a film that stages, then combines. It is something very different: a film composed entirely of *remakes* (including a remake of *Casualties of War*).

This allows de Palma to take a number of liberties. For instance, when he presents images that are framed as if we were watching a French television reportage about Iraqi cars arriving at a checkpoint, he suddenly films from the passenger seat of a car that is attempting to force its way through the roadblock. For the alert spectator, this breaks the illusion of the documentary nature of the images, but it also enhances the scene's dramatic dimension. There is no doubt that de Palma is aiming for this dramatisation and that he is willing to bring his 'documentary' images closer to the conventional action film in an attempt to further destabilise and assault the body of the spectator. We are invited to immerse ourselves in the images, before they pull us in opposing directions.

Another example of this dramatisation is found towards the end of the film, when the hero-protagonist McCoy (Rob Devaney) – who plays the character Michael J. Fox had played in *Casualties of War* – has returned to the US and gives a confessional speech to a group of friends. As he narrates the story of the rape, we suddenly have a non-diegetic soundtrack with music from Puccini's *Tosca* coming in under the emotional images, and then continuing into a slideshow that ends the film. It is obvious that de Palma not only collects the images, he 'interferes'. In this scene, viewers familiar with de Palma's voice will furthermore notice that at the beginning of the scene he makes his presence explicit by taking on the role of an off-screen friend shouting to McCoy: 'give us a war story!'

The most complex example of this tampering with the logic of 'it's all out there' can then be found in the slideshow that ends the film. This montage of still images is introduced with a title – 'Collateral Damage' – and a title card specifying that these are 'actual photographs from the Iraq War'. What follows is a series of horrific photographs: Iraqi bodies, victims screaming in pain, mutilated children. American media were not allowed to reproduce these images, but de Palma has simply pulled them off the Internet. And as in many of the other such slideshows about the war – which could also be found on the Internet – he has added a soundtrack of classical music (Puccini). The producers of the film, however, were worried that relatives of the victims might see the film, which could lead to court. Therefore the eyes of the victims have been redacted. This is not a gimmick by de Palma; he was strongly opposed to this redaction and felt censored. However, within this series of 'actual photographs from the Iraq War' de Palma includes *two staged photographs* that relate to incidents depicted in the film. He does not single these photos out as fictional, and if the producers had not redacted the documentary images by drawing black bars over the eyes of the authentic victims, the fabricated images – in particular the first of these – would have been difficult to distinguish from the rest. In the middle of the montage appears the body of a pregnant woman killed in a check-point scene earlier in the film (this is an actress), and as the very last image in the slideshow we find the staged photograph of the burnt body of the 14-year-old girl who was raped by the soldiers (this is a carefully crafted doll). This is the first time we see the corpse of the girl, earlier we only saw bloodstains on the floor of the house; de Palma clearly wanted this shocking revelation to be the last image in the film. So even if de Palma is claiming that he is simply combining what is already available, even if he is introducing the montage as 'real photos from the Iraq War', he is clearly working in a tradition radically different from that of Farocki. Indeed, it is hard to be further removed from Farocki: *Redacted* is an uneasy combination of staged images and a claim to authenticity.

At this point we are reminded of the slideshow at the end of *Dogville* (which I ignored in the earlier analysis). Five years before de Palma, von Trier had already finished his film with a series of documentary photographs, most of them from the Danish photographer Jacob Holdt's *Amerikanske billeder* (*American Pictures*) – a socially engaged 1970s photo reportage about American poverty. To this montage von Trier added a soundtrack of David Bowie's *Young Americans*. *Dogville*'s ending is at odds with the rest of the film. It creates a shift from the theatrical *mise-en-scène* to the photo reportage. It narrows down the critique that we have found during the previous two hours and forty minutes, pulling the spectator towards the anti-American reading and away from a more general investigation into the power and dangers of the inner bastard. Some viewers may appreciate this move from ethics to politics, arguing that the critique becomes more precise, more politically poignant. Other viewers (me included) will feel that this montage is at best unnecessary and reductive. Once again (as with the 2011 press conference), von Trier seems to be letting himself be 'egged on by a provocation', reducing the distance between the movie theatre and reality in a particularly problematic way. Nevertheless, in von Trier's film the end sequence *does* stand out: it not only introduces what is a very different pictorial universe, but also a very different musical universe from the one that has previously dominated the film (from Vivaldi to Bowie, suddenly the film rocks). In *Redacted*, on the other hand, the ending does not stand out. It can even be argued that it follows almost seamlessly from the film as a whole: the tension between documentation and fabrication dominates the film throughout, and this tension logically culminates in the concluding – and confusing – slideshow.

On the one hand, *Redacted* is therefore combining, confronting, thinking its way through material that is out there, and thereby reframing the war, as well as working on the body of the spectator. De Palma makes a strong claim to authenticity, the images represent reality, and it would be wrong to completely ignore this claim in discussions of the film. On the other, *Redacted* – to put it too generously – refuses to be restricted by any ethics of the authentic document. De Palma does not seem worried about manipulating the images at hand. And he also chose to fill some gaps in the narrative from Iraq by drawing on the Vietnam reportage that inspired *Casualties of War*. The result is a film that is difficult to take as fiction and is impossible to take as documentary. This produces a form of epistemological feel-bad. It becomes difficult for the spectator to find a footing and establish the terms on which to evaluate the film.

To clarify, I am not arguing that artists should have no freedom to play with the relation between fiction and reality. This relation can be established in many ways, and it can even be instrumental for raising the critical awareness of the spectator. However, if a director systematically works to blur the lines between fiction and reality, the argument for considering art as an 'experimental activity' with norms that are different from those found in everyday life is also weakened. My point therefore is that 'feel-bad' artists should be careful not to have their cake and eat it by taking advantage of the liberties that only the movie theatre affords while undermining the distinction between cinema and 'real life'.[21]

To illustrate the complexity of these questions of authenticity and manipulation, it is helpful to briefly consider the discussion of the acting in *Redacted*. Many critics agreed that this cast of unknown actors was *amateurish*. But what does this mean? A nuanced description could be found in Roger Ebert's review:

> The acting is curious. Some of it is convincing, and some of the rest is convincing in a different way: It convinces us that non-actors know they are being filmed and are acting and speaking slightly differently than they otherwise would. That makes some try to appear nicer, and other try to appear tougher or more menacing. That edge of inauthentic performance paradoxically increases the effect: Moments seem more real because they are not acted flawlessly. (http://www.rogerebert.com/reviews/redacted-2007)

This is a sensitive and accurate description of two forms of acting that can be found in *Redacted*. According to Ebert, the first is convincing in a conventional, professional way; the second is convincing in a non-professional way. Although he does not give these references, his description of the second form of acting invites comparisons with performances commonly found in reality television, on YouTube videos and in the selfie. But the ending of

Ebert's passage also demonstrates the problem the film poses for anyone who is keen to stick to criteria of verisimilitude and authenticity: now the 'inauthenticity' of the amateurish acting is said to produce something 'more real'. It can therefore be said that the film produces a clash between two regimes of 'authenticity' that cannot sit harmoniously together. This clash works to disturb and annoy the spectator; it works *because* it disturbs the spectator. Going back to the quote from James Monaco, I would say that in many scenes the acting is both poor and effective – effective, in part because it is poor.

Nowhere is this peculiar logic of 'feeding on its own inconsistencies' more apparent than in the already mentioned confession scene where McCoy narrates his experience of the war (including the rape) to his friends in a bar. The scene rings false at almost every level. The acting is 'curious' in the sense described by Ebert; de Palma adds a non-diegetic soundtrack to the home-video images, and he continues this soundtrack into the final slideshow; furthermore, the unconvincing story line has McCoy's friends applauding and shouting 'war hero' when he has told us the rape story. The scene ends with a close-up of McCoy's strained face (next to that of his girlfriend), a freeze-frame that gives us time to consider the artificiality of the whole set-up. However, the scene is still highly effective in so far as the curious combination of inauthenticity and the very forceful attempt to lay claim to the spectators' empathy only increases the destabilising effect on the viewer, ensuring that this becomes an extremely unpleasant scene.

There is no doubt that de Palma would object to this reading. When confronted with the widespread criticism of the acting, he responded with the argument he also used to counter other points of critique: *this is precisely how it is*, there is no inconsistency, this is how the soldiers act on the videos that can be found on the Internet. More generally, his view, as far as it can be reconstructed from interviews and other statements, is that the film gives the truth about the war. These are the images the American mainstream media have denied the general public, the reality on the ground: 'all these documents tell the truth' (in Burdeau 2008: 16).

The artist as warrior

At this point, let me introduce a short, thought provoking article by Boris Groys, first published in 2005 (reprinted in *Art Power*, 2008). This text, 'Art at War', can help to bring out the ethico-political ambiguities of de Palma's film more clearly.

Groys first presents what he describes as the widespread contemporary idea that artists and terrorists are rivals. Historically, 'the warrior did the actual fighting, and the artist represented this fight by narrating it or depicting it', the division of labour was well established and if anything the warrior needed the artist more than the artist (who could always choose another topic) needed the warrior. However, in recent times it has often been argued that the warrior (or the terrorist) no longer needs the artist, because he produces the images and the narratives himself. 'Bin Laden', Groys provocatively writes, 'we all know him in the first place as a video artist' (Groys 2008: 122). When we further consider that these terrorist videos are endlessly circulated, interpreted and recycled by the media, it would seem that there is little space for the contemporary artist to engage with war. The avant-garde artists – who have always worked along Bakunian lines ('creation is destruction') – may feel particularly marginalised, because they 'cannot compete with the terrorist in the field of radical gesture' (Groys 2008: 124). As Don DeLillo suggested in *Mao II* (1991): when it comes to the production of images and narratives, the radical artist has been outdone by the terrorist.

According to Groys, however, 'this very popular way of comparing art and terrorism, or art and war, is fundamentally flawed' (Groys 2008: 125). The reason is that avant-garde artists are iconoclasts. They shock and provoke by *attacking the image*. As Groys writes in a different essay ('Iconoclasm as an Artistic Device'): 'in the avant-garde, the image is – in both symbolic and literal terms – sawed apart, cut up, smashed into fragments, pierced, spiked, drawn through dirt, and exposed to ridicule' (Groys 2008: 70). In that process new icons are produced, very often exulting in the materiality of the image. The terrorists, on the other hand, are not iconoclasts. They seek to produce real, true images:

> The terrorist, the warrior is radical – but he is not radical in the same sense as the artist is radical. He does not practice iconoclasm. Rather, he wants to reinforce belief in the image, to reinforce the iconophilic seduction, the iconophilic desire. And he takes exceptional, radical measure to end the history of iconoclasm, to end the critique of representation. (Groys 2008: 125)

It is important to understand what Groys means when he is criticising terrorists' desire for the true image, their 'iconophilic desire'. He is not denying that the terrorist and counterterrorist images circulating in the contemporary mediascape have some 'elementary, empirical truth', but the question of empirical truth is not the main issue in the media. The function of these 'images of terrorism and counterterror' is to 'show more than this or that concrete, empirical incident; they produce the universally valid images of the political sublime' (Groys 2008: 126–7). This is what Groys calls iconophilia: the attempt to produce the real and true icons of the politically sublime.

To further explain this new desire for the 'icons of the politically sublime', Groys suggests that after many years dominated by the critique of representation, we are now willing to 'accept these photographed and videotaped images as unquestionably true'. This general move towards the 'acceptance of the icons' is therefore both a reaction to the earlier 'critique of representation' *and* the logical extension of this critique: the critique of representation 'was driven by a suspicion that there must be something ugly and terrifying hidden behind the surface of the conventional idealized image . . . the contemporary warrior shows us precisely that – this hidden ugliness, the image of our own suspicion, our own angst' (Groys 2008: 126). In that sense, the terrorist image-maker gives us exactly what we want.

Groys's response to the challenge of the new iconophilia is to go back a step and insist that the modern artist continue to investigate – and critically analyse – the image. Via Edmund Burke he emphasises that 'an image of terror is also produced, staged – and can be aesthetically analyzed and criticized in terms of a critique of representation' (Groys 2008: 127). Contemporary visual culture therefore has two tasks. The first is to oppose all forms of censorship; to oppose the sanitisation of the representation of war that is currently legitimised by arguments about the defence of moral values. The second is to analyse 'the use of these images of violence as the new icons of the political sublime', and to analyse 'the symbolic and even commercial competition for the strongest image' (Groys 2008: 128). Art is, Groys optimistically concludes, particularly well suited to do this task. The media cannot do it themselves because they are caught up in the proliferation of these images, they cannot step back, and they cannot avoid being tautological. But art can step back from our own present, it can historicise, take advantage of its institutional marginalisation, relate to the past and help to deliver the critical analysis.

Groys's arguments allow us to develop the analysis of *Redacted*. First of all it is clear that de Palma shares with Groys the ambition to oppose the censorship that seeks to sanitise the representation of war. He wants to show the images that the American mainstream media did not circulate – these images are out there, can be pulled off the web, and given to the American public. As such, we may consider de Palma's film as an attempt at what George Lakoff (2004) among others would call 'reframing': moving the terms of the debate, watching the war outside the parameters of embedded reporting. There is little doubt that this ambition partly explains why *Redacted* was met with a critical reception that included hysterical calls for de Palma to be deported as a traitor.

But does de Palma allow for the distance that Groys (like Rancière) clearly sees as a precondition for critique? I am not sure he does. As previously explained he pulls us in, heightening tensions, creating a film that 'embodies' war. But in addition to this, he also makes a claim about the truthfulness of his images – thereby destabilising the distinction that I have been insisting on between being inside and outside the movie theatre. Even if we have sympathy for his political agenda (and I do), the combination of emotional feel-bad and epistemological uncertainty may leave us sceptical.

Pushing the dialogue between Groys and de Palma a bit further, it is difficult to determine, for instance, if *Redacted* is iconoclastic or iconophilic: is de Palma delivering 'a critique of representation'? To some extent 'yes'. When playing different image sources out against each other, he is inviting a critical reflection on representation. But when he ends his film with a montage of photos introduced as 'real images', adding to these one of the most emotional passages from *Tosca*, and including the photo of a carefully fabricated wax doll of the burned rape victim without singling it out as fictional, it would seem that de Palma is, to reuse Groys's words, 'engaged in the symbolic . . . competition for the strongest image' (Groys 2008: 128). One might also wonder if the description that Groys gives of a contemporary shift from the 'critique of representation' to 'the acceptance of icons' (and perhaps even to a 'production of icons') is applicable to the case of Brian de Palma. In other words, when he mixes documentary photos and fabricated images, blurring the distinction between the two and confusing the spectator, it is tempting to conclude that here we have the case of a director who for so many years has been associated with a questioning of the image, an interest in the powers of falsification, manipulation and obsessional hallucinations, but who now engages in the production of an icon of the political sublime. In this way Groys's text provides us with a way to explain why this master of illusion – and of the critique of the indexical value of images and sound (*Blow Out*, 1981) – can suddenly insist so strongly on the reality and indexicality of his images. De Palma: 'If I want people fully to realise what is happening over there, well then, everything is there: it's there for them to see. We can only hope that this has an effect on them' (de Palma in Burdeau 2008: 12).

We can compare de Palma's strategy to that of Elem Klimov in the equally overwhelming *Come and See* (1985). Klimov's film is based on the Second World War memoirs of Alexander Adamovich, and focuses on the battles between German troops and Soviet partisans in Belorussia. For obvious historical reasons, *Come and See* does not consider the relation between war and mass media, but there are other good reasons to relate it to *Redacted*. Like de Palma, Klimov worked with a non-fiction source and cast non-professional actors in many scenes; his desire for maximum authenticity allegedly also meant that real ammunition was used during the *shooting* of the film. At the same time, Klimov's stated desire to 'recreate the sensual experience of war'

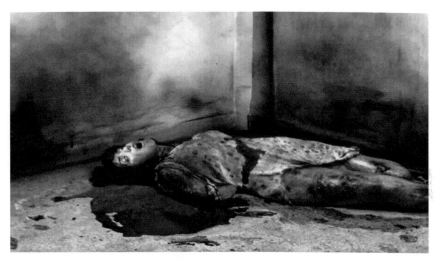

Figure 4 *An icon of the politically sublime? (*Redacted*)*

(in Chapman 2008: 103) resulted in a stylistically inventive film that contains scenes with subjective sound, rapid camera movements, unnaturalistic editing and many other kinds of formal experimentation. It is therefore not surprising that critics have emphasised both the documentary nature of the film and its nightmarish, surreal quality: its 'unreal realism' (Goodman in Chapman 2008: 203).

The combination of documentary aesthetics and avant-gardist experimentation can be said to culminate at the end of the film when the 12–14-year-old protagonist, Florya, finds a photograph of Hitler on the muddy ground. He loads his rifle, fires at the photograph, and sets off a montage of archival footage; after further shots, this montage begins to play in reverse. We see Hitler at his peak, airplanes seem to suck up bombs from the ground, buildings suddenly rise from the ruins, the Nazi army marches backwards out of the images; we recede further into history, witnessing Hitler's ascent to power in reverse, the First World War . . . Florya keeps shooting while Klimov cuts between the archival footage and close-ups of Florya's face. The scene ends when Florya has shot his way back to an image of baby Adolf sitting on his mother's lap; Florya hesitates, but decides not to shoot.

This scene can be (and has been) read in many ways, but it is safe to say that Klimov does not seek to let the archival documents speak the truth. Instead it can be argued that this very obvious form of visual manipulation serves to unravel the conventional historical narrative and instead produce a speculative, counterfactual scenario: if given the chance, would you (would Florya) have killed baby Hitler? Such a free – and fictionalising – approach to documentary images differs greatly from the approach of *Redacted*. Brian de Palma's attempts to provoke the spectator never lead him to give up on indexicality; unlike Klimov, he does not veer towards 'unreal realism'. Even if he *does* interfere with the (web-)archive when he produces his remakes, neither his film nor the many interviews relinquish the claim to reality. Instead de Palma insists on the absolute and very questionable distinction between collecting and inventing: I am collecting, not inventing.

I formulate this critique with caution because there is a risk of overstating the importance of the two fabricated images in the final slideshow and the manipulative dimension of the many remakes. It is worth noting, however, that when de Palma talks about the film in the quotations above, and when the *Cahiers* critics celebrate this film as the beginning of a new era for cinema, they are using the precise arguments that Boris Groys criticised. For example, in his review of the film – a text simply called *Là* (*There*) – Emmanuel Burdeau writes that *Redacted* 'marks the end of one rhetoric and the beginning of another. We will no longer search for the images under the images, we catch those that fly by' ('nous attrapons au vol celles qui se présentent'; Burdeau 2008: 10). In this bewildering text, Burdeau also talks about 'images zéro', completely setting aside that *Redacted* is a montage of *remakes* (some of which have been blatantly dramatised). Instead the critic excitedly concludes that 'finally the image returns to the realm of the real. What a liberation' (Burdeau 2008: 11).[22]

Ultimately, it is a question of how willing we are to let emotional manipulation combine with epistemological uncertainty. In this book, I am arguing that we should allow for different ethical standards depending on whether we are inside or outside the movie theatre; much too often we do not, and that reluctance to let art work in an area beyond (Hegelian) recognition can be ethically problematic (as argued by Kristeva: it is problematic if we suddenly have no means to think the complexities of the human psyche). Von Trier's manipulations and games stimulate ethical thought, even if they set out in a violence against the (Hegelian) ideal of recognition, and therefore initially appear anti-humanistic. However, this argument obviously rests upon the ability to distinguish between what is 'inside the theatre' and 'what is outside', between fiction and reality. The case of von Trier's press conference demonstrated the difficulty of maintaining this distinction, but de Palma's film and his slideshow in particular bring these problems into the cinema (*this* is the epistemological uncertainty). There is little doubt that this is precisely what this complex and fascinating film is aiming for, and that it thereby becomes more unpleasant. It not only provides us with an example of a visceral anti-war film stimulating our desire 'to get out of there', it also makes a claim to reality, while keeping the manipulation going. Some might say that this only educates us into being critical. However, this does not seem to be the ambition. What rather appears to be the case is that de Palma is trying to outdo manipulative image makers on their own terms, confusing reality and fiction, all the while claiming to be in the field of the real. This, I believe, is a way of taking spectatorial manipulation one step too far.

NOTES

1. Grace's status as an ambiguous victim is one of several good reasons to compare her with the Marquis de Sade's *Justine*. Indeed, von Trier himself has pointed out this parallel.

2. This is not the place to analyse the humour and self-mocking that can be found in so many of von Trier's films (since the time of the television series *The Kingdom*, in particular). Nevertheless, I believe that this is one of the most neglected aspects of von Trier's work, and this neglect sometimes leads to a misrepresentation of his work. Other aspects of this self-ironical play in *Dogville* can be found in the film's engagement with various genres: noir (Grace as femme fatale), gangster and vigilante (I shall return to this); and for almost everyone involved this will turn out to be a nightmare – set on Elm Street.

3. At the point of introducing Artaud and Bataille, let me clarify that I am not arguing that von Trier consciously borrows from either of these two authors. The logic I am about to describe (a logic that links immersion, transgression, catharsis and emancipation) can be found in many of the texts we associate with twentieth-century avant-garde art, and the reader may therefore prefer to substitute *avant-garde* for *surrealism*. If I have chosen to prioritise Artaud and Bataille (and not Jerzy Grotowski or *Tel Quel*, for example), it is because their ideas about art, theatre, cruelty, sacrifice and their interest in the Marquis de Sade seem particularly relevant to the study of *Dogville*. The reference to Artaud and surrealism is not – I should add – entirely original in von Trier criticism (see for instance, Murray Smith (2003), Linda Badley (2010) and Angelos Koutsourakis (2013)).

4. One of the clearest indications of this common ground between von Trier and the unorthodox surrealist thinkers is their shared interest in sacrifice. Unfortunately, I cannot offer a detailed discussion of this theme in the present context (it will return briefly in Chapter 3), but it is well known that this is a crucial theme in the work of Bataille – and of von Trier (most explicitly in *Images of Liberation* (1982), *Medea* (1988) and his 'Gold Heart' trilogy (*Breaking the Waves* (1996), *The Idiots* (1998) and *Dancer in the Dark* (2000)) (see also Bainbridge 2007: 15)).

5. In fact, Leth is closely associated with the Danish avant-garde. However, this is the more cool, minimalist neo-avant-garde of the 1960s, not the transgressive avant-garde that we find in the 1920s and 1930s. I shall return to these distinctions in Chapter 3.

6. Angelos Koutsourakis's recent monograph *Politics as Form in Lars von Trier: A Post-Brechtian Reading* (2013) offers the most systematic and extensive reading

of the relation between Brecht and von Trier to date. It also includes a section about the parallels between Brecht and Artaud (Koutsourakis 2013: 37–43). Despite the sophistication and intelligence of Koutsourakis's arguments for the thoroughly Brechtian dimension of von Trier's work, I still believe Brecht would have been sceptical about the manipulation that takes place in *Dogville*. It can be argued that von Trier ends up in Brechtian territory when he has pushed the spectator to respond critically to his inner bastard, but the *way in which* this goal is achieved seems to me at odds with a Brechtian tradition. To reach his goal, von Trier is inviting identification and exploiting the spectatorial desire for catharsis.

7. When I cite non-English texts (as I do here), translations are my own.

8. For instance, I strongly disagree with Horsley when he describes von Trier as a filmmaker who is 'militant and austere, perhaps the most austere filmmaker that ever was' (Horsley 2005: 12).

9. http://www.youtube.com/watch?v=QpUqpLh0iRw, last accessed 25 August 2013

10. As John David Rhodes argues in an excellent short article on Haneke, Bazin and the long take, there very often is a coercive dimension in the long take: 'The *freedom* that Bazin relishes in neorealist cinema (and in the cinema of Welles and Renoir) is actually a *coercion* to discern, to judge, to interpret' (Rhodes 2006: 19).

11. For an in-depth analysis of the central role of this scene see Brinkema 2014.

12. In 2007 Haneke remade the film for the American market, moving the action to the US and replacing the original cast with well-known English-speaking actors (*Funny Games US*). Although Haneke stressed how meticulous the reconstruction of the original had been (for instance, he went out of his way to find a pair of trainers that had been used in the original version), this change of cast resulted in two very different films: by replacing the excellent actress Susanne Lothar with the excellent movie star Naomi Watts, Haneke introduced a sexual, scopophilic dimension into the remake that had been largely absent from the Austrian version.

13. After having been tortured and terrorised, the mother of the family finally manages to grab a rifle from her tormentors and shoots one of them. The other tormentor knocks her back into an armchair, picks up a remote control, and rewinds the film to the point just before this cathartic release. The action resumes, but when we get to the point where the mother tries to snatch the rifle, the tormentors react so quickly that she fails.

14. Michael Haneke would disagree: he underlines that no violence is shown in *Funny Games*, and that the film is very different from the films he criticises. This is obviously true, but I am focusing on the experience of the film, and this experience is as violent as anything criticised by Haneke.

15. It is hardly surprising that Rancière dislikes *Dogville*. In *Aesthetics and Its Discontents* (2004) he offers a brief analysis of *Dogville* and Clint Eastwood's *Mystic River* (2003) in order to deliver a general critique of the ethical turn in the humanities. This analysis of *Dogville* is radically different from mine, as Rancière does not write about the *mise-en-scène* and how the film positions the spectator. He con-

cludes his analysis with what I think is a complete misreading of the film, arguing that von Trier's message should be that 'you can only retribute evil with evil' (Rancière 2004: 147).

16. This is not the place for an in-depth account of Rancière's 'partage du sensible', how the aesthetic experience can help us rethink politics. On this topic, see Geil's excellent article: 'The Spectator without Qualities' (2013).

17. To some extent Rancière is polemicising against a Brecht/Artaud tradition rather than against Brecht and Artaud themselves. He has written about Brecht in many texts, often in much more positive terms.

18. A later essay in the collection – 'The Paradoxes of Political Art' – explicitly takes issue with Nicolas Bourriaud's attempts to think the aesthetic experience as 'active forms of community' (Rancière 2008: 77).

19. This self-ironical play reached a (temporary?) high point in the recent *Nymphomaniac* where von Trier repeatedly quotes and mocks his previous films: he includes an *Element of Crime*-like opening scene, repeats (and distorts) *Breaking the Waves*'s idea of a husband asking his wife to engage in sexual relations with other men, and, most obviously, delivers an ironic reworking of the opening scene from *Antichrist*. He also plays with his own public persona by featuring discussions that respond to the common criticisms of von Trier being misogynist, racist and anti-Semitic.

20. This willingness to leave the directorial reins to someone else can be found in many places in von Trier's work; for instance with the creation of the so-called automavision for *The Boss of it All* (2006). The most extreme example must be *The World Clock*; an installation and theatre performance in which actors in Copenhagen were supposed to act in accordance with the activities of an ant colony in the Mexican desert.

21. Precisely how to find the proper balance between reality, fiction and the provocation of the spectator is difficult to say, and I shall make no attempt to offer a general theory about this. The problem will return in the coda following the next chapter as we consider Ruben Östlund's *Play* (2011). Most of the films analysed in this book, however, are heavily stylised works that do not make a claim to reality in the way de Palma's does.

22. In the original: 'L'image réintègre enfin la patrie du vrai. Grande libération'.

CHAPTER 2

Unease

2.1 BUYING A BUNCH OF RADISHES? VAN SANT'S *ELEPHANT*

The first chapter focused on a series of films in which the director established an oppositional relation to the spectator. In many of these films the director was aiming to tell the spectators something that they supposedly did not want to hear. This particular stance explains why it was possible to sum up in small (and schematic) formulas the directors' confrontation with the spectators. It also explains why the analysis of the films led to Rancière's critique of the stultification that the traditional pedagogue performs: these directors are not ignorant schoolmasters, but appear instead as all-knowing masters. However, as suggested in the discussion of Lars von Trier, things can be more complex and paradoxical than that. Rather than simply embodying the all-knowing master, thereby producing a form of 'authoritarian fiction' (Suleiman 1983), von Trier, in particular, tends to *play* the role of the master in a more ironic manner. This irony does not reduce the manipulative nature of his films, but it opens a breach in the didactic discourse, inviting us to implicate the director in the critique the film delivers. I do not think that something similar can be said about Simon Staho's or Brian de Palma's films; Haneke, however, does have a dry irony – so dry that in the violent climate of *Funny Games* it can be overlooked.

The films that take centre stage in this second chapter speak from a very different directorial position. They are much less direct in their confrontation with the spectator, they produce unease and disturbance in a subtler manner, and they even contain an element of seduction. Both of my key examples are heavily aestheticised films, and are therefore often pleasing to the spectator. As a result of this more oblique approach, these films produce varied responses. To some viewers they might be beautiful and sad, others might find them uneventful and disappointing, and still others might find them hugely offensive, not least on ethical and political grounds. I shall maintain that they belong to the feel-bad category in so far as they appeal to the spectator's desire for catharsis, only to refuse it. As mentioned earlier, my primary examples in this chapter will be Gus Van Sant's *Elephant* (2003) and Lucile

Hadzihalilovic's *Innocence* (2004). In both examples, we wonder what the director is aiming for, and – in the case of *Innocence*, in particular – we wonder how far we wish to follow her.

Being elephant

It is well known that *Elephant* is a film loosely based on the Columbine High School massacre, a school shooting in which Dylan Klebold and Eric Harris killed twelve of their fellow students and one teacher. The massacre took place in 1999, and was just one of eight North American high school shootings in the period between 1997 and 1999. Van Sant's film was the second major film about Columbine. In 2002, Michael Moore had released his documentary *Bowling for Columbine*, provoking much debate. Moore's film, to which I shall return, was awarded the Golden Palm in Cannes. *Elephant* was originally a television project for HBO (this is one reason it was shot in a 4:3 format), but the project developed into a feature film that premiered in Cannes one year after *Bowling for Columbine*. Van Sant won both of the most coveted prizes: best film (Golden Palm) and best director (leaving Lars von Trier a bit disappointed that only Nicole Kidman picked up one of the major prizes for *Dogville*).

Dealing with a major national tragedy, *Elephant* was under scrutiny from the beginning. Van Sant approached the difficult task from the point of view of the protagonists of the traumatic event. His film seemed to start out from the questions: What is it like to be a student in an American high school? Can I put myself in the mental shoes of the teenagers? Can I thereby begin to understand why an event like Columbine could happen? It addressed these questions via the establishment of a particular perceptual universe offering the spectator an experience of embodiment. *Elephant* is a formalist and minimalist film (just like *Dogville*), a film that is not only difficult to watch because of the harrowing events it engages, but also, quite literally, because it is difficult to see and hear. One might say that the film thrives on provoking our phenomenological desire ('can I know what it feels like . . .?') and our cognitive apparatus ('can I understand the mindset . . .?'). As will soon become clear, this does not mean that the film mocks these frameworks; on the contrary, they are among the ones it most logically engages. But the specificity of the *Elephant* experience comes partly from the fact that the film invites the spectator to share a bodily experience in the search for an explanation – while at the same time frustrating the desire we have to occupy the position of the teenagers and understand their experience. My contention is that Van Sant is aiming for this frustration, and that he thereby brings the viewer to the point where she no longer knows what to think, what to feel.

In the following analysis I will explain why this is the case, beginning with a description of the *Elephant* experience.

Approximately seven minutes into the film we encounter Nathan (Nathan Tyson), the handsome boy in the school. This happens in a typical scene that has attracted a fair amount of critical commentary (see for instance, Backman Rogers 2012 and Boillat 2011). The scene is composed of only two long takes: at the beginning of the scene Nathan interrupts his football practice, and for the next eight to nine minutes the camera tracks him from the back as he walks from the training ground to the school, through its many long corridors, before meeting his girlfriend Carrie (Carrie Finklea).[1] This non-eventful scene (shot in a style inspired by Béla Tarr's *Sátántangó* (1994)) is a good example of the *Elephant* experience. Let me begin with the use of sound.

The soundtrack is dominated by Beethoven's 14th piano sonata, opus 27 no. 2; the piece known as the *Moonlight Sonata* (a name given by the music critic Ludwig Rellstab, not by Beethoven himself). In other passages Van Sant uses the equally famous *Für Elise*, also in a minor key. These are two of the best-known piano pieces by Beethoven, and they are obviously rich in connotations. They are exceptionally beautiful, and a part of their beauty has to do with their ability to marry calm and tension. They are also well known to the point of being commonplace. Both pieces play with repetition and can therefore be related to the overall narrative structure of the film (more about this shortly).

The *Moonlight Sonata* is overlaid with diegetic and non-diegetic sounds eating away at the piano music. No music was composed for the film; instead Van Sant and his sound designer Leslie Schatz combined already existing material. For this particular scene they use a composition by the sound artist Hildegard Westerkamp, appropriately named *The Gates of Perception* (*Türen der Wahrnehmung*, 1989).[2] They also include excerpts from a recording of Allen Ginsberg reading aloud, and they manipulate a number of diegetic sounds from the school – voices, music and noises. Apart from the sonata, these many sounds are barely audible (few spectators will recognise the recording with Ginsberg, for instance) and the result is a muted and multi-layered sound design in which no element really stands out. We have the impression of hearing everything from beneath a bell jar: a guitar-playing student, some distant church bells, the voice of a teacher in a classroom, noises from trains, some hip-hop dancers . . . the sounds Nathan traverses all remain 'out there', disconnected from him, often with no obvious diegetic motivation. Therefore the sounds do not allow a clear sense of positioning, a distinct awareness of his and our bodily position. In addition, Van Sant recorded (muffled) sound with three different microphones at the same time: one at the feet of the characters, another at the head and a third above the heads. All of this makes it difficult for us to place ourselves in the images – and more generally, in the universe the film is establishing.

Forty minutes after this early scene, we discover that the *Moonlight Sonata* and *Für Elise* are the two pieces that Alex, one of the killers, practises on the piano. This gives the music in this early scene a semi-diegetic character – retrospectively (retro-acoustically?) it is *almost* possible to imagine that Alex is playing in this sequence. The suggestion seems to be that the mental universe of the killer is bleeding into the film: this is a claustrophobic universe. But not quite – the pianist we hear in the early scene is, after all, more professional than Alex.

We can therefore say that the manipulations with sound allow for a blurring of perspectives. The sound is associated with the perspective of Nathan since he is the one walking past the hip-hop dancers, the open classroom from which we hear bits of lecturing, the guitar-playing student, and so on; it is also associated with Alex since he is the one who practises these piano pieces;[3] and it is associated with a third perspective we could call 'Gus Van Sant' and 'the spectator/listener' – the one (in)capable of bringing these different layers together. Instead of using sound to anchor the images, as is generally the case in narrative cinema, Gus Van Sant works with an ungrounding of the characters and the spectator via the sound design.

All these elements (beauty, multiple perspectives, blurring, the feeling of being unanchored) can also be found in the visuals. There is very little depth of field in Van Sant's images. Only at a very specific – and reduced – distance does the outside world come into focus. For the most part we are given a 'myopic perspective' that leaves the background amorphous. This is done throughout the film, including during the last ten to fifteen minutes when we follow the killers in the corridors, shooting away at sometimes very indistinct body shapes that are trying to get away. The myopic perspective is one reason why the interplay between images and sound design takes on such an important role: because we cannot really see, we listen. But the listening, as already explained, only furthers the destabilisation, sending us back to the blurred images in search of a stable ground that is nowhere to be found. In this circular manner sound and image work together to produce the ungrounding.

Another characteristic of the cinematography is the combination of a subjective point of view with the long takes. Van Sant does not jump between different perspectives – at least not as quickly as most films do. He rarely bridges the distance between the characters via shot reverse shots, for instance. Instead he divides the film into different sections, so that at regular intervals we have a title card with the name of a student (or a group of students), whom we then mainly follow around. Because these long takes go hand in hand with the lack of depth of field, and with the subjective camera angles, they work to separate characters: there is no interaction between the characters, they each belong to their private universe.

But even that may be too much: do the teenagers really belong to their own universes? Rather, they seem to float around. As mentioned, this feeling has to do with the sound design and the blurs, but it also comes from the manipulations with tempo. Van Sant includes slow-motion and fast-forward sequences that lift the characters out of a more conventional time/space matrix. The same could be said about the recurrent images of the clouds moving across the sky. These shots have been interpreted in many ways: Van Sant himself suggests that 'it is almost as if the weather was responsible', and some critics have associated the sky with a post-9/11 sense of doom: when will the aeroplanes appear? (see Bouquet and Lalanne 2009: 154). However, it also makes sense to consider these brief interludes with moving clouds as a subversive take on the conventional establishing shot: rather than grounding the action in a particular setting (as an establishing shot would do), Van Sant leaves actions, characters and spectators floating in the air.[4]

A last important dimension that needs to be mentioned from the outset concerns the narrative structure of the film. *Elephant* does not progress in a linear way. A first interruption is found eight minutes into the film, where the alert spectator will notice that the film is 'looped'. We 'rewatch' an episode that we had previously seen from the perspective of a different character (something that again creates distance between characters). As the film continues, the loops become more easily identifiable. Again, this narrative technique adds to the disorientation. We suddenly realise that – temporally – we were not where we thought we were; and that we no longer know exactly where we are. These manipulations give the film a labyrinthine character that mirrors the space of the school corridors, where we also lose our way.

In cognitive film studies, there has been a lot of interest in 'puzzle films' or 'mind game films': works such as Christopher Nolan's *Memento* (2000), inspired by a text by Antonio Damasio; Michel Gondry's *Eternal Sunshine of the Spotless Mind* (2004); and Nolan's *Inception* (2010). These all engage in very sophisticated manipulations with time and narrative structure. *Elephant* is different: Gus Van Sant is also interested in time, in consciousness – and to some extent his film does have a puzzle character. But in *Elephant* there is little narrative to sort out. This film is not about piecing events together in order to understand what happened. Quite the contrary, we know what happened, and it seems there is no way to put the pieces together. It is thus a film moving away from narrative and time. Nathan's walk, significantly, is framed by two identical shots of the headmaster looking at another teenager, John (John McFarland), in a patronising way. This clearly communicates that even if Nathan has been walking for nine minutes, we have not progressed. But it is important to add that the move away from narrative progression does not take us towards stasis. It would be more accurate to say that there is nothing but movement. Kinesis, but no progression. Like clouds across a sky.

It is thus clear that Van Sant is working very carefully with a number of relatively simple but highly effective stylistic devices that allow him to create a singular perceptual experience. But what is he aiming to achieve?

Whose consciousness?

Van Sant does not seek to make a psychological or a sociological film, at least not in the conventional sense of these terms. There is no expressive acting by this cast of mainly non-professionals, which Van Sant found in some local high schools, there are no probing close-ups (in many scenes we do not even see the faces of the teenagers), and there is no revealing dialogue (large sections of the dialogue were improvised, and some of it is barely audible). He does allude to the various socio-psychological explanations of the tragedy that were presented at the time – the killers watch a programme about Nazi Germany (but they do not pay attention), they play a first-person shooter game, one of them gets bullied in school, several parents are depicted as irresponsible – but these different psychological and sociological explanations are cited as if mainly to be robbed of their explanatory power.

It is tempting to argue that this is an epistemological film in the sense that it attempts to make us perceive from a different point of view, and as already mentioned this particular point of view is commonly associated with the mind-set of the teenagers. Van Sant is allowing us to experience how they do *not* really interact, how they do *not* belong. Their everyday lives resemble a labyrinth in which they are lost – one of the students even wears a t-shirt with a Minotaur! They cross paths, but all seem to be living under a bell jar. Van Sant creates a 'structure of feeling' (Raymond Williams) that resembles a form of existential jet lag: a particularly unanchored way of being in the world, in which you are no longer sure about the limits of your subjectivity but seem to be floating between a position as subject and object. Presumably, such relations, such a structure of feeling, are among the reasons why the tragedy could occur?

In an interview with Amy Taubin for *Film Comment*, Van Sant, using a slightly different vocabulary, emphasised the importance of this experience of non-connection:

> I find it interesting that there's one thing no one has mentioned about the film. The thing you're actually watching all the time is a dislocation and a non-connection. It's visible, it's in the representation. It's what the film represents.

The connections aren't there between the students or between the students and the authority figures. It's all askew and whacked out. I tend to think our life is like that, and that's why I think the answers lie within us. (Van Sant in Taubin 2003: 33)

This reading can be developed along Merleau-Pontian lines: 'cinema shows us thought through gestures' (Merleau-Ponty 2011: 335), or we can speak in the phenomenological–cognitivist language of Vittorio Gallese and Michele Guerra and argue that the film offers the spectators an exercise in 'embodied simulation' (Gallese and Guerra 2012). Obviously, the specificity of this particular experience of embodiment is that we are invited to share an experience of *dis*-embodiment, but after all, disembodiment is also a form of bodily experience. This is a universe that contemporary phenomenology and cognitive theoreticians are trying to think with notions such as hapticity, affectivity, mood, and various concepts exploring what is called lower-level consciousness. To indicate how much the film depends on the particular phenomenological experience, it is helpful to compare it to one of its sources of inspiration: *Elephant* (1989) by the British director Alan Clarke.

Clarke's *Elephant* is a forty-minute television film about IRA revenge killings in Northern Ireland. This is another minimalist film with virtually no dialogue; the camera simply follows the characters. It consists of eighteen murder scenes composed in a deliberately repetitive way: typically the camera is placed just behind a man, and it then follows him as he walks through corridors or other nondescript spaces; he then encounters some other person, and either shoots him or gets shot. It is clear that Van Sant has been impressed by the extensive tracking shots and he often films from the same angle as Clarke did.[5] Nevertheless these two *Elephants* are completely different animals. In Clarke's film there is no out-of-focus cinematography – the images are sharp. The footsteps, the banging of doors, the gunshots can all be clearly heard, and we find nothing like the muted and disharmonious sound design of Van Sant's film. In comparison with Van Sant's *Elephant*, it is as if the bell jar has been lifted: Clarke wants to make evident, make us feel that a catastrophe is ongoing in Northern Ireland. He films with a desire to make the spectator confront – head-on – a problem that no one is dealing with: the 'Elephant in the room'. If we simplify a bit, we can say that in comparison with Clarke, Van Sant blurs all sounds and images – the result is a radically different film, also ethically and politically (I shall return to this).

All this being considered, it must nevertheless be said that the above interpretation of Gus Van Sant's film – *Elephant* puts us in the mental shoes of the teenagers – does not fully capture the experience of watching the film. It may sound strange, but it is an overly optimistic reading of the film because it suggests that via film, via art, we can experience the point of view of the teen-agers in an almost unmediated way. In the aforementioned article by Vittorio Gallese and Michele Guerra ('Embodying Movies'), we find this optimism in full force. On several occasions, the authors go as far as to suggest that the film's form of embodied simulation gives us 'direct access to the world of others' (such expressions recall Sartre's description of the reading process as presented in the introduction above).[6] However, even if *Elephant* may *seek* access, it certainly does not share this form of optimism. Instead, an impor-tant reason for the unease produced by the film has to do with Gus Van Sant's ability to put the spectator in a position where we precisely *cannot* reach the teenagers. We do not know from which point of view we are experiencing the events.

So let me complicate the immersive reading by returning to the scene I described above. Most of this scene is shot from an angle just behind Nathan, with a shallow depth of field. As suggested, critics often associate this angle with the perspective of the high school students. Obviously this does not mean that Nathan is myopic, that we are literally watching with his eyes, but it does mean that the film communicates something about his 'being in the world'. This is not untrue, but there are complementary ways to talk about the camera angle.

As an intermediate position, it could be said that the camera – instead of inviting immersion or identification – encourages us to *accompany* the student: we are being put in the position of a witness.[7] We do not always stay close to the students; when Nathan walks from the football pitch to the school, for instance, the camera stops twenty-five metres before he reaches the door. At other times this act of accompanying comes across as more menacing, and critics have written about how camera seems to be *stalking* the high school students. Moving even further away from the immersive, we can note that sometimes our perspective is partially blocked by the character we are fol-lowing. This simple observation prompts us to reconsider whether this is also a film about how the spectator is *unable* to interact with the world of the teenagers.

It is tempting, here, to compare *Elephant* to Maya Deren's *Meshes of the Afternoon* (1943). Towards the end of her film, Deren uses loops to shift between her male and female characters, includes slow sequences to lift her protagonist out of a conventional time–space matrix, and (also as in *Elephant*) combines the deconstruction of narrative with a forward moving structure leading towards a violent, traumatic event. Unlike Deren, however, Van Sant does not probe the psyche of the teenagers. If Deren's film is vertical, inviting us into the depths of the human psyche, Van Sant's film works laterally: we drift but do not gain access.

There are moments in which Van Sant clearly highlights our distance from the teenagers, as when, for instance, sunlight gets caught in the lens of the camera. This may have been the unintended result of filming in long glass corridors where reflections are difficult to control, but Van Sant not only leaves these reflections in the final cut, he also makes the most of them. The result is a number of scenes with light effects played out on the bodies of the characters. These moments suggest that we too are under a bell jar. Rather than being with the teenagers, or in their minds, we are cut off from them. From this position we may feel less confident saying that the teenagers do not interact – or at least we may want to add that the lack of interaction is a much wider problem that also includes ourselves.

A very different kind of argument for a distance between spectators and teenagers has to do with the beauty of the film. The film displays a marked tendency towards aestheticisation, towards idealisation. In particular, we find an idealisation of the young boys. Sometimes idealisation can further immersion, sometimes it makes us aware of a directorial presence. Here is it is important to bring in sexuality. It matters that Gus Van Sant idealises the boys in such a way that many heterosexual viewers (and undoubtedly some homosexual viewers) will be distanced. In the above-mentioned interview for *Film Comment*, Amy Taubin asked Van Sant about this sexualisation of the

Figure 5   *The bell jar: light effects on the back of Elias (*Elephant*)*

boys – and about the absence of a corresponding sexualisation of the girls (in particular in a girl's locker scene, which Taubin perspicaciously saw as a subversion of the conventional, sexualised locker scene that we often find in horror films). Van Sant replied that he had not tried to differentiate between the boys and the girls, and that to him all these young students possessed different forms of beauty. To some extent this answer does correspond with the experience of watching the film, but only to some extent: one group of girls is clearly satirised, but none of the boys are. This has led to what I think were unfair accusations of misogyny (see for instance Courcoux 2011: 85–100). In any case, Van Sant's answer ('they are pretty much all alluring and interesting looking', in Taubin 2003: 31) makes clear that idealisation is woven into the film's fabric. When putting the teenagers under glass, Van Sant also puts them on display, and through his particular form of idealisation he pulls them away from us: we do not have access to a simpler, unmediated 'experience of the teenagers'.

To corroborate this point about idealisation it is helpful to bring in Van Sant's slightly later film, *Paranoid Park* (2007). Here the aestheticisation was taken to heights that made reflections such as the ones above inevitable. We follow a slightly younger teenage boy – another Alex (Gabe Nevins) – who has accidentally killed a security guard while train-surfing. Much of the film heavily aestheticises Alex and his friends in the local skater park (Paranoid Park). We see these boys skateboarding in slow-motion sequences set to a non-diegetic soundtrack of Elliott Smith's romantic indie-rock tunes. Van Sant is clearly flirting with video-clip and advertising aesthetics. Reversing the chronology and watching *Elephant* through *Paranoid Park* it becomes apparent how idealisation – consciously or unconsciously – holds the spectator in a slightly distant relation to the images of the high school students.[8]

These observations are not meant to deny that *Elephant* is being offered as exercise in embodied simulation – it is. But Van Sant also manages to demonstrate that those bodies can never become ours. Instead we have a film with multiple points of view that do not fully come together (just like the heterogeneous soundtrack that accompanied Nathan), and it is precisely the experience of being caught between these multiple perspectives without ever being able to fully embrace any of them that creates the unease.[9] Here the title comes into play. Gus Van Sant explains that in addition to Clarke's film he had in mind a Chinese tale when naming his film. Five blind men are sitting in front of an elephant, all touching a different part of the animal. Each man believes that he alone knows what an elephant is: the one sitting at the trunk compares it to a snake, the one at the ear to a sail, and so on. In the end, the five men leave the animal, quarrelling about what an elephant is. This is a story about the singularity of perception, the absence of a common point of view. If *Elephant* is a feel-bad film — and to many viewers it is an extremely powerful and depressing film — it is not only because it concerns a terrible tragedy and because the teenagers do not interact. It is also because *Elephant* puts a glass wall between the spectator and an understanding of the traumatic incident. Therefore 'traumatic' is the proper term to use: we cannot access the event, it remains 'unclaimed' (Caruth 1996); rather than simply feeling something (despair), we feel that we should be feeling something. These complexities culminate at the end of the film.

Even if we know what happened, the ending still keeps us suspended. And Van Sant plays with our expectations: halfway through the film we see the killers arrive at the school, loaded with weapons and wearing army outfits. We assume the massacre is about to commence, but then Van Sant cuts off, and only twenty minutes later — after a new loop — do the shootings begin. These loops disappear during the last fifteen minutes of the film; instead we have a straightforward chronological development. We now get the ending we have been dreading and expecting. As in previous scenes, the camera often stays out of focus, but the shots are loud and clear. There is an element of suspense (who will get away?), but there is also — as many critics noted — something profoundly anticlimactic about the ending. For instance, Roy Brand writes that 'the movie ends with the scene of the massacre, which is horrible but also alarmingly calm' (Brand 2008: 194). This is undoubtedly the moment where our emotional engagement with the film will be most personal, viewer responses at their most diverse.

We can describe the ending as a moment of meta-emotions. The spectator begins to think about what she is feeling and what she *should* be feeling. The film is at once powerful, unpleasant and undramatic. It is powerful and unpleasant because it shows the horrific shootings and the emotional deadness of the killers. Eric and Alex do not run, they do not shout; they walk, shoot and show little interest (apart from a detached play with some of the victims before killing them). It is also true that the ending is more 'askew and whacked out' (Van Sant in Taubin 2003: 33) than any of the previous scenes: the colours have been enhanced in post-production, the soundtrack is now largely dominated by the (non-diegetic) sounds of running water and chirping birds, one of the killers quotes Shakespeare in the middle of the shootings, and another scene offers a very stylised variation on the police's shooting of Michel at the end of Godard's *À bout de souffle* (*Breathless*) (1960). Despite all these excesses, the ending appears dramatically inadequate rather than extravagant. The hallways are almost empty, there are few shocks (apart from the moment when Alex kills Eric), some screams, but only just enough of them for the overwhelming silence not to defamiliarise. We thus get caught in a circularity of emotions: the climax is anticlimactic . . . but it has no right to be so . . . therefore it becomes very unpleasant . . . but still not properly climactic . . . The result is a soft, and fundamentally anti-cathartic disarray of affects.

Long before trauma- and affect-theory became well-established and productive fields of humanistic enquiry, Georges Bataille delivered a description that to some extent anticipates the experience of watching these last fifteen minutes of *Elephant*. In his late book on Édouard Manet (*Manet*, [1955] 1983), he analysed the experience of Manet's *The Execution of Maximilian* (1867, and 1869), a reworking of Francisco Goya's *The Third of May 1808* (1814). Whereas Goya's execution scene horrifyingly depicts a screaming man who emerges from the depths of darkness only to die; Manet's version sublimates everything that Goya gives. Bataille describes the painting and its effect on the viewer in the following terms:

> On the face of it, death, coldly, methodically dealt out by a firing-squad, precludes an indifferent treatment; such a subject is nothing if not charged with meaning for each one of us. But Manet approached it with an almost callous indifference that the spectator, surprisingly enough, shares to the full. *Maximilian* reminds us of a tooth deadened by Novocain; we get the impression of an all-engulfing numbness, as if a skilful practitioner had radically cured painting of a centuries-old ailment: chronic eloquence. Manet posed some of his models in the attitude of dying, some in the attitude of killing, but all more or less casually, as if they were about to 'buy a bunch of radishes'.[10] Every stain of eloquence, feigned or genuine, is done away with. There remain a variety of colour patches and the floating impression that the subject ought to have induced an emotional reaction but has failed to do so – the curious impression of an absence. (Bataille 1983: 48, translation slightly altered)

As already mentioned, Van Sant aestheticises the teenagers, and therefore his film is less 'impersonal' than Manet's best paintings. But Van Sant clearly shares with Manet (as described by Bataille) the ambition to eliminate discourse and drama. The social, political, psychological discourses all fall away, and what appears is 'the curious impression of an absence'. Like Manet, Van Sant moves his spectator towards what Bataille, in the following paragraph, calls the 'definitive silence' (p. 50). Furthermore, the two artists also share the ability to produce the disturbing meta-emotions that Bataille writes about: rather than the rush of emotions that von Trier aimed for with the killings at the end of *Dogville* and de Palma with the final image of *Redacted*, and rather than simply feeling empty, we feel very strongly that we should be feeling something – we are left with 'the floating impression that the subject ought to have induced an emotional reaction but has failed to do so'. Because of this disturbing, silent, emotional complexity, many critics wondered about the ethics of Gus Van Sant's film. Were they right to be worried?

Figure 6 *Buying a bunch of radishes (*Elephant*)*

Figure 7 *Buying a bunch of radishes II (Édouard Manet: The Execution of Maximilian, 1869)*

An ethics of frustration

In order to answer this question it is helpful to contrast *Elephant* with Michael Moore's *Bowling for Columbine*. In his documentary, Moore investigated the phenomenon of high school killings, looking for the reason why they happened, seeking to prevent future tragedies. In the end Moore's explanation was socio-political: he argued that the killings largely resulted from the combination of a gun culture supported by the powerful National Rifle Association and a media-landscape frightening Americans of the society in which they live. In comparison with this, we have seen that Van Sant never produces a socio-political argument, and he does not make suggestions about how the problems can be solved. The film appeals to our desire to understand, to rationalise, and thereby come to terms with the tragedy, but it also frustrates these desires. Van Sant draws us close to the teenagers, we get to walk with them, but he also cautions us against any belief that we might fully understand them.[11] And unlike Alan Clarke's call for action (we need to face up to the situation in Northern Ireland!), Van Sant's film rather works to postpone the moment of action and conclusion. This might upset the spectator.

It *did* upset many spectators. Sophie Moore's review article from *Film Quarterly* is a good example. In many (but not all) respects, Sophie Moore's experience of the film resembles the one I presented above. For instance, she describes the ending of the film in the following way:

> There is a sense of anticlimax to the actual shootings that is the film's strength as a social commentary and its weakness as a narrative film. The waiting is over and the inevitable shooting takes place; students are fleeing and dying. And yet, we continue to wait – wait for it to register. We wait to feel sadder, more horrified, more unsettled. The killers themselves are not just mechanical and numb but despondent – underwhelmed by the enormity of their own actions. And in this moment of viewing, so are we.
>
> Or are we? If we were truly insensitive to terrible events like the Columbine shooting, we would not continue to pry at their mystery. (Moore 2004: 48)

Sophie Moore continues this passage by comparing *Elephant* and *Bowling for Columbine*, favouring the latter because it does not 'set aside the burden of interpretation' (Moore 2004: 48). As she explains, we need not agree with the thesis of *Bowling for Columbine*, but there will be something to argue with, and the film will therefore help spectators to get started on the process of working through the traumatic events. Van Sant's film, on the other hand, does 'not giv[e] us quite enough material to work with, with the result that the power of his film ebbs along with its refusal to proffer neither the bracing effects of an unexpected turn nor the comfort of traditional closure' (Moore 2004: 48). In Bataille's terms, we could say that Sophie Moore regrets that Van Sant's film is silent. She concludes that Van Sant 'sidesteps the moral tension inherent in both his decision to make the film and our decision to view it . . . we are relieved of our complicity, and Van Sant of his' (Moore 2004: 47).

It is one thing that Sophie Moore has misgivings about *Elephant*'s lack of narrative, unexpected turns and traditional closure; this is clearly the wrong set of expectations to bring to the film. The main problem for her is that the film does not sufficiently interpret the events. She suggests that this failure is cowardly and unethical, and she was far from alone in this reading. In *Artforum*, Geoffrey O'Brien concluded that 'Elephant comes up fairly empty; it has little to offer in the way of analysis or explanation, and one is left with nothing but the same numb response produced by newscasts of the event: it happened, it was terrible' (O'Brien 2003: 39). And in *Variety*, Todd McCarthy summed up the anti-*Elephant* sentiment by calling the film 'pointless at best and irresponsible at worst' (McCarthy 2003).[12]

But even if we think that *Bowling for Columbine* is 'the natural comparison that we reach for in considering *Elephant*' (Moore 2004: 48), this does not mean that we need to play one against the other. Moore's film is a piece of politically committed filmmaking. It contributes to the debate about high school shootings, engages with the social reality, and is certainly a film with a discourse. It does what many social films do when dealing with contemporary political events: offers explanations, searches for solutions, and works with causality. *Elephant* does something else: it brings in the teenagers. It invites us to understand their situation: we get to walk with them, but we also experience our inability to put ourselves in their place. *Elephant* therefore reminds us that our judgements and acts should be informed by a careful effort of empathy – *and* that they should be tempered by the knowledge that we do not have full access to the world we will be judging. Visually, the film brings us to the space of the blur, aurally, to the ambient noises eating away at the *Moonlight Sonata*; in terms of conceptual geography this is where the Chinese elephants live. Our natural inclination will be to turn the lens, bring the events into focus, eliminate the noises, and come to a conclusion about Columbine that allows us to move on. But *Elephant* works against this inclination, and thereby also suggests that sometimes the desire to draw conclusions can be dangerous. This obviously does not mean that we should (or more accurately, *can*) give up judging, nor does it mean that social analysis will bring us nowhere. But the film encourages us to remember that we may not fully understand the situation we wish to judge.

This attempt at putting the spectator in a position where she is forced to delay the moment of judgement has nothing to do with irresponsibility, cowardice or taking the easy way out: indeed, in a situation where everybody craves an explanation – to agree or disagree with – the refusal to satisfy this

desire and let people move on may well be the most difficult (and provocative) of all positions. Thereby *Elephant* belongs to a group of what we might
call 'suspension films'. Let us consider a few more examples of such films,
before briefly returning to *Elephant*.

2.2 AN ETHICS OF SUSPENSION: *I CAN'T SLEEP, HIDDEN* AND JUDITH BUTLER

Another suspension film is Claire Denis's *I Can't Sleep* from 1994. Like
Elephant it tackled a fairly recent, traumatic event: the Thierry Paulin Affair.
Between 1984 and 1987, Paulin – known in the popular press as the 'granny
killer' or the 'monster from Montmartre' – killed at least twenty older women
in the Montmartre neighbourhood in Paris. He committed many of these
crimes together with his boyfriend, Jean-Thierry Mathurin. Paulin was not
only a young homosexual mass murderer; he was also an immigrant from
Martinique and a drug-using, HIV-positive transvestite. He succumbed to his
illness before the end of his trial.

A film about a homosexual, immigrant, HIV-positive mass murderer
sounds like a very sensationalist project. Add to this that the Paulin affair was
one of the most notorious French *faits divers* of the 1980s and we seem to have
a director aiming for headlines in the most obvious way. But even if *I Can't
Sleep* is based on a spectacular story, it is very subdued. It *is* a serial-killer story
like so many other films, French or not, art films or not, from the mid-1990s,
but as Thierry Jousse writes in the *Cahiers du cinéma*, 'the climate is absolutely
anti-dramatic' (Jousse 1994: 22). In the American film quarterly *Cinéaste* Steve
Erickson calls it 'one of the least sensationalistic films ever made about serial
killing' (Erickson 1994: 64). Of course it is this anti-dramatic way of filming a
dramatic story that makes the film so intriguing and provocative. As was the
case for *Elephant*, it led some critics, Alain Riou for instance, to blame Denis
for refusing to take a moral stand (see Reisinger 2007: 46).

Like Gus Van Sant, Denis teases us by offering a series of psychological
and sociological explanations for the crimes. For instance, she follows Jean
Baudrillard in suggesting that Paulin – Denis gives him the androgynous
name Camille – needed the money because he was fascinated by a world of
fashion and luxury.[13] But she never gives the spectator enough material to
fully establish a psychological or a sociological explanation. To some extent
we can therefore only draw the conclusion Denis reached when commenting
upon the Paulin case: 'the opacity remains.' Instead of explanations we get to
walk with Camille, just like we walked with Van Sant's teenagers. Denis has
explained that she was interested in bodies during the filming of *I Can't Sleep*.
When trying to find an actor for the role of Camille, she looked for someone

who was able to become a 'floating body' (Denis in Jousse and Strauss 1994: 25), and this is precisely what Richard Courcet succeeds in being. This float- ing sensation is of course very much a product of the cinematography. *I Can't Sleep* is perhaps the first film in which we find all the trademarks of Denis's style: the long takes, the numerous tracking shots, the scarcity of dialogue, the understated acting, an introspective soundtrack, the elliptic narrative, the absence of shot reverse shots; this is the style brought to a high point in a film such as *Vendredi soir* (*Friday Night*, 2002) and still very much on display in the recent *Les Salauds* (2013, see Chapter 3). With these techniques (also encoun- tered in *Elephant*), Denis unties dialectic relations, pulling the characters (and the spectator) away from the sphere in which intersubjective conflicts are played out. Furthermore, she has chosen to shoot during those hours of the day that are most likely to undermine any idea of a clear identity (evening, night and early morning). The title of Denis's film alludes to this floating sensation. The characters seem to have reached that state of drowsiness that occurs when you go beyond the normal fatigue of sleep deprivation. Camille, in particular, strolls around in what I called a state of existential jet lag. But perhaps the most provocative of all Denis's decisions is to turn *I Can't Sleep* into a multi-plot story in which the loudest French *fait divers* of the 1980s is no more important than the story of Camille's brother Théo (Alex Descas) who is longing to go back to Martinique, and that of a young Lithuanian girl, Daïga (Yekatarina Golubeva), who is trying to make a name for herself as an actress in Paris.

I Can't Sleep can be viewed in many ways. Elsewhere (Lübecker 2007), I have argued that it works to uncouple the association of violence and truth; that the film is seeking to challenge the well-known (Hegelian – and, in par- ticular, Kojèvian) idea that a conflict reveals something essential and truthful about us (an idea we found in 'the Lars von Trier moment', for instance). Here I simply want to emphasise the paradoxically *interventionist* dimension of the film, in order for this reading to reflect back upon *Elephant*. Therefore it is important to understand the socio-political context of the Thierry Paulin affair. This was a *fait divers* that had kept the French media busy for several years; it was also a case that had been used by politicians who wanted more police on the streets, better conditions for the elderly and other social provi- sions. The politicised nature of the affair then exploded when Paulin was finally arrested. Now, the Front National argued that the only reason Paulin and his lover had not been captured much earlier was that anti-racist organi- sations such as SOS Racisme had created a climate in which the police no longer dared to do their job for fear of being charged with racism. And the conservative newspaper *Le Figaro* accused the socialist newspaper *Le Monde* of suddenly ceasing to cover the affair once the racial and sexual identity of the killers had been revealed. In short, there was no shortage of people wanting to act, accuse and judge responsibly.

Filming *I Can't Sleep* in this context obviously cannot be viewed as an apolitical gesture: Denis – like Van Sant – could have chosen to make a film about so many other things. Hers was the deliberate politics of increasing the distance from observation to judgement, expanding the terms of debate by making – as Denis said – a film that even Paulin's mother would be able to watch. Just like Van Sant, Denis at the same time *shows* and helps us *undergo* an experience of dissociation (while Jean-Louis Murat's melancholic voice fills the soundtrack with 'Le lien défait' (The broken tie)). But why this insistence on an ethics of frustration, an ethics of suspension?

One answer can be given if we consider a more recent, very celebrated example of how contemporary film works with suspension: Michael Haneke's *Hidden* (2005). As many readers will know, this is the story of a well-to-do Parisian family that suddenly receives a series of videocassettes and drawings on their doorstep: someone is spying on them. It soon transpires that the drawings point to an incident in the life of the father, Georges (Daniel Auteuil). When he was a small boy, his parents adopted a young Arab boy, Majid (Maurice Bénichou), whose parents had been killed during the Algerian war of Independence, in the massacre of 17 October 1961.[14] Georges became jealous of the attention Majid received, and he invented a scheme (including the killing of a cock – the French national symbol) that led to Majid being sent to an orphanage. Now, forty years later, the mysterious videocassettes and drawings force Georges to confront these past events.

Haneke's mysteries are never explained. We will never know *who* sent the drawings and the cassettes, and we will never know *why*. Furthermore, we will never know with certainty *what* happened between the boys in 1961, nor will we be able to determine the relation their sons have today. What we *do* understand, however, is that the story of Georges, Majid and their families is tied to the relation between France and Algeria. Haneke is inviting us to address a series of larger political conflicts and questions (the Algerian war, the massacre of 17 October 1961, the Papon affair,[15] and the question of how to negotiate the relation to a major national trauma) via the melodramatic conflicts between the two families.

Haneke's suspensions are more directly confrontational than those of Van Sant and Denis. He is working in a logic that can be summed up as a form of anti-cathartic tease: 'so you want to know, so you want to know . . . I will not tell you!' But *Hidden* shares with *Elephant* and *I Can't Sleep* the attempt to increase the distance between traumatic events and a judgement that would provide closure. Again, this suspension provoked critique and debate. Some critics found that France's relation to Algeria was being used as a decorative element giving intellectual gravitas to what was basically a thriller. Some of these critics accused Haneke of being uninterested in the characters of Majid and his son – they suggested that he was exploiting the Arab characters in a cavalier way. Paul Gilroy, for instance, wrote the following in *Screen*:

> The film seemed to offer only a shallow, pseudopolitical, or perhaps more accurately an antipolitical, engagement with profound contemporary problems that deserve – or demand – better treatment than an elaborate exercise in mystification can provide . . . We leave the theatre jolted but with no clear sense of how to act more justly or ethically. (Gilroy 2007: 233)

Gilroy may be right to state that Haneke does not seek to engage 'systematically' with the political questions he brings up. He is indeed mystifying. But this mystification does not mean that he is cavalier. It seems clear that what Gilroy asks of Haneke is precisely what the filmmaker set out *not* to deliver. As Haneke has explained on several occasions (for instance on the DVD extra material), he never reveals *who* is terrorising Georges because this would pull attention away from Georges and his guilt. If we knew that the culprit was Majid or his son, for instance, we would think less about Georges and his guilt. We would be discussing whether Majid or his son were justified in terrorising Georges, whether they were going too far, what else they could have done. We would see the film as a battle between two characters, two families, two sets of moral reasoning, and that dichotomy would have helped to let Georges off the hook.

Haneke's reason for not giving us all the elements is to prevent us from putting the story aside with the feeling of 'I've got it.' We have to establish a relation to the film that takes the insecurity into account. This is obviously a way of putting the spectator in the same situation as some of the characters in the film – something has happened, now we have to negotiate our relation to these events, and that is a job that cannot (very easily) be finished. In this respect Haneke is doing exactly what Alain Resnais had done in 1963 when he made *Muriel, or the Time of Return* about the Algerian war (see my introduction): creating a climate for paranoia and inviting us to reflect upon how we relate to events that partially escape us.

Haneke's stated intentions with *Hidden* are very similar to the way in which Gus Van Sant presented *Elephant*. In the interview in *Film Comment*, Van Sant talked about the necessity of eliminating the easy explanations – the ones that would make it possible for the spectator to think not only 'I've got it . . .', but also 'I've got it and it has nothing to do with me.' Van Sant explained:

> The way I thought the film is supposed to work is that it leaves a space for you to bring to mind everything you know about the event. It doesn't give you an answer. There's no one-stop solution. And if you think there's an

answer you can isolate – maybe it's video games, maybe it's the parents – then that lets you think that the problem is somewhere else and that you aren't part of it. And that's a mistake, because we are all part of it. (Van Sant in Taubin 2003: 33)

But at the same time, Haneke's film has a different emphasis from those of Van Sant and Denis. Whereas the latter films almost exclusively work to suspend, Haneke's film is also thematising the problems that may arise when a subject refuses suspension. In this manner it becomes more explicit in its ethical message.

Georges is a desperate man with a strong desire for closure. He feels entitled to know the truth about the cassettes. *Hidden* demonstrates how this sense of entitlement produces a world of lies, violence and death that destroys both his own and Majid's family. In this way, we can say that the film chronicles the violence of a desire for closure. It is therefore not true that Haneke gives us 'no clear sense of how to act more justly or ethically' (Gilroy). There is a clear ethical lesson in *Hidden*, perhaps even two: we should relate to our mistakes; and also: a strong longing for clear answers and positive solutions can be dangerous, because sometimes the desire for closure may be inextricable from a desire for repression. The film is not saying that 'we cannot know anything', but rather that 'we cannot know everything.' By destabilising the spectators – possibly even confusing and annoying them – this and other suspension films remind us that judging is best done on the basis of the acknowledgement that occasionally things escape us. As Judith Butler writes in *Giving an Account of Oneself*:

> It may be that only through an experience of the other under conditions of suspended judgment do we finally become capable of an ethical reflection on the humanity of the other, even when that other has sought to annihilate humanity. (Butler 2005: 45)[16]

In order to conceptualise the difference between the politics of a film like Michael Moore's and the interventions of Van Sant, Denis and Haneke – and to stress that these different forms of interventions should be considered as *complementary* rather than mutually exclusive – let me stay with Judith Butler for a moment, and introduce two concepts that she has developed in her more recent writings: the scene of address and the idea of unframing.

The scene of address and unframing

The notion of 'a scene of address' is found in the book I quoted from above: *Giving an Account of Oneself*. In this text Butler establishes a soft distinction between the scene of address and the scene of recognition. We have already encountered the Hegelian scene of recognition (see the introduction). This is where subjects face other subjects, negotiating relations of intersubjectivity, passing judgements on each other, becoming aware of themselves as subjects (and therefore also as objects for the other). Underneath this scene (but the distinction is weaker than such a formulation suggests), Butler situates the scene of address. This term refers to the many less clearly defined elements that help to establish the 'layout' of the scene of recognition. For instance, Butler is interested in how gestures, body movements and voices influence the ways in which the intersubjective relations are being negotiated on the scene of recognition. It is noteworthy that when Butler presents the scene of address she often draws on literature – more specifically Kafka. She looks at certain disembodied voices in Kafka's prose, at movements, at various elements that precede the more clearly defined intersubjective relations we find in the struggle for recognition.

The key point is that on the scene of address we do not have a clear subject–object relation. Here the subject is already, always, inextricably bound up with the other:

> I, the subject, am appealed to by the Other, and this appeal actually divides or produces a rift in me, so that I am never fully coincident with myself. I am always in some sense constituted by this demand that the Other puts upon me to respond. The division that constitutes me is neither fully internal nor fully external, but becomes precisely the interlacing of the two. (Butler in Murray 2007: 420)

As mentioned, there is no strong distinction between the two scenes, but the scene of address allows Butler to emphasise that we are bound up with one another to such an extent that we can never fully know ourselves. The process of becoming (something like) a subject is set in motion by the experience of being ungrounded by the address of the other. And only if we remember that no subject can therefore fully understand and give an account of itself, may we then be able to relate to the other (and ourselves) in an ethical way. In other words, our relative self-opacity is neither a tragic condition nor an excuse for acting irresponsibly; it is instead 'a chance':

> To be undone by another is a primary necessity, an anguish, to be sure, but also a chance – to be addressed, claimed, bound to what is not me, but also to be moved, to be prompted to act, to address myself elsewhere, and so to vacate the self-sufficient 'I' as a kind of possession. If we speak and try to give an account from this place, we will not be irresponsible, or, if we are, we will surely be forgiven. (Butler 2005: 136)

It seems to me that these predialectic regions (that Butler also associates with the psychoanalytic scene of the transfer) are the ones we are pulled towards when watching the films by Gus Van Sant and Claire Denis. Both directors interrupt the socio-political discourses that we commonly – and with very good reason – deploy when we are faced with tragedies such as high school shootings and cases of extreme human evil. Instead they draw us closer to the bodies and the movements of the perpetrators and the victims, while at the same time reminding us that we cannot fully understand them (just as we cannot fully understand ourselves). The aim of this is not to refrain from judging, but rather to postpone the moment of judgement, and invite us to (eventually) judge in the acknowledgement that there is no such thing as a fully self-conscious subject. As demonstrated by the case of Georges in *Hidden*, the combination of a strong desire for closure and the power to act can sometimes be a dangerous cocktail. To use another example of the dangers of seeking closure – this time from Butler's *Precarious Life* – on 21 September 2001 (only ten days after 9/11!) George W. Bush declared that the time for grieving had ended, and that now was the time for action to replace it (Butler 2004: 29).

If *Giving an Account of Oneself* is a work of moral philosophy, Butler's *Frames of War* (2009) is a more socio-political set of essays, concerned, among other things, with the politics of representation. Once again, Butler is interested in the structures that determine the layout of the scene of recognition, but this time the structures she has in mind are of a more explicitly ideological nature. For our purposes, it is enough to mention Butler's distinction between 'social norms' (in the Hegelian sense of *Sitten*, customs), and the 'frames' (the 'staging apparatus') that determine the field of visibility. For instance, she offers Donald Rumsfeld's rules for embedded reporting during the Iraq War as an example of a 'staging apparatus' that seeks to determine social norms. What this distinction makes clear is that in the current media landscape it is not always enough to ask whether someone deserves recognition, we also have to question whether we have the 'norms of recognisability' that allow us to consider this question of recognition: who and what can we actually see?

Not surprisingly this relation between norms and frames is dynamic. We can say that the norms determine the frames, but we must straight away add that the repetition of particular forms of framing helps to consolidate and/or produce the norms that govern the criteria that determine which lives are deemed worthy of recognition. This analysis leads to the more normative dimension of Butler's argument. She suggests that one of the key roles for contemporary visual culture must be 'to learn to see the frame that blinds us, to thematize the forcible frame, the one that conducts the dehumanizing norm' (Butler 2009: 100). How can this be done? Butler is interested in how to un-frame, how to de-frame (Butler uses both these terms), and how a 'meta-framing' ('frame the frame', Butler 2009: 8) can lead us to reflect critically upon the politics of recognisability. Regardless of the prefix, the point is that visual culture must try to expose how framing is done. What Butler invites us to consider, then, is the question of how norms are being translated into visibility (and vice versa), and how bodies and subjectivities are being constituted in this process: 'the "frames" ... not only organize visual experience but also generate specific ontologies of the subject' (Butler 2009: 3).

To return to the feel-bad films, it is obvious that *Redacted* attacks the official framing of the War on Iraq. As already mentioned, Brian de Palma wants to show the images that the Bush administration sought to obliterate; he is aiming to reframe. Furthermore, he invites the spectator – at least to some extent – to establish links between the various image sources, he creates shocks, provocations and disturbances that work on the body of spectator, and thereby aims to produce what Butler called new 'ontologies of the subject'. Nevertheless, in this attempt to oppose the framing done by the Bush administration, a number of presuppositions about the grammar of political conflicts, and the war of images, remain in place. For instance, the interviews with de Palma clearly suggest that in order to convince, he believes it is a question of finding 'the right' images rather than producing analytic distance from the images.

Van Sant, Denis and other directors of what I have called suspension films work on elements of this grammar – the visual grammar of social conflicts. *Elephant* and *I Can't Sleep* allow us a glimpse into the depressing 'disconnected' existence of their protagonists, but they do more than offer a critique of thorough alienation. They also seek to slip below the oppositional, confrontational logic that dominates the scene of recognition, and from this position raise the question of whether our desires to judge, act, oppose and seek closure sometimes help to consolidate the frames the directors wish to oppose. They do this by playing with the various framings that determine the conventional representation of socio-political problems (for instance by inviting – and then challenging – the sociological reading), and they thereby make us aware of the various norms that govern contemporary debates. Schematically put, we could thus say that even if de Palma is aiming for a reframing, his film, like most of Michael Moore's film, largely engages in a political battle of a dialectic nature. Van Sant and Denis, on the other hand, pull back from this dialectic scene and seek instead to engage with the conflicts outside the parameters of a conflictual logic. Obviously, that refusal of the dialectic scene will in itself provoke (and it is undoubtedly meant to provoke). Many spectators and critics are therefore sceptical about the politics and ethics of such a position (Why not move to action? What difference will it make that we spend time with Van Sant's teenagers?). However, I believe that the confusion and frustration that these suspension films produce can be an excellent way of opening up the political sphere. The suspension films should therefore be allowed to operate *alongside* the more traditional forms of political filmmaking in a relation that will necessarily be disharmonious and tense.

2.3 EMBRACING CHILDHOOD: HADZIHALILOVIC'S *INNOCENCE* AND BRAKHAGE'S *KINDERING*

The films considered so far in this chapter (*Elephant*, *I Can't Sleep*, *Hidden*) were all 'interventionist'. As mentioned, they walked onto different political minefields, sought to destabilise dialectic relations, and thereby tried to extend the distance between observation/experience and judgement. Toying with the cause–effect logic that dominates the self-understanding of political reasoning, they were sometimes met with the reproach of being mystifying, and therefore reactionary. Yet these films *chose* to enter the scene of politics and dialectics, and this situates (and therefore stabilises) the interventions. They challenge the conventional socio-political discourses, but they do this in view of developing and renewing these discourses, and not in order to escape the sociological sphere. Without wanting to make too strong a distinction, the next films of unease are different in so far as the ungrounding is less defined. For instance, we may still think of Lucile Hadzihalilovic's *Innocence* (2004) and Stan Brakhage's *Kindering* (1987) as 'suspension films', but what exactly is being 'suspended'? What are we watching? And how far do we want to follow the directors?

The elegant and the clumsy approach to *Innocence*

Innocence is Hadzihalilovic's first and so far only feature film. As mentioned in the introduction, it is based on a late nineteenth-century novella by Frank Wedekind, *Mine-Haha, or On the Bodily Education of Young Girls* (first published in 1903). Readers familiar with the writings of Wedekind will not be surprised to find that this is a provocative, and perhaps perverse film. Schematically, it is possible to distinguish between two different approaches to the film: one is elegant, the other less so; this analysis will seek to be both – in the proper dosage.

Innocence follows the lives of a group of young girls – about 5–12 years old – in a boarding school. The school is situated in a big black forest, and the forest is surrounded by a high wall. The young girls arrive in coffins through underground tunnels – for all this, as for so many other things, no explanation is given. They undergo an education consisting mainly of dance classes and biology lessons focusing on topics such as the transformation of caterpillars into butterflies. A few teachers and some older female servants are discreetly present, but mostly the camera concentrates on the girls as they interact. They inhabit a richly textured and very sensuous universe. Hadzihalilovic has worked meticulously with colour, sound design and various forms of visual manipulation. For instance, the film was shot on Super 16 and then framed in CinemaScope, and colours were enhanced in postproduction (see Romney 2005). These elements, and others such as the settings, props and costumes, give to the film a deliberately outdated and very painterly quality. This helps to bring the film closer to the realm of the uncanny (as Walter Benjamin has argued, the uncanny is often tied to the outdated).

Like Van Sant and Denis, Hadzihalilovic seems to move away from the world of psychology and sociology, preferring instead to show bodies that move and interact. *Innocence* has therefore also proved particularly appealing to phenomenologically inclined scholars. Among such analyses we find (for instance) a long review article by Vivian Sobchack (2005), a journal article by Emma Wilson (2007) and another by Davina Quinlivan (2009) focusing exclusively on the very sophisticated sound design. These texts emphasise the mystery, the sensuousness and the ineffable nature of the film. Sobchack, for instance, investigates how the film works to seduce, and modify, the body of the spectator – she explains that it offers a very precise, sensuous universe while at the same time withholding any explanation that would allow us to translate what we see and feel into a definite meaning:

> Precise, rigorous, meticulous, Hadzihalilovic's films are simultaneously oneiric, haunting, and disconcertingly vague. Indeed, watching her work, one has the sense that both everything and nothing is given. What we see and hear is thoughtfully chosen and intensely meaningful, but at the same time, it absolutely belies (and belittles) any interpretation that would go beyond (or beneath) its own literal premises and presence before us. (Sobchack 2005: 46)

By suspending meaning, the director makes us stay with the sensorial experience; the link to the films of Denis and Van Sant should be obvious.

This phenomenological reading of the film can be backed up with quotes from the director herself. Hadzihalilovic explains: 'I like films that take you into a particular physical world by playing on sound and sensorial perception' (in Sobchack 2005). Commenting on *Innocence* she stresses that the spectator 'shouldn't try to explain anything. Just as there are no answers to the question, there's no moral to the story either.' Instead, she encourages her spectators to simply immerse themselves in the film. *Innocence* therefore seems like a perfect illustration of what is often called a cinema of the senses.

As an example of this type of engagement with the film – the 'elegant approach' – let me briefly follow Emma Wilson's sensitive and perspicacious analysis, published in 2007 in *French Cultural Studies*. Two things in Wilson's reading deserve to be highlighted in the present context. The first concerns politics and ethics. Wilson is interested in Hadzihalilovic's exploration of the girls' universe. Or rather (and to jump straight to one of Wilson's main points), she is interested in how Hadzihalilovic allows the spectators to watch and sense from the girls' perspective. The camera is often positioned at the height of the girls, and there is a focus on the materiality of objects such as the hair ribbons and garments. Most importantly, *Innocence* unfolds in a universe that partly escapes us (as it escapes the girls). This is a worrying, mysterious, captivating and uncanny world – 'a polymorphous perverse world warped and coloured by infant elaboration and enchantment, distortion and enhancement' (Wilson 2007: 172). As Wilson further writes: 'What *Innocence* achieves is the impression that this film is a shared projection, managed and motivated by the children themselves' (Wilson 2007: 173).

Wilson then asks: can the girls' community help to suggest new forms of being together? Her key reference for the discussion of this question is the philosophy of Jean-Luc Nancy. There is no triumphant answer to the question, but the article nevertheless manifests a certain optimism about how these young protagonists present a less fixed, a more floating form of subjectivity that can 'allow different perspectives on identity and subjectivity'. With the girls, we are in a world that has not yet been locked into clear subject–object relations; we are in a floating space where identities – individual and collective – remain open to negotiation. A pre-dialectic world where intimacy and intrusion (as in Nancy's *L'intrus* (2000)) are inextricably intertwined, where metamorphosis (as in the child's growing body) is continuous, and relations between the inner and the outer, the social and the private are in flux: 'Here identity is non-self-identical, shifting, unsettled and future-oriented; the mutable matter of child bodies offers a choice illustration of identity with otherness, in transaction and process' (Wilson 2007: 181).

It is important to add that this insistence on the child's perspective and the sensorial universe – this softening of dialectic relations that allows identities to be in a flux – does not amount to an abandoning of politics. On the contrary, like other writers focusing on the phenomenological experience of the film, Wilson is interested in the political and ethical potential of the pre-dialectic sphere (it should be obvious how her interests overlap with, among others, those of Judith Butler). Pulling the girls away from separate identities, and pulling the spectator into this more floating universe, can be a risk, but as Sobchack, Marks, Beugnet and many others have argued, that universe also holds ethical and political potential.

The second point to highlight is that Wilson – like Sobchack in her much shorter text – remains acutely aware of the 'other reading'. So much so, that Wilson's very first sentence not only presents the framework she will use for the analysis of the film (she insists on the 'embodied experience'), but also makes clear which framework she feels that contemporary representations of childhood is seeking to leave behind – that of the 'scopophilic or maternal gaze' (Wilson 2007: 169). Wilson acknowledges that the film sometimes invites a psychoanalytic reading, and she notes that by focusing on the sensual nature of the interaction between the girls, she risks overlooking the sexual dimension; nevertheless, in this text her interest lies elsewhere. She therefore continues, 'to focus exclusively on sexual interpretation serves to set the film squarely within the ambit only of adult interest and attention' (Wilson 2007: 173–4). In this manner, she decides largely to set aside the sexual dimension and instead stay with the girls and their interactions in order to tease out the potential their polymorphous world may hold for the rethinking of how to live together, how intimacy and openness can co-exist.

As this shows, a more sexual, psychoanalytic and power-oriented reading of the film is possible. An example of this approach can be found in a brief review article in *Cahiers du cinéma* where Sylvain Coumoul (2005) dispelled all mysteries, focusing instead on how the girls were presented to the gaze of the spectator. Instead of finding a subtle sensuous exploration of the girls' universe, he argued that the film positions the spectator as the bearer of a paedophile gaze in an attempt to deliver an all too well-known critique of patriarchal society – but first of all, in a sensationalist attempt to attract attention via this form of 'provocation chic' (Coumoul 2005: 53). To better understand this reading, let us return to the plot.

After many scenes with physical exercises (girls on swings, swimming in lakes, using hula-hoops, doing gymnastics and ballet-classes), and after a series of classroom sessions that seem to focus mainly on a peculiar form of evolutionary biology, we discover that at night the oldest girls dress up as butterflies and give dance performances in an underground theatre. The performances are clearly received as a form of sexual entertainment by a public that is male-dominated, but not (as several critics have written) all male. We learn that the income generated by the performances of the older girls contributes towards the running costs of the school.

This plot development encourages us to think about the film in terms of gender, perversion and prostitution. *Innocence* depicts young girls who are fashioned for the pleasure of (mostly) men. Other plot elements add to the ideological reading – inviting us to think of the institution as a form of prison, and the film as a feminist critique of a patriarchal, almost totalitarian society. We see a girl who tries to escape the school in a small rowing boat but drowns. Soon, the teachers and schoolgirls gather around a bonfire with a coffin, sending her off in an unsettling pagan ritual. When another girl falls ill, a mysterious doctor – a rare male presence – arrives to give an even more mysterious injection; in a third scene a teacher tells the girls that obedience is the only way to happiness. It is also worth noting that some scenes play with sexualised imagery in deliberately clichéd ways (thereby, as Comoul suggested, pushing the spectator towards a viewing position we will not find comfortable). One such scene shows two of the youngest girls alone in the forest, in their white jackets, short skirts and ankle socks. They begin to quarrel, Selma (Alisson Lalieux) pushes Iris (Zoé Auclair) to the ground, and Iris hurts her ankle. With Iris momentarily unable to move, the frustrated (and sadistic) Selma takes advantage of the situation and whips her with a thin branch. We witness a regular spanking scene ('you are too nosy!') that only stops when Iris's legs are bloody.

At the end of the film, the oldest girls go to a train station underneath the forest, and are transported to a big station-like building fronted by a plaza with fountains (the journey takes place in trains that some critics compared to those used for the deportation of Jews during the Second World War). The girls say farewell to their teacher, and for the first time in the film they are confronted with young boys. One of our protagonists, Bianca (Bérangère Haubruge), now 'graduates' in a scene where the film arguably moves towards the satirical register: she gently lifts her skirt as she slides into a fountain, she flirts with a young boy, and the film ends with the camera going into the very phallic jet of water, delivering close-ups of the water that Sobchack likens to spermatozoids. Coumoul suggests a subtitle for the film: 'la fabrique de salopes', 'the production of sluts' (Coumoul 2005: 53).

Hadzihalilovic's previous work can be construed to support Coumoul's analysis: apart from having worked on the feel-bad films of her husband Gaspar Noé (to whom *Innocence* is dedicated), Hadzihalilovic had directed two short films in her own name: a short humorous anti-AIDS film called *Good Boys Use Condoms* (1998), and, more interestingly in the present context, the fifty-two-minute film *La Bouche de Jean-Pierre* (1996). This last film depicts a roughly 11-year-old girl in skirt and semi-long socks (like the girls of *Innocence*), who is sexually harassed by the partner of her aunt – no ambiguity here. To escape this situation, she follows the example of her mother, who is in hospital after a suicide attempt, by swallowing a lot of pills. Although the escape plan succeeds, and the film therefore offers some element of relief, this is still a disturbing film unambiguously centred on the theme of paedophilia.

'Listening to the hushed words of life'

We now have two very different readings of the film. The elegant reading proposes that *Innocence* is a mysterious, sensitive and dark film that challenges the spectator to give up on fixed meanings, and follow the girls into a subtle universe that may inspire new ways of being together beyond the most tired conceptions of identity and community. The other reading offers the film as a perfect case study for an introductory course on psychoanalysis and feminism. In the first reading the spectators are invited to give up on distance, immerse themselves in the sensuous experience, and live the film from the perspective of the young girls; the less elegant reading, on the other hand, argues that this satire of our patriarchal society specifically pushes the spectator into a quasi-paedophilic position. The tension between the two readings seems to crystallise in the question of how to read the title. Elegant critics will often understand the title literally – not because they ignore the possibility of a sexual reading of the film, but rather because they believe Hadzihalilovic provocatively marginalises the sexual; the less elegant readers will generally consider the title ironic – the film clearly demonstrating that there is no such thing as innocence. How do we reconcile, balance or choose between the two analyses? Wilson offers one possible answer:

> Perhaps what is necessary is the open, distressed acknowledgement that representations of children and relations to children may be conceived by certain viewers in sexual terms, and equally that they may not be; that there are infinitely various shapes, motivations and intents within and in front of these images. (Wilson 2007: 174)

Without denying the fact that the film offers ambiguous images that viewers will respond to in very different ways (something clearly demonstrated by the literature on the film), I will argue that what Wilson describes as a divergence between *groups* of viewers is precisely a tension that needs to be internalised in the individual spectator. It is this disturbing ambiguity that Hadzihalilovic is aiming for.[17]

I therefore believe that *Innocence* should be seen as a deliberate play between the two approaches. Obviously, there can be other ways to engage with the film, but I think that Hadzihalilovic invites, on the one hand, a phenomenological, haptic, cinema-of-the-senses reading that insists on *Innocence*'s capacity to create a form of imbrication between spectator and film; and on the other, a reading – psychoanalytic and/or ideological – that reinstates a more firm dialectic and presents *Innocence* as a film about sexuality, education, power and the play with the spectator's gaze; a film in which education is depicted as a process of sublimation that produces subjugated subjects. The result is disconcerting. It is problematic to marginalise the sexualisation – and at the same time it is impossible to deny that Hadzihalilovic's film is more than 'the production of sluts'. The interplay between the two readings works in such a way that one cannot help but feel clumsy when delivering the sexualised, the 'adult' reading. But at the same time, the film *does* invite us to be clumsy – in

Figure 8 Innocence

the most elegant of ways. The relation between the two readings recalls the flickering experience of duck/rabbit images: both are visible, but never at the same time. And yet we must try to have this double vision.

To exemplify the challenge of double vision, let us consider a typically ambiguous scene that occurs early in the film. Though this moment hardly lasts for a second, it deserves our attention. The girls are in the forest, doing gymnastic exercises, turning cartwheels, playing with ribbons, going on swings. The camera floats gently between the trees and the girls, and on the soundtrack we hear the discreet sounds of a glockenspiel and the soft diegetic noises from the scene of play. We then see a little blonde girl with a hula-hoop – remarkably this hula-hoop looks identical to the one found in the coloured publicity photographs for Kubrick's *Lolita* (1962): it has the exact same pale blue colour, the exact same flat form. Suddenly, the girl looks straight into the camera, smiling in a way that awkwardly expresses a childish form of sexuality.

This moment encourages a detour via Roland Barthes – it offers something like a 'punctum'. In the first part of *Camera Lucida* ([1980] 1981) Barthes's well-known (but enigmatic) notion refers to the one detail in a photograph that holds his attention. This detail engages his body (and his personal history). Typically it will not have been staged by the photographer but is placed with the spectator. In the case of *Innocence*, it is unlikely that the girl was instructed to look in this way. In the second part of *Camera Lucida*, Barthes modifies his initial presentation, and now focuses on the specific temporality of the punctum. The punctum makes visible the 'cela a été', the 'this has been'. What the photograph shows may still exist, but on the photograph it already appears in its quality of 'having been'. The temporality of the punctum is therefore complex, but Barthes's argument will be that rather than capturing time, rather than bringing us back to the fullness of the represented moment in a Proustian way, the punctum captures a death to come. When Barthes, in the second part of the book, looks at a childhood photograph of his recently deceased mother, his gaze is arrested by the image of a girl that will die.

Something equally complex is at stake when the gaze of the blonde girl catches the camera. This gaze displays a form of sexuality that the girl herself may not be aware of, and that she certainly would not be able to articulate. As in Barthes's photo, this is a curiously a-chronological incident: the girl is not simply there at the time of being filmed – her subjectivity is already running away from her. It is this link between achronology (or: double chronology), death and the bodily engagement of the spectator that makes me think of Barthes and his punctum. Perhaps this curious chronological structure allows us to opt for *neither* the literal *nor* the ironic reading of the film's title? Based in Barthes's notion of the punctum we may instead say that the film presents an innocence that is real, but always already anachronistic. This curious temporality – we are both in the past and in the future, both with the girls and with the adults – seeps through the entirety of the film.

With this little reading, I have now reintroduced sexuality and the gaze. I have also introduced a notion (the punctum) often associated with the psychoanalytic tradition that many phenomenologically inclined film scholars have been eager to set aside. There are reasons for this relative marginalisation of the psychoanalytic in many areas of contemporary film studies (having to do with, among other things, the Anglo-American reception of Christian Metz and a certain form of Lacanian psychoanalysis);[18] but it is surprising to have psychoanalysis at large cast as having completely forgotten the body and the material world in order to prioritise only the distant gaze, the disembodied spectator, power, ideology, and so on. It is possible to argue that 'the genius of Freud is in his contact with things, his polymorphous perception of words, acts, dreams, their flux and reflux, their repercussions, echoes, substitutions, and metamorphoses' (Merleau-Ponty 2000: 277). It is possible to argue that 'Freud is sovereign in his ability to listen to the hushed words of life' (Merleau-Ponty 2000: 277–8). *Innocence* seems to me very Freudian – in this Merleau-Pontian sense.

Furthermore, the punctum need not be construed as exclusively psychoanalytic. It is generally presented as a variation on Lacan's theorisation of the *tuché*, the moment in which Barthes becomes a victim of the Real of the image (see for instance Foster 1996: 132). And Barthes's metaphors are indeed full of violence – he talks about being hit by an arrow, and later about catastrophes and terror. The phallic reading is therefore logical. However, it is worth remembering that Lacan's presentation of the *tuché* (in the seminar on *The Four Fundamental Concepts of Psychoanalysis* ([1964] 1973)) leads to a discussion of Merleau-Ponty's *Le Visible et l'invisible*, and reading these pages alongside Barthes's own text it is therefore not surprising that Jennifer Barker more recently suggested the punctum can be thought in proximity with the haptic (Barker 2009: 31). Barker insists on the tactile dimension, and more importantly she emphasises that the punctum is not merely, not primarily, a quality of the image but lies in the subjective *experience* of the image. Looking at the various examples that Barthes's text gives, it is noticeable that there are puncta whose origin he cannot situate. And furthermore: some puncta do not institute stable dialectic relations, but instead go well with the idea of more floating relations. Barthes clearly communicates this ambiguity when writing about the punctum as a 'floating flash' (Barthes 1981: 53).

Introducing the Barthesian punctum, I am not arguing against Emma Wilson's ambition to tease out the potential of what she calls 'non-self-identical, shifting, unsettled and future-oriented' identities. Rather, my point (and I don't think any phenomenologist would disagree) is that we do not need to set aside the sexual in order to carry that reading through: indeed, it is difficult to find a more efficient way of ungrounding identity than through the sexual. We should therefore be able to follow these girls, to meet their gazes, and to think and be affected by their sexuality as an essential part of this shifting, unsettled and future-oriented identity. If we do not try to respond to both the psychoanalytic and the phenomenological dimensions of the film, we run the risk of robbing the girls of their sexuality. But these children *have* a sexuality, almost all of Wedekind's famous writings (*Mine-Haha* included) make this point again and again; so does *Innocence*.

At the same time, there is little doubt that Hadzihalilovic knows very well how difficult it is to meet the gaze of the girls. More than a hundred years after *Mine-Haha, or On the Bodily Education of Young Girls* (1903), more than a hundred years after the *Three Essays on the Theory of Sexuality* (1905) prompted accusations of paedophilia making Freud a *persona non grata* in the Viennese bourgeoisie, we still have not found a way in which to talk about childhood sexuality. It could even be argued that this topic is more taboo than ever. It is *this* situation – the lack of vocabulary – that Hadzihalilovic exploits. But why?

Innocence and education

Like *Elephant* and *Dogville*, *Innocence* is a story about education. Such stories produce in the spectator a very strong expectation that a moral or political message will be communicated – either positively, as in the classic *Bildungsroman*, or negatively, as in many satires. What happens to these expectations in the case of *Innocence*?

It is possible to satisfy them. As mentioned, we may think that the girls' universe presents ideals that are worth teasing out – for instance, about non-self-identical subjectivities, the expansion of the field of sensuous experience, and the new ways of being together that these sensual explorations suggest. A second option, as we saw, is to consider the film along the lines of a satire of patriarchal society, a satire that unveils the intimate relation between education and sublimation by showing us how the girls are being educated into mastering their sexuality so it can secure them a future in a patriarchal society (in this sense, the film's stunning beauty becomes indicative of the intense process of sublimation). This is a satire that positions the spectators in an ethically uncomfortable position in order to make us feel that we are complicit with the system. A third option would be to say that the film is 'educational' in so far as it runs these two previous tracks together in such a way as to demonstrate that we still do not have a language in which to talk about childhood sexuality. In this way, *Innocence* ambiguously demonstrates how far we have to go before children's sexuality will cease to disturb us. Finally, a fourth possibility – at first less 'educational' – has also been mentioned: we can take Hadzihalilovic seriously when she says 'there is no moral to the story.' As Sobchack and Wilson suggest (seemingly in line with Hadzihalilovic), the film has the power to restore in us the experience of childhood. To a child, the world is mysterious – sometimes marvellous and magical, at other times disturbing or outright terrifying. This mystery, this sensitivity, never fully leaves us, but as adults we tend to marginalise it: *Innocence* works against the forgetting of the experience of being overwhelmed (by the world and by one's own body). This fourth approach to the film therefore does not need to eliminate the other analyses. On the contrary, the combination of sexual and ideological 'mysteries' with the enchantment of the physicality of everyday experience helps to build this universe where the spectator will feel uncertain about the events on screen and, perhaps, regain the feeling of being overwhelmed.

These various readings (and the fourth 'total'-reading) all have their merit, and they all demonstrate that *Innocence* is a seductive, worrying and thought-provoking film. But in my view they cannot fully 'domesticate' the film, and pull it inside the *Bildungstradition* that it so ambiguously flirts with. In this respect *Innocence* differs from the films addressed in the first part of this chapter. *Elephant*, *I Can't Sleep* and (in a different way) *Hidden* mystified and produced anxiety in the spectator. They demonstrated how unease can put pressure on – and even undermine – the sphere of clear subject–object relations, and thereby disturb the autonomous political subjects that seek to judge, act and achieve closure. I argued that the destabilisation took place for good and ethical reasons; for instance it was instrumental in inviting us close to the situations and the characters we would – eventually – be judging. It is therefore possible to include these films within a broader understanding of the Enlightenment tradition (just as it was possible to do with *Dogville*, *Daisy Diamond* and *Funny Games*), and it is not entirely surprising that in France *Elephant* became the subject of a pedagogical CD-Rom for high school students. The relation between *Innocence* and the Bildungstradition, on the other hand, seems more ambiguous, and it is very difficult to imagine that *Innocence* could become a pedagogical CD-ROM for American high school students. Of the key examples discussed so far in this book, *Innocence* is in the paradoxical situation of being at once the film least likely to upset the sensibility of spectators (there is no in-your-face confrontation of the spectator and no controversial political event at the heart of the film) and the most ethically elusive. This is not just because it deals with an area more clouded by taboos than any of the other occasionally incendiary films (children's sexuality), it is also because of the tender and possibly perverse way in which it deals with this taboo. As mentioned, we may be tempted to say that the film reawakens in us the child's experience of being overwhelmed, and we may think that this experience brings back a sensitivity that adults often lack. However, due to the ambiguous interplay between power and sexuality, we should be careful not to idealise the girls' experiences: whatever its charms, this is not a school you wish you had attended.

In words now familiar to us: it is again essential to keep a strong distinction between the ethics inside and outside the movie theatre. It is fascinating for the spectator to go into the woods, and the film does reawaken our sensibility by letting us relive the disturbances that occasionally haunt the child. This experience, however, should not make us forget the difficulties that would be involved in importing to our society what happened in the woods. Perhaps we simply have to conclude that *Innocence* is not a film the spectator should approach with the expectation of finding a productive ethical (or political, for that matter) position? I shall return to this hypothesis in my conclusion.

To my knowledge, *Innocence* is a unique film. It is true that we have films such as Kubrick's *Lolita* (1961) and Peter Weir's *Picnic at Hanging Rock* (1975) (not to mention soft-porn films such as *Laura* (1979) and other David Hamilton titles) about young girls and their sexuality, but in all these films the girls are older, they have a different level of consciousness, and the ways in which they face the no longer quite so mysterious world is therefore radically different. The same can be said of John Irwin's *The Fine Art of Love* (2005); another *Mine-Haha* adaptation released just one year after *Innocence*. Again, the girls are much older (about 14 years old); the narrative less elusive, and there is no sense that sexuality escapes the consciousness of the girls.[19] Many critics (and Hadzihalilovic herself) have found the closest 'relatives' to the film in the photography of Sally Mann and in the disturbing surrealist art of sculptors and painters such as Bellmer, Balthus and Magritte. But perhaps the most appropriate context for Hadzihalilovic's film is a strand of recent French fiction that includes writers such as Christine Angot, Caroline Thivel and Jean-Pierre Enard. These writers, discussed in Victoria Best and Martin Crowley's *New Pornographies*, are part of a cultural situation that is 'hopelessly entangled' (2007: 216) and that 'display[s] a fascination with infantile eroticism that is ambiguous, ethically uncertain, pervasive and utterly persistent' (p. 213). However, I would like to stay with the filmic, and conclude this analysis of the films of unease with the short analysis of a bewildering experimental film by Stan Brakhage that offers a somewhat comparable experience.

Brakhage's avant-garde horror

Like *Innocence*, *Kindering* (1987) is an unsettling film with very young children: a girl and a boy approximately 3–5 years old. At first, little seems to warrant the comparison with Hadzihalilovic's film. *Kindering* is an avant-garde film with a running time of only two minutes and fifty seconds. It is largely filmed through an anamorphic lens that distorts the images to such an extent that it becomes difficult to determine what we see (a technique used in several Brakhage films); there is none of the 'excessive' clarity that we find in *Innocence*. But despite the abstraction, *Kindering* is historically, geographically and sociologically much easier to situate than *Innocence*. Brakhage describes the film's setting as the typical 'Americana backyard': we see a washing line with pegs, a green lawn where children play with their plastic toys while a dog minds its own business. Unusually for Brakhage, there is a soundtrack to the film – and this has none of the subtlety of Hadzihalilovic's hushed sound space with glockenspiels, grandfather clocks, birdsong, and discreet mysterious train rumblings; in *Kindering*, a young child, probably a girl, is play-singing over an orchestral track. Like the images, the soundtrack is distorted (the tempo goes up and down), electronic sounds have been added, and the result is a sound space that would fit a low-budget horror film from the seventies or eighties. However, it is the complex and troubling nature of the 'contract' between director, children and spectators that brings *Kindering* closer to *Innocence*. To explain, let me describe the longest scene (forty seconds) in Brakhage's film.

In this scene the camera dwells on the little boy standing in the background of the out-of-focus image: he is whipping a metal swing frame with what appears to be a rope or a thin branch. His upper torso is moving from side to side, making the same movement that Selma did in the flagellation scene in *Innocence*. In front of the metal frame, the little girl appears to have jumped off the swing, and is now crouching on the ground. She has her back to the camera and sometimes bends forwards towards the grass. She is wearing a short, pink princess dress. After a moment we notice that some form of leash is tied to her upper left arm, pulling her towards the left of the screen. Who is pulling? Why is she on a leash? At the end of the scene the camera pans and these questions are at least partially answered: we realise that the leash (perhaps from the dog?) is tied to a swing that goes back and forth thereby pulling on her arm. Throughout the scene, the camera is at some distance from the children. More than that: Brakhage is filming from behind the thin branches of a bush, using a zoom. Occasionally, these branches are taken by the wind, blocking our view and thereby also making us aware of our position as peeping Toms (why are we hiding behind a bush?). On the soundtrack the voice of a child is singing 'ah-ah-ah's over an atonal mix of string instruments, computer manipulated sounds and percussion instruments – at a certain point a male opera singer can also be heard. The voice of the child does not have any obvious relation to the other sounds, and the soundtrack as a whole is constantly on the verge of tipping into noise.

It is difficult to avoid being mystified and troubled by these images, and in particular by the relation between the camera and the children. We seem to be spying on the young children who clearly have not noticed us. They are playing with cultural and sexual archetypes – princess dress, swings, flagellation – in a series of blurred images accompanied by a horror-like soundtrack. Is Brakhage *using* the children to deliver a critique of the sexual and ideological structures that dominate adult society? Or is it our gaze that projects an inappropriate discursive framework onto these *innocent* scenes of play?

In fact, Brakhage is filming his grandchildren. Even if *Kindering* is shot on 16 mm (and not 8 mm), and even if the film is filtered through its maker's highly advanced technical knowledge and unique avant-garde sensibility, the film therefore relates to the many home videos that parents and grandparents all over the Western world (including the Americana backyards) were making in the 1980s. Does this family relation make the film less or more unsettling? Do Brakhage's avant-garde techniques enhance the objectivisation, furthering the distance to the grandchildren?

Watching these anamorphically distorted images calls to mind Hans Holbein's *The Ambassadors* (1533). This famous painting contains what must be the best-known example of anamorphic art in the Western world. In the centre of the image we find the rich and stately ambassadors, dressed up in their imposing fur-trimmed gowns and standing in front of a panoply of symbolic objects referring to their cosmopolitan lives and the historical situation. In the foreground floats a seemingly abstract form; an anamorphically distorted cranium, visible only to those standing to the very right of the painting. This *memento mori* suggests that despite their richness and opulence, the ambassadors remain acutely aware of their own mortality and the true values of life (represented also by the profile of a very slender crucifix hanging in the top left corner of the painting). Holbein's *The Ambassadors* (famously analysed by Jacques Lacan in the already mentioned seminar on *The Four Fundamental Concepts of Psychoanalysis*) thereby plays material wealth and earthly achievements against the distorted skull, the ever-present death. The background of the painting is made up by a richly draped, green curtain that increases this destabilisation by catching the ambassadors between a distorted skull and a curtain whose secrets remain hidden. It would be inexact to describe the skull as a punctum – Barthes's analysis of the punctum is inseparable from the mechanics of the photographic technique: you therefore cannot *paint* a punctum – nevertheless, the skull introduces the same form of temporality as the one Barthes wrote about: it brings out, in its own carefully crafted way, the death to come.[20]

Brakhage's own understanding of *Kindering* is worth citing. In a short written presentation, he insists on the curious temporality of the film. He notes that his grandchildren are 'seen, as in a dream, to be already caught-up in – yet absolutely distinct from – the rituals of adulthood'. Again, this is the temporality of the punctum (and of *Innocence*): the children are in two temporal universes at the same time. We also have a short audio-commentary by Brakhage that accompanies the film. Given the fact that Brakhage is taking his grandchildren and distorting them, bringing out the ritualistic dimension of their play, it is not surprising that this commentary emphasises the extreme emotional difficulty of making the film. He explains that '[*Kindering*] takes an unsentimental look at grandchildren, which is really, really a hard thing to do.'[21] It thus seems likely that for Brakhage the experience of making the film was one of transgression. Maybe this explains why he feels compelled to emphasise that he hopes the grandchildren's 'sense of beauty and wonder' is visible in the film (I am not sure it is). This, finally, leads to an interesting parallel between *Kindering* and Pierre-Auguste Renoir's many paintings of children. Brakhage explains that Renoir's paintings can provoke one of two responses in him: when Renoir gets it right, they inspire a strong sense of admiration; on the other hand, when Renoir 'ends up with something like a candy box, I want to throw up – like practically any sane human being'.[22] In order for a Renoir painting to provoke admiration, the beauty needs to be sharp and precise. Brakhage talks about 'beauty as darts' and thereby almost seems to quote from some of Barthes's more phallic passages on the punctum. It is logical to assume that in *Kindering* the anamorphic lens and the distorted soundtrack are key for Brakhage's attempt to go from 'candy box' to 'beauty as darts' – towards Barthes's 'floating flash'.

All this suggests that the grandchildren are being objectified. Brakhage is spying on them, catching them in a scene of flagellation whose many possible meanings (social and sexual) escape the innocent children, but not

Figure 9   *A floating flash (*Kindering*)*

Brakhage and his spectator. In this way the film produces a clash between different perspectives, different temporalities (the children's and the adults'). Furthermore, Brakhage is playing with both visual and aural distortions. Most viewers will agree that this brings us closer to the register of the horror film, and as the reference to Holbein suggested, we might say that these manipulations bring out the death in the scene. In all these games, the children seem like objects for manipulation – and for our gaze; the result is an unease that Brakhage seems to share (and the constitution of a cinematic universe that reminds us of *Innocence*'s temporality, as well as its rituals, beauty and horror).

But maybe this is an overly 'adult' and 'cultured' analysis of the film? What happens if we instead – like in *Innocence* – try to put ourselves in the position of the children? We can imagine how they must have laughed at the distortions.[23] We can imagine that they would have loved to create these visual and aural effects, and that they would be less concerned about being 'objectified' and played with (because they are less anxious about being subjects, being fixed identities). In this way, it is possible to say that Brakhage embraces the perspective of the children: this is a very 'childish' film, bringing out the director's sense of play and wonder (and horror). Is this what the title *Kindering* means? To do like a child would do, to play like a child, to be like child? It seems likely that this neologism is meant to reduce the distance between children, director and spectators.

Nevertheless, what *Innocence* and *Kindering* share is the ambiguity of the relations between children, director and spectator. In neither case can these relations be fixed in such a way that the 'contract' between the director, spectator and film ceases to perturb us. The spectator senses a clash between consciousnesses: the children see things in one way, the director and the spectator will at least in part see them differently. The result is uncertainty about how to relate – to the films, to the children, to the directorial stance. This insecurity may 'reawaken' the sensorial apparatus of the spectator, it may expand the limits of our subjectivity, letting us gain access to some of the deeper recesses of our childhood experiences, to a world like 'a dream' (Brakhage); but it is difficult to draw too strong conclusions about the positive nature of this experience. The film is reminding us of our vulnerability, reminding us of how we are (still) overwhelmed by life; it would be unreasonable to ask for more.

From confrontation to silence

Chapter 1 considered a number of films that establish a particularly antagonistic relation to the spectator, forcing us into an almost sado-masochistic relation, pushing the master–slave dialectic to its limit. Most of the films in the present chapter instead work with indeterminacy and 'floating flashes' in order to destabilise (and occasionally undermine) any binary set-up. Rather than a battle with the films, or the directors, we grasp for elements to cling to. Once again, the result is disturbing.

There is, however, a difference between the various films discussed in the current chapter. Van Sant, Denis and Haneke challenge a socio-political sphere that we expect to be dominated by responsible, active, self-sufficient subjects; this gives their films an interventionist character. With *Innocence* and *Kindering*, the destabilisation is taken one step further: it becomes difficult to determine what these films are unframing. In Hadzihalilovic's and Brakhage's films the contract between director and public, and that between director and actors, is fraught. In his comments, Brakhage seemed somewhat anxiously to acknowledge the ambiguity of these relations when he noted how difficult it was to present an unsentimental look at grandchildren, how much he hoped the film showed the children's sense of beauty and wonder. In the next chapter, we shall find other such films that impress themselves upon us (almost) without indicating their aims.

It is hardly surprising that the films in this second chapter 'speak and sound' very differently from the ones I wrote about in Chapter 1. In *Dogville* we had a narrator, instances of direct address to the spectator (sometimes aural, sometimes visual), and a fairly rich dialogue – not least in a number of scenes where moral questions were being debated between the characters. In *Funny Games* we also found the direct address to the spectator, an occasionally dense dialogue, and a peculiar 'overload' that results from Haneke instructing the family to play tragedy and the villains comedy. An 'overload' could again be found in *Daisy Diamond*. Even if Anna is alone with her baby in large parts of the film, there is a lot of sound: during the first thirty minutes of the film Daisy cries and cries; throughout the entire film Anna delivers numerous monologues, not least from Bergman's *Persona*. Finally, *Redacted* was an extremely loud film. Not only is there a lot of talking and shouting, the many confrontations between various image sources, discourses and acting styles also work to assault the spectator.

In comparison with these assaultive films, *Elephant*, *I Can't Sleep* and *Innocence* are almost silent.[24] The main characters are bodies, and we are invited to listen carefully to the hushed words of the films. The 'silence' (created also by highly sophisticated soundtracks) is key in the softening of oppositional relations. By this I mean not simply that the characters do not speak as much as they did in the assaultive films (although this is certainly true) but also that the films as such do not impose themselves on the spectator in a way that requires an answer. Instead, they gently push the spectator towards what Bataille described as the definitive silence: the point where our social, political, psychological and other rational discourses fall away. This silence is sometimes appealing and idyllic, but in these cases it is mostly worrying and disturbing.

The experience of sliding towards silence goes hand in hand with a move away from the identificatory logics that dominated the films in the first chapter. The assaultive films very often invite the spectator to identify with on-screen characters who are facing what we perceive to be evil characters: Grace v. the citizens of Dogville; Anna and Georg v. the nameless sociopaths in *Funny Games*; Anna and Daisy v. representatives of the evil film industry; McCoy v. the reckless soldiers Reno and Flake. The films presented in this second chapter tend not only to avoid such binary set-ups, but also more generally to bypass the appeal for spectatorial identification. Indeed, the point of Van Sant and Denis's films is precisely that such binaries – and the identificatory logics that accompany them – must be resisted.

The various films of unease therefore prompt the following clarification of what is meant by a 'deadlock on catharsis': the production of a spectatorial desire for catharsis does not necessarily go together with the more traditional (psychological) patterns of identification with characters. The experience of 'being Elephant' is intense and disturbing, but it is not an experience that can be reduced to identification with either victims or killers (in part because this dichotomy no longer works); to be in Hadzihalilovic's forest and in the backyard with Brakhage's grandchildren means being unable to determine what is at stake while at the same time remaining deeply affected. Some might wish to theorise this change between the first and second chapters as a move from emotional investment to affectivity, and Brian Massumi's distinction between emotion and affectivity does indeed seem helpful when distinguishing between the assaultive films and the films of unease (Massumi 2002: 23–4). Steven Shaviro provides a succinct summary: 'for Massumi, affect is primary, nonconscious, asubjective or presubjective, asignifying, unqualified, and intensive, whereas emotion is derivative, conscious, qualified, and meaningful, a "content" that can be attributed to an already constituted subject' (Shaviro 2009: 47). In many respects this distinction captures the move from emotion films in Chapter 1 to the affective films in Chapter 2. This being said, the distinction between emotion and affectivity, between films of assault and films of unease, is so sufficiently weak that many feel-bad films combine the two ways of producing unpleasure. To conclude these two first chapters of the book, I will now introduce the example of a film in which the logics of assault and unease seem particularly interwoven.

NOTES

1. Nathan wears a red jumper with a white cross, the label 'lifeguard' underneath; because of the framing this cross becomes a fix-point in the image. Several characters wear 'meaningful' t-shirts and jumpers, and many of them are associated with a specific colour. In Nathan's case the reversal of the Red Cross logo suggests that this is a man who will not be spared in the final massacre.

2. In other scenes they use Westerkamp's soundwalk *Beneath the Forest Floor* (1992) and Frances White's *Walk through Resonant Landscape No. 2*, 1992. (For detailed analyses of the sound design, see for instance Vignon 2011 and Kulezic-Wilson 2012.)

3. As other critics have noted, one of the most famous, violent characters in film history was another Alex, who fetishised Beethoven: Malcolm McDowell's character in Kubrick's *A Clockwork Orange* (1971).

4. Moving clouds can be seen as Van Sant's signature shot. In his (almost) shot-by-shot remake of Hitchcock's *Psycho*, one of Van Sant's few variations is to introduce a series of moving clouds in the shower scene. As other critics have noted there is a romantic, sublime dimension to these shots – we are clearly in the realm of that which exceeds rationalisation (see Laguarda 2011).

5. Another source of inspiration for *Elephant*, Frederick Wiseman's black and white documentary *High School* (1968), also contains scenes where the camera tracks characters from the back as they walk through seemingly endless school corridors.

6. Gallese's and Guerra's argument is not about *Elephant* specifically, but about film-viewing in general. On the basis of Gallese's theory of the mirror mechanism (MM), which includes the famous mirror neurons, the authors write: 'Summing up, according to ES [embodied simulation] theory our brain–body system re-uses part of its neural resources to map others' behavior. When witnessing actions performed by others, we simulate them by activating our own motor system. Similarly, by activating other cortical regions we re-use our affective and sensory-motor neural circuits to map the emotional and somato-sensory experiences of others. *By means of ES we have a direct access to the world of others'* (Gallese and Guerra 2012: 185, my emphasis). This extraordinary idea (and the expression 'direct access to the world of others') can also be found on page 193 of their article.

7. For an excellent analysis of *Elephant* as an exercise in witnessing see Brand 2008.

8. My analysis here overlaps with Anna Backman Rogers's analysis of Sophie Coppola's *The Virgin Suicides* (1999) and Gus Van Sant's *Elephant*. Rogers draws on Deleuze to analyse how the two directors very deliberately work with clichés and stereotypes from advertising and fashion photography to bring out a sense of crisis, death and decay (see Backman Rogers 2012).

9. Many viewers have rightly emphasised the play with videogame aesthetics. These references demonstrate that the film borrows both from first- and third-person shooter games (see for instance Krichane 2011).

10. The 'bunch of radishes' is explained earlier in Bataille's text. As a young student in the workshop of Thomas Couture, Manet complained about the unnatural postures of the models. Annoyed, he told them to adopt the posture they had when buying a bunch of radishes at the grocery store.

11. My cautioning against the most optimistic versions of 'empathetic spectatorship' is not unlike the one that can be found in Lisa Cartwright's *Moral Spectatorship*: 'both the projecting subject and the recipient of the projection may "feel for" the other. But this is not to be the other or to feel "like him" (to feel as and what he feels)' (Cartwright 2008: 34).

12. In Gary Bettinson and Richard Rushton's textbook *What Is Film Theory?*, *Elephant* features in a chapter on Screen theory. Here it is used as an example of the type of apolitical film that Colin MacCabe would not have liked in the 1970s. Bettinson and Rushton explain: 'the film . . . fails to provide an adequate social or political context within which the events of the film take place. The film cannot provide an underlying logic which would allow us to understand what is at stake politically in the shootings that are the film's central event. Instead, in accordance with an inherently realist logic, we are merely shown what things there are, as if all we have to do to understand the world is to see those things. Such a strategy would be entirely ineffective for a scholar like MacCabe. For him, we can assume, *Elephant* is incapable of delving into the wider structural issues which could further inform us as to why these shootings have occurred' (Bettinson and Rushton 2010: 74–5).

13. Baudrillard commented on the Paulin affair on several occasions both before and

after *I Can't Sleep* (for an account of the Paulin case in French media see Reisinger 2007). Denis made reference to Baudrillard in various interviews at the time of the film's release.

14. On that date there took place a legal, announced demonstration in Paris to support Algerian independence. The demonstration developed into riots; many historians agree that the police provoked the demonstrators. The number of victims is highly contested, but it is likely that between 100 and 300 Algerians lost their lives. Some were killed in the streets and simply thrown into the Seine, others were murdered in the police stations where they had been taken for interrogation.

15. The prefect of Parisian police in 1961 was called Maurice Papon – he was responsible for the behaviour of the police. During the Second World War he was the secretary general for the police in Bordeaux, and in that position he was one of the most important civil servants in the government of the occupied zone of France (the Vichy government); he was overseeing the deportation of thousands of French Jews. In the 1980s and 1990s Papon was fighting legal battles with historians and relatives of the victims of the events he had been involved in, but it was not until the mid-1990s that he was finally put on trial in one of the most famous legal affairs in recent French history. In 1998, the 87-year-old Papon was convicted of crimes against humanity.

16. This quotation appears in the context of a series of references to Simone de Beauvoir's *Must We Burn Sade?* The 'other' who may have sought to 'annihilate humanity' is a general other, but it is also Sade.

17. It is worth adding that the source text for Hadzihalilovic's film, the novella by Wedekind, is itself a highly ambiguous text. It can be argued that it contains a relatively clear, feminist critique of the school as a social institution, but Wedekind then confuses this critique with a decadent eroticisation of the young girls. An early critic of the text – Leon Trotsky, writing in 1908 – mockingly suggests that Wedekind is the perfect writer for an intelligentsia that only two to three years ago was high on revolutionary hopes, but today is losing its way in decadence. Trotsky's critique of Wedekind's reactionary politics, moral cynicism and perverse nihilism is not incompatible with Comoul's critique of Hadzihalilovic (see Trotsky 1975).

18. See Vivian Sobchack's remarks in Scott Bukatman 2009.

19. One can also think of other films with child protagonists such as Victor Erice's *The Spirit of the Beehive* (1973). Erice also invites us to rediscover the sensibility of the child, but in Hadzihalilovic's film the 'contract' between spectator and film is much more ambiguous than the one we find in Erice's film. In the case of *Innocence*, we have reasons to hesitate in giving ourselves over to the film.

20. One of the larger arguments in Barthes's book is that the invention of photography in the mid-nineteenth century coincided with the disappearance of death from the public space. One way to read Barthes's book is to say that it details how death found an outlet via the photographic punctum.

21. In the work of Brakhage the experience of children – the perspective of the

newborn, for instance – is often presented in much more idealising terms. Most famously, the ideal of the child's 'untutored eye' is a perspective the adult should seek to emulate via a process of de-culturation (see for instance, *Metaphors on Vision* in Brakhage 2011).

22. All quotes from *by Brakhage: An Anthology* (Criterion Collection, booklet and audio-commentary).

23. Like the many local children who joyously laughed when Brakhage showed them his 1971 film about autopsies, *The Act of Seeing with One's Own Eyes* (a film most adults find very difficult to watch).

24. Because *Hidden* is largely about Georges's *refusal* to live with insecurity, his desire for closure, it is distinct from the other suspension films, and therefore also less silent than the films of Van Sant, Denis and Hadzihalilovic.

Östlund's Play – *Between Assault and Unease*

Play (2011) is a Swedish film directed by Ruben Östlund. Like Östlund's previous feature, *The Involuntary* (2008), it can be described as a sociologically oriented film that concentrates on everyday conflicts in Swedish society. It may be less visceral than *Dogville* and *Funny Games*, and less elusive than *Elephant* and *I Can't Sleep*, but it certainly engages the body of the spectator in a confrontational and non-cathartic way. It deals with highly controversial subject matter in a manner that postpones judgement, and more generally it seems grounded in the idea of the movie theatre as an experiential venue: it is a feel-bad film.

Like the films in the beginning of the second chapter, *Play* is based on real events. These took place between 2006 and 2008 in central Gothenburg where five 12–14-year-old boys of African descent had developed a scheme to harass and con slightly younger boys. They implicated the younger boys in an elaborate ploy during which the black boys played on racial stereotypes, eventually deceiving their victims out of money and other belongings. *Play* focuses on one such con episode in which three younger boys (one of them of Asian descent, the other two, typical, blond Scandinavian boys) are tricked into giving away their mobile phones and wallets, and one of them even his trousers. Östlund works with non-professional actors. He bases part of the dialogue on transcriptions from the court case against the five boys, interviewing the perpetrators, the victims, the psychiatrists and some of the policemen involved in the case. Even though he makes a stylised film, Östlund is clearly concerned with realism.

Thematically and stylistically *Play* is first of all inspired by the films of Michael Haneke. The title resonates with *Funny Games*, and just as in Haneke's film we watch a very unpleasant set-up punctuated by shorter scenes of sadistic play. In Haneke's film the mother is forced to play hot/cold and recite prayers by heart, while in Östlund's film the boys race each other, and one of the blonde boys is tricked into doing eighty-six push-ups. It can be argued that these humiliations eventually allow the black boys to con their victims, but as in *Funny Games* these incidents are also just a perverse way of passing time.

A substantial part of the film takes place on various forms of public transport. These scenes strongly recall the powerful metro scene from Haneke's *Code Unknown* (2000) where Anna (Juliette Binoche) is attacked by a couple of Arab teenagers. In Haneke's film the other passengers look away, until an older Arab man (Maurice Benichou, who was later in *Hidden*) stands up for her.[1] In Östlund's film the train, the tramway and the bus also allow an investigation into group dynamics. The various transport systems become metaphors for Swedish society, and they allow the director to make two observations. On the one hand, we see that fellow passengers mostly look away when the black boys harass their victims, just as they did in *Code Unknown*. On the other, the public transport scenes in which there is no imminent threat of physical violence suggest how thoroughly Swedish society self-polices. For instance, one plotline concerns a cradle travelling on a train, seemingly without an owner. This generates much frustration for the train personnel, who repeatedly use the communications system to remind the passengers of the codes of conduct: 'do not block the aisles', 'do not leave your belongings unattended.' The personnel move the cradle around, they call for the owner, eventually also making the announcement in broken English (much to the amusement of the first-class passengers); clearly, they are obsessed with regulations and order. Similarly, one of the most unpleasant scenes takes place towards the end of the film when an overzealous train attendant delivers a moralising lecture to the three boys who have just lost all their belongings. The train attendant (whose face we never see) does not know what has happened to the boys, he only knows that they have no tickets, and he now explains to the boys, in excessive detail, what he believes to be the larger social and ethical ramifications of not buying a ticket. Taken together these various public transport scenes underscore that everyone has to stick to the rules, pay for their ticket, clear the aisles, move in the same direction – and when conflict arises, we all look the other way. The film thereby also suggests the intimate relation between moralising and looking away: sometimes moralising is precisely a way of not looking. What Östlund wants, however, is to look without moralising.

Östlund's cinematography also recalls the earlier films of Michael Haneke. For instance, he prioritises static shots, long takes and a framing that leaves essential elements off-screen. These choices combine to make sound a key component for the reception of the film. A typical scene gives a mid-range shot of the eight boys sitting in a bus. As the bus pulls to a stop, one of the black boys, Anas (Anas Abdirahman), announces to the others that he has to go home and help his mother. A heated discussion between three of the black boys follows: quitting in the middle of the play is not an option. The camera remains static; in most of the scene Anas is alone in the frame, his two friends shouting at him from outside the bus. At a certain point they step back onto the bus (and into the frame) to check if Anas's mother did indeed text him to come home. Finally, the aggressive boys (and their three victims) leave the bus, and the doors close. But when the doors then open for a late passenger, the two boys come racing into the frame and kick Anas in the head. He falls from his seat to the ground, the kicking continues and now only the aggressors are in the frame. This is followed by the confrontation – at the back of the bus, in largely blurred images – with a (rare) passenger who seeks to intervene. On the internal radio the bus driver (another authority that remains unseen) asks if he should contact the police. The aggressive boys leave, the bus begins to move, and we hear panting and crying from the floor. The other passengers are silent. Slowly, Anas crawls back onto his seat, into the frame, and Östlund cuts.

The visceral nature of this scene results from the combination of physical violence and the interplay between (in particular) framing, shot duration and sound. It is obviously important that Östlund's camera stays fixed – for a long time. When Anas gets beaten up, we want the camera to move, we want it to register emotion, but it doesn't. This enhances the confrontational nature of scene and makes it feel much longer than the two and a half minutes I described (in total this shot lasts for five minutes and twenty seconds). There is little depth of field, so even if this a fixed shot and a long take our eyes cannot wander freely in the image. We are locked into a frustrating viewing position, and the sound constantly reminds us that essential elements escape us. In this way Östlund plays sound against image to create a claustrophobic and non-empathetic viewing position. All this is very much in the Haneke vein.

The specificity of Östlund's film is not only to take Haneke's approach to a new socio-political setting (Sweden), but also to seek a confrontation with the liberal spectator. This brings us to von Trier (and to Korine, as we shall shortly see). With von Trier, Östlund shares the desire to provoke a humanist discourse that both directors would probably associate with a privileged bourgeoisie. More generally, he provokes any viewer keen to reach a clear conclusion about the events on screen.

Östlund sets off in a personal anecdote when trying to clarify his ambitions: 'We could say that the film *Play* originates in an image. An image inspired by real events. Five black kids rob three white kids' (Östlund 2011). The director was provoked by this image . . . and then wondered why. Östlund had understood the image as an attempt to trigger a fearful response – as an attempt to make him conclude that Sweden is getting flooded by immigrants. But now he wondered: why do I think this is an image about race relations? Is it *me* who is projecting race relations onto the image? In this manner the image became the springboard for a confrontation with what might be his own prejudices.

Figure 10 *'We could say that the film* Play *originates in an image . . .' (*Play*)*

It is this self-reflexive viewing experience that Östlund strives to create for his spectators. Like Hadzihalilovic (and Brakhage), he requires a form of double vision, but this time the best analogy is no longer the duck/rabbit image. Rather, if the experience sounds familiar it is because it recalls the analysis Roland Barthes developed in the theoretical afterword to *Mythologies* ([1957] 1990): 'Myth Today'. Here Barthes presents the myth as a sign system that highjacks an already existing sign system. The example he gives is so close to *Play* that it is worth recounting. Barthes considers the photo of an African boy in a military uniform who salutes the French tricolour. On the one hand, this is just an image: a black boy in front of the French flag, an everyday scene from one of France's African colonies. On the other hand, this cover of the weekly magazine *Paris Match* also communicates that in the African colonies, healthy, young soldiers are freely supporting the idea of the French nation as it is embodied by the Fifth Republic. This play between 'literal meaning' and 'surplus meaning' functions in such a way that the myth can always claim its innocence. The surplus meaning can hide behind the literal meaning and pretend that no pro-colonial message was intended (*this is just a soldier saluting the flag*) – but at the same time it will be smuggling into the public sphere an ideological image that normalises the colonial politics. Taking on the role as 'mythologue', Barthes's intention is not to bring about that utopian situation where a society would be freed of myths (he does not think that this would be possible), but rather to make us aware of the myths;

in the vocabulary of Butler, he wants us to consider the norms conveyed and produced by the myth's framing.

Östlund's experience of the image that inspired *Play* can be theorised with the Barthesian model for the myth. But the task Östlund sets himself is more complex than the one Barthes performs in *Mythologies*. Barthes's writings are a meta-discourse delivered at critical distance from the myths that he is writing about. Östlund's ambition is to create the images that can trigger the mythical reading, and, at the same time, invite the spectator to step back and engage with the images in a self-reflexive and critical way. *Play* thus has to evoke the myth without fully being a myth. This demands a lot of the director – and a lot of the spectator. How can the director at once activate and suspend the mythical? How can he create the moment of suspension or delay on which the self-critical reflection depends? How can Östlund be sure that the spectator does not simply see the images as a racist would?

The main part of the answer to this question lies in the details of the plot. For instance, it should be clear from the remarks above that *Play* is keen to avoid being reclaimed for the purposes of conservative nationalism. The portrait of Sweden and its citizens is too negative for these images to serve a populist nationalist party such as Sverigedemokraterna. Other elements also work against the nationalist reading. For instance, the film defuses the dichotomy between the African and the white boys by including an Asian boy in the group of three. It is not that Östlund dissolves the dichotomy (he needs it to stimulate the race reading on which he wants us to reflect), but the inclusion of the Asian boy allows him to discreetly expose the racial thinking of the two blonde boys when, at the beginning of the conflict with the black boys, they somehow feel it would be most natural for their Asian friend to negotiate with the aggressors. Add to this a number of other elements (such as a near-end sequence that explicitly deals with the question of whether race and/or class matter when deciding what is just and right), and it is obvious that Östlund is seeking to make a film so complex and multi-layered that it produces a hesitation in the spectator who therefore cannot jump to the racist reading.[2] Nevertheless, it is a very difficult task that Östlund has set himself: he needs to stimulate the stereotypes that he wants us to consider.

After *Play*'s premiere at the Cannes festival in 2011, the very first question came from a Francophone journalist of African descent: 'So you don't like black people?' (Östlund 2011). One might hasten to think that the journalist's misreading of the film demonstrates that the film presupposes a fine-tuned awareness of Swedish cultural politics. And there is no doubt that *Play* will be received very differently in different cultures; the balance between political correctness, free debate and stigmatisation is a very sensitive and a very local one (which is why Freud describes nationalism as 'the fetishisation of small differences'). However, back in Sweden Östlund would soon find that his countrymen were equally eager to extract one single message that they could then condone or condemn. The positive responses came from both the political left and right, as did the negative (see Stigsdotter 2013). Östlund himself contributed to the debates, repeatedly underlining that his intention was to confront the spectators with their own prejudices, and arguing that the real problem lay with our refusal to confront the economic disparities in which the *fait divers* originates.

It is not my intention to draw conclusions about all of the complex issues raised by the film and the heated debate it provoked. In the present context, I simply want to insist on three reasons why *Play* became such a controversial film. First, the film deliberately frustrated the spectators' desire for closure. In *Play* there are no clear suggestions about how to solve the socio-political problems presented in the film, but as we have already seen in the discussions of films of unease such *Elephant*, *I Can't Sleep* and *Hidden*, many spectators expect films to suggest solutions to the problems they engage. As Ingrid Stigsdotter writes, the case of *Play* therefore clearly demonstrates that if a film deals with a sensitive topic 'then the open text is not pleasurable, but frightening' (Stigsdotter 2013: 46). The same could be said about all the other films of unease. Secondly, the many visceral, Haneke-inspired scenes work to assault the spectator. This mode of address is always likely to challenge the spectators. When these first two dimensions combine, Östlund maximises the potential for disturbance: because the film provokes an intense feel-bad emotion in the spectator, the desire for closure and moral clarity is increased, and the open-endedness will come across as all the more frustrating. In this manner the combination of a confrontation and the complex mythical images puts the spectator under pressure. A third element raises the stakes even further: the faux-documentary style of the film. It is not the case that Östlund rigs the distinction between documentary and fiction like de Palma did, but because Östlund uses non-professional actors (who keep their real names), and because he more generally models the action of the film so closely on real events, it is not surprising that spectators might find it difficult to consider the movie theatre 'an experiential venue' (Bishop 2012) whose ethical norms may be asymmetrical from those that dominate everyday life. However, this is clearly a view that Östlund shares: he seeks to construct his film as an experiment that can allow us to gain awareness about our own relation to racist stereotypes. His titular 'play' therefore not only refers to the 'funny games' the black boys play with the other boys, but also to the relation between spectators, film and director as they negotiate their differences in the public sphere.

NOTES

1. In a conversation with Gunnar Bergdahl (2010) and Roy Andersson, Ruben Östlund discusses this particular scene from *Code Unknown*. He is fascinated by Haneke's ability to stage the clash between the private (everyone minding their own business) and the public (the metro being a public stage).

2. Finally *Play* can also be read in a more optimistic manner, on the basis of the last scene. We are now in a school where two 12–14-year-old children are performing. The first is a blonde Swedish girl who is dancing what seems to be an African dance. She is performing for her school friends – we do not see them – but also directly for the camera. She is enjoying the music, and it is a pleasure to watch her dance. This is followed by the performance of one of our protagonists: the Asian boy who was mugged. He is playing a piece of Western European music on his clarinet (Michael Bergson: 'Scene and Air' from *Luisa di Montfort*, op. 82). These performances (which are far from being virtuoso) give to the word 'play' its more pleasurable meaning, and thereby suggest that playing (in the proper ludic sense of the term) could be one way to 'mediate' intercultural conflicts.

CHAPTER 3

Transgression, Transgression

INTRODUCTION: THIRD-GENERATION AVANT-GARDE?

When Peter Bürger published his seminal *Theory of the Avant-Garde* in 1974, it was met with well-deserved praise – and some strong criticism. One of the most controversial ideas in the book concerned the relation between the historical avant-garde (1910s–1930s) and the neo-avant-garde (1950s–1960s). Bürger understood the relation along the lines of the famous Marxian statement about how history occurs first as tragedy, then as farce: the neo-avant-garde was a travesty of the historical avant-garde. In the historical avant-garde, Bürger found a radical desire for emancipation; he emphasised the avant-garde's attempt 'to do away with the distance between art and life' (Bürger 1984: 50), and thereby allow a reordering of the real in which man would finally be reconciled with the world. Admittedly, the historical avant-garde did not succeed in its ambitions (therefore it was a tragedy), but the revolt against 'the institution of art' was nevertheless sufficiently successful to make visible many of the ideological structures that dominated society and the art world. In this way the 'tragedy' of the historical avant-garde could be seen as a productive failure allowing a critical interrogation of both art and society.

By the 1950–1960s, Bürger argued, things had changed. The revolutionary and anti-institutional ambitions of the historical avant-garde were now being repeated in movements such as pop art and Fluxus. Via these repetitions, 'the neo-avant-garde institutionalize[d] the *avant-garde as art* and thus negate[d] genuinely avant-gardiste intentions' (Bürger [1974] 1984: 58). This paved the way for the cooptation of the avant-garde by the culture industry, with transgressions now eagerly awaited by the art market (and therefore pre-empted). The desire for the new was subsumed into a capitalist logic of fashion and the marketable.

One of the best-known responses to this narrative of decline was delivered by Hal Foster in a 1994 article reprinted in 1996 as 'Who's Afraid of the Neo-Avant-Garde?' (in *The Return of the Real*). Foster's argument was that 'rather than cancel[ling] the historical avant-garde, the neo-avant-garde enacts its project for the first time' (Foster 1996: 20). According to Foster, the somewhat intuitive anti-institutional outbursts of the historical avant-garde were now being worked through and comprehended in the works of the neo-avant-garde, and in this process of creative reflection (a 'return in the radical sense'; Foster 1996: 3) more subtle and efficient logics of resistance and critique were being invented. A similar prioritisation of the neo-avant-garde at the expense of the historical avant-garde could be found already in Rosalind Krauss's ironically titled essay on 'The Originality of the Avant-Garde' in which she offered Sherrie Levine's appropriation art as the example of a radical return (Krauss 1985). Now, the heroic romanticism of the historical avant-garde (the mythical image of an artist blowing the world to pieces) was being replaced by what were perhaps more discreet but also more efficient forms of repetition and critique.

I begin my third chapter with these well-known debates because they allow us to conceptualise and historicise one of the discussions about contemporary art cinema that has taken place in recent years. In 2004 James Quandt published an oft-quoted article ('Flesh & Blood: Sex and Violence in Recent French Cinema') on what he hesitantly described as the 'New French Extreme' (Quandt 2011: 18). This short, poignant text reads as a diatribe against recent films by Claire Denis, Marina de Van, Philippe Grandrieux, Catherine Breillat, François Ozon, Bruno Dumont, and others. Quandt's argument has a very Bürger-esque character. He suggests that contemporary French film inscribes itself in the tradition of the historical avant-garde, and of surrealism in particular. In film historical terms, this tradition of transgressive and emancipatory art – a tradition that Arthur Danto calls the 'intractable avant-garde' – was prolonged in the sixties in the work of directors such as Godard and Pasolini (see Danto 2003). Quandt, thus, does not distinguish between a historical and a post-war avant-garde. Instead he distinguishes between these two earlier avant-gardes and the contemporary French art film: The New French Extreme is a travesty of the twentieth-century avant-gardes. There is no longer any emancipatory project; instead, directors wallow in pseudo-transgressions, and recycle avant-garde topoi in a way that allows a seamless recuperation by the culture industry. Grandrieux's *La Vie nouvelle* (2002), for instance, delivers 'a fashionista vision of the apocalypse' that 'suggest[s] not ethnic cleansing but a St. Honoré catwalk' (Quandt 2011: 22). More generally, Quandt suggests that these contemporary French films 'attempt to meet (and per chance defeat) Hollywood and Asian filmmaking on their own *Kill Bill* terms' (Quandt 2011: 25). This argument exists in more or less critical versions. Although Hampus Hagman does not 'mean to suggest . . . that the aesthetics of the New French Extreme evolve solely out of cold calculations of reception' (Hagman 2007: 38), he nevertheless argues that in these films 'transgression' is a form of 'branding' that (also) originates in a desire to reach an international (and, in particular, American) public.[1] Unlike Quandt, however, Hagman does not present this argument in normative and moral terms: the mixture of exploitation and art cinema that he finds in the New French Extreme is not used to make a point about the decline of French cinema.

Many film scholars responded critically to Quandt's article, prompting him to write a second essay in response to the critique (Quandt 2011: 209–13). In these debates the label was internationalised and directors such as Haneke and von Trier were now also associated with extremism. In the present context it is therefore relevant to make clear that 'feel-bad film' is *not* another name for 'extremism'. Quandt focused on graphic depictions of violence; he was interested in how images of gore and explicit sexuality had found their way into French art cinema, and how these images had become depoliticised in the process. The definition of the feel-bad film does not depend upon how 'graphic' or 'gory' the images are. The films considered in Chapter 2 would generally not be associated with extremism, and even the assaultive films in Chapter 1 contain less explicit violence and sex than many mainstream genre films. Furthermore – as we shall see later in this chapter – even if extreme films often make for uncomfortable viewing, some of them present narratives that are (ultra-)cathartic and thereby far removed from feel-bad cinema as I define it.

This being said, the overlap in director names and film titles also suggests that feel-bad films and extremism *can* overlap. This is why Quandt's diatribe against recent French art cinema (and its capitulation to capitalism) raises a number of relevant questions. So let me insist on a point that most critics – Quandt and I included – agree upon: many of these contemporary films (both the extreme and the feel-bad films) stand in a relation to the intractable avant-garde. They share with the avant-garde an interest in confronting the body of the spectator, and they also explore whether transgression and unpleasure can lead to emancipation. It is therefore not surprising that both the filmmakers and many of their critics have mentioned Marcel Duchamp, Antonin Artaud, Georges Bataille, René Magritte and Luis Buñuel in the discussion of these films. Other figures also play a role (Bresson, Dreyer, Duras and Hitchcock, for instance), but Quandt is right in suggesting that many of these films – in particular the European films – gravitate towards surrealism and other aspects of the historical avant-garde.

The question, then, is whether Quandt describes this relation accurately. Is he right to suggest that these directors demonstrate the inanity of contemporary reworkings of avant-garde shock tactics because there is no emancipatory project? Could it be that the recent films represent a self-reflective engagement with the historical avant-garde, and therefore (along the lines of Foster's argument) reveal new progressive elements via the reworking of the avant-garde? Should we, in fact, say that both the idea of travesty and that of critical self-reflection are misleading when it comes to describing the relation? What happens when we repeat transgression? Should we add a 'third stage' to this move from 'revolutionary heroics' to 'subtle logics of critical return'?[2] The films chosen for this last chapter will open a discussion of precisely such questions.

This chapter therefore changes the approach to the filmic corpus slightly. The titles studied are still feel-bad films, and like many of the previous films they have been accused of recklessness, anti-humanism and nihilism. I will argue that while the films in the first two sections of the present chapter originate in a feeling of despair, those in the third section – 'the feel-bad farces' – display a particularly intransigent form of irreverence that makes it difficult to pull them into the social and ethical sphere. However, as indicated above, the questions that inform these various analyses are more historical, more contextual. The two key examples in this chapter are being brought together, because both can be taken as investigations into the status of transgression in contemporary film culture. I shall begin with the film that inspired Quandt's article, Bruno Dumont's *Twentynine Palms* (2003), and then turn to Harmony Korine's *Trash Humpers* (2009).

3.1   THE AVANT-GARDE AS TRAGEDY? DUMONT'S *TWENTYNINE PALMS*

Twentynine Palms is a powerful and unpleasant film. From its initial screening at the Cannes Film Festival in 2003, to reviews in newspapers and journals, and user comments on various websites, reactions have varied from walkouts and outrage to enthusiastic statements of admiration. The negative reactions reveal that viewers often feel assaulted; the film is a kick in the gut, and many viewers find no justification for the provocation. Let me begin by investigating the three main hypotheses about the film that are encountered in the relatively modest amount of critical commentary the film has generated.

First, it can be argued that this is a film about a passionate love affair, *un amour fou*. Most of the film focuses on the relation between David (David Wissak) and Katia (Katia Golubeva) as they drive David's Hummer through the Californian desert in the area surrounding the small town of Twentynine Palms.[3] David is an American photographer scouting locations for an unspecified project, and Katia is his Russian girlfriend; both are in their late twenties. Katia speaks very little English, and he speaks no Russian, so their dialogue consists mainly of trivial remarks in broken French, exchanged within the limited space of the Hummer. David's hair is consistently in front of his eyes, so that two of the most obvious means of communication – language and eye contact – are eliminated, and the relationship between the characters instead becomes a body-to-body one. Dumont is therefore right when he explains that the film functions via regression (see DVD extra material): to a large extent, it strips away discourse, intellect, psychology and civilisation to leave us with bodies that interact by fighting, screwing, crying, shouting and being consumed by their passion (these bodies in constant collision are *not* the floating bodies we encountered in the second chapter of this book).

At this degree zero of psychology and individuality, a second hypothesis about the film becomes possible: the process of regression is so radical that we enter a 'sacred' and 'mythical' space. 'Sacred', here, should be understood in Bataille's sense of an experience that destabilises subject–object relations; the 'mythical' refers to the narrative ordering of such experiences. As we shall see this space may connect to the religious, but it does not have to. In *Twentynine Palms* the sacred space is largely produced by the way in which the film exploits the natural environment. The impressive Mojave Desert appears as an overwhelming organism, the most powerful 'character' in the film. In the first place, there is the vastness of the landscapes (which Dumont films in a scope format). Then there is the manipulation of the sound: we have the wind in the microphones throughout large parts of the film, and when the Hummer drives over stones in the desert the sound is strongly amplified. The rock formations in the desert assume an anthropomorphic form, and the Joshua trees resemble otherworldly creatures. In short, the impressive landscape breathes, cracks and appears to live; accordingly there is little difference between the animate and the inanimate, between subject and object. As Martine Beugnet writes in a very good analysis of the film, characters are 'becoming . . . mineral' (Beugnet 2007: 131); at the same time, we may add, minerals and plants become anthropomorphic. *Twentynine Palms* is thus set in a landscape very different from the Northern French countryside that Dumont explored in his previous (and many of his subsequent) films. If *Twentynine Palms* is dominated by a process of 'becoming mineral', the other films (and in particular, the opening sequence of *L'humanité* (1999)) are dominated by an almost Sartrean logic of 'becoming mud' (as in *La Nausée*). However, these formulations also indicate that generally Dumont's films tend towards the destabilisation of the relation between subject and object, between figure and ground.

The flirtation with the mythical is accompanied by a number of elements that explicitly invite an engagement with the sacred. Dumont (director of *La Vie de Jésus* (1997), and later *Hadewijch* (2009) and *Outside Satan* (2011)) plays with religious references: the trees, being Joshua and Palm, could hardly be more biblical, and in many shots David and Katia appear as twenty-first-century versions of Adam and Eve as they wander naked in the desert (for a reading that insists on the importance of situating Dumont within a religious framework, see Clark 2006). To some extent this mythico-religious world is turned on its head: the raw and unfriendly desert is clearly no Garden of Earthly Delights, and when the protagonists explore the rock formations, David keeps on his military boots, thereby reminding us that Twentynine Palms is also the site of the largest US Marine training camp. However, the film does not offer an ironic treatment of religious themes; rather, it pushes the spectator from a world of biblical references to a rough and mythical version of the sacred. Dumont takes us to the point at which the physical intertwines with the metaphysical.

If for some the film plays with a sacred and religious dimension, for those advancing the third hypothesis it moves around American archetypes, and in the process it delivers a cultural and political critique. More specifically, the play on American iconography can be perceived as anti-American. The settings are typically American: the freeway, the gas station, the vast land-scapes, the Hummer (a car designed for the US army), the motel where the characters watch inane Jerry Springer shows. Furthermore, this European art film combines elements from some of the genres most consistently explored by American filmmakers: the road movie and the horror film are here set in the landscape of westerns. Clearly in line with the anti-American reading, these genres are largely subverted: *Twentynine Palms* is a road movie that goes nowhere, since the lovers return to the same motel every night, and a horror film that will frustrate all thrill-seeking viewers during the first one hundred uneventful minutes.

One of David and Katia's few conversations merits particular attention here. In a café scene, David asks Katia if he should shave his head in the style of a marine sitting at a nearby table. 'It's beautiful', she answers, then laughingly adds that *he* should not try it. David takes offence at her apparent mocking of his masculinity, and this sets off a minor argument. The incident may be relevant for the ending of the film. As the absence of story unfolds, the ambience becomes increasingly tense; a storm approaches, there are outbursts of hostility from the locals, and in a drawn-out scene the lovers accidently run over a three-legged dog. Despite these signs, however, the ending still comes as a shock. First, David and Katia are attacked on one of their desert drives. The Hummer is rammed from behind by a much bigger pick-up. David and Katia crash and are dragged out of the car by three men. One man hits David in the face with a baseball bat, another sodomises him, and the third ensures that Katia is watching the assault. The rapist has a shaven head, like the soldier encountered in the café; the viewer is thus invited to think that he might be a marine from the nearby camp. After the assault, the lovers make it home to their motel. Eventually, Katia goes to buy food, and when she returns David has locked himself in the bathroom and is refusing to respond. Suddenly, he comes screaming through the door and brutally stabs her to death (in a deliberately blatant variation on the stabbing in *Psycho* (1960)). In this scene, David has cut his hair in a rough fashion, and the spectator is left to wonder if it is *this* kind of masculinity the American marines represent. The film thus presents a violence that, despite its mythical character, also appears as more specifically American.

Each of these three readings – the *amour fou*, the sacred, and the political – deserves a fuller development. For the political reading, it would be interesting to draw on *America*, in which Jean Baudrillard argues that the Californian desert mirrors the social desert that (he believes) defines American society (Baudrillard 1988). For the sacred reading, it seems natural to probe the relation to Dumont's other films, which all so clearly investigate this dimension, and to move in the direction of a more systematic engagement with the physicality of the viewing experience. For instance, one could consider the general destabilisation of subject–object relations, and thereby pursue the project that Martine Beugnet began with *Cinema and Sensation* (Beugnet 2007). Finally, the reading focusing on the all-consuming desire of the protagonists would benefit from a careful investigation of the libidinal logic that takes us from the anal rape of David, to his killing of Katia, and ultimately to his death. After David's horrendous murder of Katia, there follows one long take (lasting two minutes), in which the viewer is offered a bird's-eye shot of the Californian desert. The Hummer is to the right of the screen with one door open, David is lying dead and naked some ten metres from the vehicle, and a policeman walks around with his radio, unsuccessfully trying to convince his colleagues to deal with the matter. Although the possibility of another murder cannot be excluded, it seems logical to conclude that David has committed suicide as a result of being unable to deal with the horrors of the rape and the murder.

However, even if these three approaches to the film could each provide new insights, one must also ask how they combine. Do they sustain each other? Do they come together to produce a rich and multi-layered film? They clearly do not; rather, these three strands interfere with each other. In the end, this is barely a film about a relationship. The reduction of the characters to their sheer physicality means that we quickly find ourselves slipping from the psychological to the physical, and then to the metaphysical. At the same time, this is not really a film about a mythical or sacred relation between man and nature: too many elements of a more socio-political character disturb such a reading. However if we evaluate the film as a political allegory (or even a post-9/11 film; see Wilcox 2005), it also disappoints: there is no political analysis, as the characters' relation to the pulsating universe and their quarrels within the microcosm of the Hummer take up too much space to allow the development of a political dimension. Instead of being a rich and multi-layered film, *Twentynine Palms* is a raw and edgy one. Instead of watching a work in which the three strands organically combine, we experience an implosion of meaning. In order to develop this argument (and to approach the question of how the film relates to the avant-garde), it is helpful to compare with Michelangelo Antonioni's *Zabriskie Point* (1970).

Undermining the avant-garde ethos?

In an interview with Demetrios Matheou in *Sight and Sound*, Dumont explained that he had *not* seen Antonioni's film before shooting *Twentynine Palms* (Matheou 2005). Even if Dumont's film may, therefore, not be regarded as a conscious play on *Zabriskie Point*, the comparison is logical and enlightening. In both cases we have a European filmmaker who travels to California to direct a film that must subsequently (at least in part) be seen as a statement on American culture. In both cases this venture into the American landscape is commercially and critically unsuccessful. Both films follow a young couple in love as they explore the deserts surrounding Los Angeles. In addition, the directors film in scope format and linger on the landscapes in such a way that these come to possess a strong mythical dimension. In the context of my argument, however, the main reason for invoking *Zabriskie Point* is that Antonioni's film also infuses a love story with mythical elements and political allusions, but it does so very differently than *Twentynine Palms*.

When *Zabriskie Point* was released, Antonioni was one of the most established European directors (unlike Dumont in 2003). He had recently directed the successful *Blow-Up* (1966), the first of three films to be produced by MGM, and his next film was eagerly awaited. It had a big budget, a high-profile soundtrack (featuring groups like Pink Floyd, The Grateful Dead and The Rolling Stones), and a complicated production history that generated expectations that proved impossible to meet. The reason for mentioning this reception history is that *Zabriskie Point* failed to satisfy on the three levels I have been discussing in relation to *Twentynine Palms*: the love story was judged to be weak (to a large extent because the non-professional actors playing Mark and Daria failed to convince), the film did not satisfy the political expectations that Antonioni – to some extent – had created himself (for instance, by the inclusion of the Black Panthers' communications secretary, Kathleen Cleaver, in the cinéma vérité-like opening of the film), and the more metaphysical scenes (to which I shall return shortly) were often derided. In other words, desire, politics and myth seemed to get in the way of each other, and the film was seen as an unintended symptom of the exhaustion of a certain emancipatory spirit associated with youthful rebellion and anti-establishment culture. However, there is little doubt that such a reading of *Zabriskie Point* lies far from Antonioni's intentions. It is true that there is a fatherly dimension to Antonioni's slightly tentative embrace of youthful rebellion (for instance, we shall see that the two famous transgressive scenes both take place in the *imaginary* of the protagonists), but at the same time it is clear that the film celebrates the anti-conformism of its young protagonists. This can be indicated through a brief analysis of the two best-known scenes in the film.

The first of these is the collective love scene at Zabriskie Point. To begin with, our young couple are alone in the moon-like landscape, where they share a first kiss. They embrace and roll around in the desert sand, to the accompaniment of a guitar improvisation by Jerry Garcia of The Grateful Dead. The love scene then develops in a phantasmagorical way: the desert gradually fills with young men and women, who all kiss and roll around in the dust, more or less naked, in constellations of twos and threes, sometimes of the same sex, always playful. Even if Antonioni's dream of bringing tens of thousands of young people into the Californian desert had to be abandoned for logistical reasons, this is still a beautiful and – for an MGM film of the early seventies – provocative scene that poetically insists on the fertilising powers of love, youth, sexuality and imagination (as the action takes place in the imagination of the central characters). Crucially, the love of the protagonists is given a collective dimension: the young people (from The Open Theatre) populate the prehistoric landscape of Death Valley and transform it into a site of play.

It is enlightening to compare this scene with one of the most memorable moments in *Twentynine Palms*. Like Daria and Mark, Katia and David leave their car and go into the desert. Significantly, they are an older couple, just a little too old, we may think, to convincingly embody any youthful

Figure 11 *Love all* (Zabriskie Point)

Figure 12   *'I don't want to go back...'* (Twentynine Palms)

revolutionary romanticism. The sun is burning as they approach the foot of some rock formations and enter into an intercourse that is far from being their first – no innocent kisses here. In Dumont's film we do not find a celebration of the fertilising powers of love: after a bit of sexual activity – he takes her from behind, and they produce a sound of clasping body parts – she stops the intercourse with 'I am too dry'. The couple laugh, then climb up onto the rocks and lie down almost naked on one of them (he keeps on his military boots). We are offered a bird's-eye shot, as they lie head to foot, her hand covering his crotch, offering protection against the burning sun. Their sand coloured bodies blend in perfectly with the rocks. On the soundtrack the shriek of a bird – a vulture, perhaps? – can be heard.

In beauty and power this shot matches Antonioni's desert scene, but if the earlier scene celebrates human harmony with nature, Dumont's scene rather shows an awe-inspiring absorption of the human into the arid landscape. Furthermore, whereas Antonioni's scene bestows a collective dimension on the love of the protagonists, Dumont's couple are alone, and before leaving the rock formations Katia twice states that she does not want to go back. The second time she delivers this line, her voice sits uneasily between laughter and crying, communicating her psychological instability. These differences are reinforced by the cinematography. Antonioni's scene has a relatively low average shot length: there are numerous extreme close-ups, and we even have a very brief loop-sequence which makes it evident that Antonioni is inviting us to join in the playfulness of his characters and the guitar improvisation. Dumont's scene, on the other hand, has a much slower pace, and is char-acterised by a complex interplay between sound and image, which makes it difficult for the spectator to establish a relation with the protagonists; audio close-ups are used throughout the scene, while the images vary between extreme long shots and extreme close-ups. With this play between sound and image, there is no place from which to watch the scene (in the first scene of *L'humanité*, we also find this spectatorial ungrounding via the combination of an extreme long shot and an audio close-up). Even if Dumont is not deliberately seeking to undermine the famous love-in at Zabriskie Point, his scene can thus be understood as a response to Antonioni's: the romantic idealism of Daria and Mark has given way to the older couple's isolation in the desert.

This contrast between the two films becomes even more apparent if we compare their endings. I have mentioned how *Twentynine Palms* shockingly implodes in rape, murder and suicide – before ending on the visual contrast between the naked, dead body of the hippy-esque photographer David, and an armed policeman with his walkie-talkie and sunglasses (who seems to have wandered off the set from Peter Watkins's *Punishment Park* (1971)). The violence in the last ten minutes of the film is so radical that it knocks the wind out of the viewer; rather than constituting a logical finale that brings together the film's themes, the violence interrupts everything. The famous ending of *Zabriskie Point*, on the other hand, offers a cathartic release. Here the three strands come together in a very different way. After Daria has learned about Mark's death at the hands of the police, the ending offers us her fantasies about blowing up the house of her boss, a real estate tycoon who is the film's main villain and (possibly) Daria's former lover. This explosion – repeated over and over again, in slow motion, and to a soundtrack of psychedelic rock by Pink Floyd – constitutes a politically revolutionary act, an orgasmic climax, and an ecstatic, almost transcendental experience that reveals the beauty of destruction. As in the love scene, the action takes place in Daria's imagination, but this does not diminish the feeling of release. When we finally return to reality, Antonioni subverts Western mythology: instead of a cowboy riding into the sunset, we find Daria in her Native American dress walking towards the sun, embodying an anti-establishment sentiment. We may therefore conclude that the scene suggests the dawning of a political consciousness and a liberation from male domination; we may also say that it highlights the powers of the imagination. In any case, the beauty of the images is impressive, the anti-consumerist message conveyed by the repeated explosions is unambiguous, and the rhythm of the music and the editing transports viewers, providing them with a cathartic release.

Overall, the juxtaposition of these two pairs of scenes suggests that Dumont is engaging in an almost point-by-point confrontation with Antonioni's optimism. Antonioni's celebration of the fertilising powers of youthful love becomes the 'I am too dry' of Dumont's tense scene;[4] Antonioni's celebration of love as a collective force is replaced by the 'I don't want to go back' of Dumont's antisocial and fragile female lead; Antonioni's cathartic, anti-consumerist and anti-capitalist violence at the end of the film

turns self-destructive in Dumont's hands; Antonioni's spectator is rhythmi-
cally transported to a region dominated by vitalism and a belief in the emancipatory potential of transgressive experiences, whereas Dumont's spectator
is left shattered with nowhere to go. In the thirty-three years that separate the
two films, the belief in emancipation has completely evaporated.

Out of the desert . . .?

Quandt argued that many recent French films are characterised by an obses-
sive interest in sex, violence and gore. These shock tactics seem related to the
avant-garde(s) (Quandt mentioned surrealism, Bataille, Godard and Pasolini),
and to the heroes of these anti-establishment traditions (Sade and Rimbaud,
for instance), but in fact the recent films owe much more to Hollywood
sensationalism in their desire to satisfy the culture industry. According to
Quandt, the fundamental difference between the contemporary directors
and their precursors lies in the fact that the new films have little to offer: they
simply wallow in blood, sex and violence, in futile pseudo-transgressions.
When Dumont is quoted for wanting to shock his spectators in order to
draw them out of normality, 'because people are way too set in their ways,
they are asleep', Quandt rhetorically asks: 'Awakened, though, to what? What
new or important truth does Dumont proffer?' (Quandt 2011: 24). Quandt
instead argues that the vacuous cult of the transgressive constitutes a 'narcissistic response to the collapse of ideology in a society traditionally defined by
political polarity and theoretical certitude', and he goes on to conclude that
'the authentic, liberating outrage – political, social, sexual – that fuelled such
apocalyptic visions as *Salò* and *Weekend* now seems impossible, replaced by an
aggressiveness that is really a grandiose form of passivity' (Quandt 2011: 25).

Quandt's critique of Dumont can be answered in many ways. For instance,
Martine Beugnet rightly observes that Quandt's approach to these films is
underpinned by a set of normative expectations that stem from narrative
cinema. This makes him unable to appreciate the inventiveness of the films at
the cinematographic and phenomenological level, and it therefore also makes
him insensitive to both the bodily and emotional explorations in which the
films engage (Beugnet 2007). Before I offer my response, let me first note
that the preceding comparison between *Zabriskie Point* and *Twentynine Palms*
seems to approach Quandt's analysis. Did I not argue that the revolutionary
optimism that still dominated Antonioni's film had been burnt away in the
sun of *Twentynine Palms*?

I *do* believe Quandt touches upon something important when he differ-
entiates *Twentynine Palms* from the provocations of surrealism, Pasolini and
Godard. The discussion is complex, but it seems accurate to say that many

of the works produced earlier in the twentieth century were propelled by a 'liberating outrage' (Quandt 2011: 25) that it is difficult to find in a film like *Twentynine Palms*. To a very considerable extent, this has to do with – and must therefore be linked to – the wider socio-historical context. Many avant-garde texts and films from both the inter-war and post-war periods were created in radical environments dominated by an anti-bourgeois and revolutionary discourse from which they cannot be separated. Dumont, by contrast, films at a time when even the last contours of a revolution – be it sexual, spiritual or political – seem absent. When neither the historical context nor the film itself suggest a positive project, it becomes possible to agree with Quandt's view that in *Twentynine Palms* we are not awakened to anything.

At this point, Bruno Dumont's own reservations about *Twentynine Palms* should also be mentioned. In subsequent interviews he described the ending of his film as being too definitive, too brutal. This should not surprise us considering that *Twentynine Palms* differs radically from most films in Dumont's filmography, stories that either deliver a final redemptive moment in which human solidarity is reaffirmed (*L'humanité* (1999), *Flandres* (2006), *Hadewijch* (2009), and *Outside Satan* (2011)), or at least hint at this possibility (*La Vie de Jésus*).[5] As such, many of these other films can be situated in the tradition of directors such as Dreyer and Bresson, a tradition to which *Twentynine Palms* definitely does not belong.

To a large extent, Quandt's disappointment with Dumont comes from the fact that *Twentynine Palms* does not (at least attempt to) present a solution to the problems associated with the contemporary socio-political situation (this is made explicit in Quandt's follow-up article: 'More Moralism from that "Wordy Fuck"' (in Horeck and Kendall 2011: 209–13)). Quandt is looking for a constructive dimension and when *Twentynine Palms* fails to deliver, he sees the film as an expression of narcissism and nihilism. To what extent, though, can we expect Dumont to offer a 'liberating outrage'? Should we necessarily want this redemptive moment (which Dumont offers in so many of his other films)? And can we conclude that the film is narcissistic and nihilistic when it does not deliver?

In contrast to Quandt, I believe the power of Dumont's film originates in its *not* offering a positive vision. What Dumont so compellingly communicates is the despair at being faced with the collapse of sexual, social and 'sacred' liberation; and by recreating this experience for the spectator he escapes both narcissism and nihilism. It may be true that this is not '[t]he authentic, liberating outrage' of Godard and Pasolini, but it is an authentic outrage at the lack of liberation – and I believe this desperation is more directly expressive of the ideological situation that dominates our time than the spirituality we find in (for instance) *L'humanité*, however interesting that film might be.

The essential difference between Quandt's reading and my own stems from how Dumont's film relates to the avant-garde. As mentioned, Quandt thinks of the relation in terms of travesty, whereas I disagree with this Bürger-esque reading. This does not mean, however, that it can be understood along the lines of Foster's analysis as a critical reflection on the status of the historical avant-garde (although it precisely does allow such reflections). The more discreet logics of repetition, grids and serialism that Foster finds in the neo-avant-garde are irrelevant to the film. Instead the film can be described as a paroxystic and tragic attempt at forcing a way from transgression to emancipation. Neither travesty nor critical reflection, *Twentynine Palms* finds its source in a form of despair that is rooted in the experience of a disjunction between transgression and emancipation. Indeed, the film is characterised by its taking the viewer all the way to the libidinal, metaphysical and political dead-end; it gives us a moment of transgression (two moments of radical vio-lence) but no subsequent emancipation. It is unsurprising that this provokes, and it is clear that the provocation comes not only from the sex and violence, but also from the absence of a redemptive moment.

We may therefore describe the film as doubly 'transgressive': first it is transgressive in challenging social and aesthetic norms. It provokes viewers with the combination of explicit images, a physical viewing experience, the deflation of genre expectations and the denial of identificatory viewing patterns. Very often such provocations against the (political and aesthetic) mainstream are found in films that embrace a progressive, anti-establishment agenda. But in this – second – respect *Twentynine Palms* disappoints; again it transgresses. Even if Dumont, in some of his interviews, embraces the rhetoric of the intractable avant-garde (and suggests that cinematic shock-therapy may produce new subjectivities that can lead to better ways of being together), this film does not even hint at an emancipatory agenda. Instead, it stands as a shocking and vibrant testimony to the impossibility of liberation – a testimony delivered without any 'end-of-century' decadence or passivity.

But it is not enough to suggest that Dumont communicates a form of desperation – that he holds up a mirror to the nihilism, and thereby allows a critique of that nihilism (to borrow from Dominic Fox's *Cold World* (Fox 2009: 47–8)). We must add that he recreates this experience of desperation for the spectator, he 'inflicts' it upon his viewer. This is a feel-bad film: it stimulates our desire for catharsis by suggesting an avant-gardist link between transgression and emancipation, but instead of the optimism we found in *Zabriskie Point* for instance, it offers an implosion, delivered in what might be described as the aggressive mode. The spectator therefore needs a very strong stomach not to direct her frustration and aggression at the director. This film is difficult to love. I nevertheless believe that Dumont has less distance to the spectator than was the case in von Trier's and Haneke's films in Chapter 1. *Twentynine Palms* is a less manipulative, less ironic, and more desperate film than *Dogville* and *Funny Games*. If we allow ourselves to anthropomorphise it, we might then say that it suffers the disconnection between transgression and emancipation – *Twentynine Palms* lives this tragedy as its passion. And it is far from being the only contemporary film that does so.

3.2 DESPERATION FILMS: *CODE BLUE, IN MY SKIN* AND *LES SALAUDS*

Let us now consider three more films that are willing to go all the way into the dead-end: Urszula Antoniak's *Code Blue* (2011), Marina de Van's *In My Skin* (2003) and Claire Denis's *Les Salauds* (2013). Like *Twentynine Palms* they do not point to a way out of the dead-end, indeed they refrain from offering any positive dimension whatsoever. After the analysis of these three desperation films, we shall evoke a counterexample: Catherine Breillat's *À ma sœur* (2001). The point is not to offer a new reading of this much debated film, but rather to make clear that the avant-gardist belief in a link between transgression and emancipation (which I will generally address with reference to the writings of Georges Bataille) has not completely disappeared.

The Polish director Urszula Antoniak's *Code Blue* (2011) is as dystopian as *Twentynine Palms*, and Antoniak has explicitly said that the ending of her film was meant to leave the spectator shattered. At the film's premiere in Cannes 2011, spectators were met with an anonymous, handwritten note posted on the door to the cinema, warning (and teasing?) that 'this film might hurt your emotions.' While this recalls Gaspar Noé's thirty-second warning in *I Stand Alone* (see Chapter 1), a more direct reference for *Code Blue*'s minimalist cinematography and mute storytelling can be found in the glacialisation trilogy of Michael Haneke, and in particular in his debut *The Seventh Continent* (1989). This also suggests that Antoniak's film belongs in the tradition of European art cinema (it contains references to Dreyer, Bresson and Bergman, among others), rather than in any tradition we would usually associate with the avant-garde. However, like the other films discussed in this third chapter, this is a film about transgression and what – if anything – follows it.

The film is set in Holland, where we encounter the fortysomething night nurse Marian (Bien de Moor) who works with terminally ill patients. At the beginning of the film, Marian spends most of her time walking around the dark and quiet hospital corridors, floating through doors that open by sensors (no need for any touch here), listening to the heavy breathing of the dying patients as it mixes with the sounds of beeping machines. This is a cold, inhuman environment. The title of the film sums up the situation very neatly – in addition to recalling Haneke's *Code Unknown*, the title provides an example of technocratic hospital jargon: a 'code blue' refers to the situation when a heart stops and the patient requires resuscitation.

From the very beginning Antoniak is aiming for strong emotions, setting the tone with a small colour-drained prologue in extreme slow motion, featuring close-ups of the face of a dying woman (set to a soundtrack of Hildegard von Bingen). This prologue does not introduce a character that we will get to know in the course of the film (as such it recalls the opening shots of Philippe Grandrieux's *La Vie nouvelle* (2002)), but instead seems driven by an almost scientific ambition: can I capture the exact moment when life leaves a body? We then watch the story of Marian as she attempts to withdraw from life, her only relations being with the terminally ill. Twice the care she gives inadvertently stimulates sexual desire in the mute, dying men she helps, and twice she reacts by preparing a fatal injection: one man dies, the other fights her off and only dies later. Marian is not simply the victim of a cold world; she is a victim that has turned into the angel of death. Clearly, she is looking for the intensity of emotion that the proximity with death allows, but at the same time she wants to remain in absolute control. And she not only struggles against *other* people's desire but also against her own. A shot of her naked body indicates that she is a cutter. This suggests that she wants to feel alive, that her retreat into purity and death is the result of a painful, internal battle.

Code Blue is so narrative-based that this self-abnegation cannot last. A major breakthrough comes halfway through the film, when from the safety of her apartment Marian watches a young woman being raped by two men in a nearby field. At the end of the rape she realises that a young man, Konrad (Lars Eidinger), whom she has previously seen in a video-store, has also been watching from his neighbouring apartment. He has not only been watching the rape, he has seen her watching the rape. When the two later meet at a party, they seem destined for each other. Marian finally opens to the world and invites Konrad up to her apartment. The result is a violent end sequence in which he beats her up. The film then ends as she goes into her bathroom, pulls out the metal handle and the lock from the door, and uses the bits and pieces to cut open her wrist. The bathroom door closes.

Code Blue can hardly be called understated but it is more open to interpretation than this summary suggests. Not least because the two most important moments of violence and transgression are highly ambiguous. The violent end scene with Konrad can be seen as Marian's tragic encounter with life – with the violence, intimacy and sexuality that she had tried to shut out. But it can also be understood as an investigation into a complex form of desire, perhaps even as the fulfilment of her desire. Marian *wants* the humiliation, she wants the sado-masochistic relation that Konrad establishes. When she first spots Konrad in the video-store, he is returning a couple of DVDs. She rents these films, which turn out to be *Doctor Zhivago* (David Lean, 1965) and a hard-core porn film. These titles schematically suggest the gap between melo-dramatic romance and extreme sexual objectification, between masochism and sadism. It is possible that this gap feeds her interest for Konrad. More likely still: just like Konrad, she does not know what she wants; she is so torn between wanting and not wanting to interact with others that the relation to Konrad almost by definition cannot satisfy her.

Further ambiguity is found in the pivotal rape scene. In an interview fea-tured on the DVD, Antoniak questions the status of the rape. The morning after the incident, Marian goes to the crime scene where she finds a condom and an orange that was used to gag the girl. These objects confirm to Marian (and the spectator) that a scene did in fact take place (whereas other scenes, seen from her perspective, are presented as imaginary); but the condom also leads Antoniak to remark 'what kind of rape is this if one of the guys was using a condom? This creates a doubt about what we saw.' Antoniak thereby suggests that maybe we watched a more consensual act, maybe Marion's pathological relation to bodies and intimacy leads her to see any sexual act as violent and transgressive. And if the condom isn't enough to make us doubt what we see (is it impossible that a rapist would wear a condom for fear of sexually transmitted deseases, or getting caught?), other elements make the scene ambiguous. For instance, a number of non-diegetic, electronic noises on the soundtrack invite us to place the incident at least partially in the psyche of Marian; furthermore Antoniak's images are blurred and grainy, making the scene stand out in a film otherwise dominated by sharp images; and finally, we may wonder about the point of view: the beginning of the scene is shot from Marian's perspective (in long shots, looking down on the rape), but the camera then moves closer to the scene, delivering a series of close-ups of the victim intercut with images of Marian, suggesting that the images are being filtered through her psyche. The scene ends as Marian discovers Konrad in the neighbouring building: she closes her curtains, almost as if to signal that the show is now over. It is therefore difficult to determine what is real and what is imagined. However it is clear that for Marian this is a traumatic experi-ence of shared, transgressive spectatorship.

This combination of ambiguity and extreme (sexual) violence not only has to do with psychological complexities (what is Marian's desire?) and hermeneu-tical challenges (is it a rape?), but also with the way in which the transgressions are placed in the narrative. As mentioned, the meeting between Marian and Konrad takes place in three stages: (1) she perceives him in the video-store, and then watches the masochistic and sadistic films he handed in; (2) she discov-ers/imagines that they share a transgressive spectatorial experience (the rape); (3) they meet at the party. In this way the narrative invites us to think that the (shared) experiences of watching extreme violence, sexuality and transgression (1 and 2) create a bond between Marian and Konrad (3). This obviously does not mean that the rape is associated with something positive, but the violent viewing experiences nevertheless prepare Marian for the encounter.

We may therefore be tempted to think that *structurally* the rape plays a role similar to that of a ritual sacrifice, especially if we consider it along the lines of Georges Bataille's readings of Marcel Mauss. For Bataille – as for Marian – the transgressive experience is one of self-loss, it is a moment in which we go beyond ourselves. In the case of the ritual sacrifice, we do this by identifying with the animal that loses its life, getting as close as possible to the experience of death. That experience is not about intersubjectivity but is a more radical form of 'communication' (to use Bataille's term) that depends on a momentary loss of subjectivity altogether. Bataille presents this as a sacred moment where we are in the world 'like water in water' (Bataille 1973a: 32); here he finds what he calls the 'community of those without community' (Bataille 1973b: 483). When Marian watches the rape, she places her hand on her pelvis, clearly identifying with the victim, and something along the lines of this radical communication seems to take place.

The sacred dimension of *Code Blue* is further enhanced by the set of cinematic intertexts that Antoniak draws upon. As mentioned, the film references the spiritually oriented European modernism of directors such as Dreyer, Bergman and Bresson. More specifically, like other contemporary directors (Lars von Trier, Carlos Reygades and Bruno Dumont for instance), Antoniak offers her variations on Dreyer's *Ordet* (1955). This is a very different tradition from Bataille's theorisation of sacrifice, but what the two traditions have in common is a belief in the transcendent potential of transgression. In *Ordet* love, religion, innocence and grace produce the miraculous ending in which Johannes (Preben Lerdorff Rye) brings Inger (Birgitte Federspiel) back from the dead: she rises from her deathbed. In *Code Blue*, Marian sleeps in a way similar to Inger's position on the deathbed (same pattern on the white pillow, same folded hands on the duvet, same camera angle from the foot of the bed). These references to *Ordet* – combined with those to the world of the sacrifice – make us look for something along the lines of 'death as a revitalising experience'. But instead the ambiguous 'sacrifice' (rape) only lures the protagonist further into the dead-end, setting up the encounter with Konrad and ultimately leading to a suicide from which no resurrection, no code blue will save her. To simplify: what *Twentynine Palms* did to the slightly romantic revolutionary optimism of Antonioni's *Zabriskie Point*, *Code Blue* does to *Ordet*.[6]

This does not mean that the film mocks the transcendental beliefs of Dreyer or the Bataillian link between transgression and community. Instead, the spectator's viewing position both mirrors and contrasts with that of

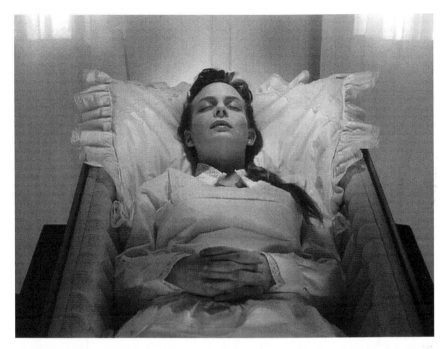

Figure 13   *Resurrection (*Ordet)

Figure 14   *Sleeping (*Code Blue)

Marian and Konrad as they witness the rape: our protagonists watch extreme (sexual) violence – just like we, the spectators, watch death and violence throughout the film. At the diegetic level this experience of transgression has catastrophic consequences for Marian: it brings her closer to Konrad, leading to more violence and destruction as she gets beaten up and, ultimately, commits suicide. The narrative thus offers no grounds for thinking the transgressive viewing experiences as a way to redemption, community or any other such positive notions. Even so, we are invited to watch these transgressions and the suicide because Antoniak believes in exposing the spectator to such unpleasant and powerful experiences. Again we therefore need to insist on the distinction between what happens intra- and extra-diegetically. Although the narrative never thematises *what* the value of transgression could be, the film still testifies to some form of belief in watching fictional transgressions. This tension recalls that of *Twentynine Palms* where – diegetically – little seems to follow the transgressions, even as Dumont's film presents itself as a transgressive experience.

In my opinion this paradoxical structure – the films communicate something like 'we want to believe in transgression, even if our narratives do not' – is not a reason to discard the films. Nor is it an entirely new structure. The relative decoupling of transgression and emancipation recalls the argument presented by Thierry de Duve at the end of *Kant after Duchamp* (1996). De Duve was also interested in the link from transgression to emancipation, and was critical of the idea of art as an 'emancipation project'. His reservations lay less with the idea of putting art and emancipation together than they did with the belief in art as a teleological activity. He therefore objected to the idea of a transitive link from transgressive art to emancipation. As de Duve put it: 'the problematic term is not "emancipation" but rather "project"' (de Duve 1996: 437). He wanted to replace the idea of the 'project' with the Kantian idea of a 'maxim', a regulatory idea that stimulates thought. In other words: we may wish to keep the idea of 'transgression as emancipation' as a maxim, we can hold it out as an ideal, but we cannot demand that art realise this ideal for us.

To a certain extent this seems like an appropriate description of the relation between transgression and emancipation in *Twentynine Palms* and *Code Blue*. However, De Duve's idea of the maxim remains too cool and analytic to capture the passionate desperation of Dumont's film and (to a lesser extent) that of Antoniak. Instead these films can be understood as bringing three moments together in their critique of the contemporary situation: (1) they attempt to force a way from transgression to emancipation, (2) they acknowledge their failure to achieve this, and (3) they communicate this failure by making the spectator experience the frustrations generated. As such, the films are not exactly expressing a 'maxim', nor are they sustained by an emancipatory or transcendental 'project'; rather, they communicate the desire for such a project. It is (the frustation of) this desire they want the spectator to feel.

Rattling the bars: Marina de Van's *In My Skin*

At this point, we might compare *Twentynine Palms* and *Code Blue* to another of the films criticised by James Quandt: Marina de Van's *In My Skin*. I believe this film takes the 'desire for a project' a step further. At first glance, these are very different films. De Van's film is more socio-political than those of Dumont and Antoniak. It opens with images of the skyscrapers at La Défense in Paris; this is where Esther (played by de Van herself) works. She is on a fixed-term contract, but aims for rapid promotion in the company. Her work is appreciated, she soon gains the confidence of her boss, and she is promoted at the expense of her old friend Sandrine, their friendship lost in the process. The company she works for specialises in market research for brands that produce luxury products, and Esther is responsible for the Middle Eastern market. La Défense, short-term contracts, Louis Vuitton for the Middle East: this is the world of high capitalism. Esther has bought into the ideology of this world: she tells her boyfriend (Laurent Lucas) that she does not want to move in with him until they have enough money to buy a big flat and lead a life of luxury. To achieve this goal she encourages him to take a more commercial job than the one he really wants, and unsurprisingly she finds him particularly sexy in a suit and tie.

This is only half the story; the other half is about cutting. In *Code Blue* we never saw Marian engaged in the act of cutting. *In My Skin* is different. Having tripped and accidentally cut herself on a piece of glass, Esther develops a pathological interest in her own body. She is amazed at how little pain she felt when she accidentally cut herself; fascinated, she now engages in a process of self-mutilation that will gradually alienate her from her colleagues, friends and partner. These scenes of self-mutilation are shot using split-screen sequences, extreme close-ups and, in one case, fast-forward cinematography: the result is a series of carefully constructed, stylistically impressive and highly 'unwatchable' (Grønstad) sequences. Most harrowing – most unwatchable in every sense of the word – are the moments when the screen goes black and only the (erotic) sounds of cutting and panting can be heard.

In My Skin stages a confrontation. On the one hand we have the glossy world of luxury products, suits, ties, pencil skirts and expensive restaurants; on the other the seedy hotel and the dark storage room in the office building, where Esther locks herself up to cut. This dichotomy is established from the opening credits: a split sequence montage in which the left half of the screen offers *Dynasty*-like cinematography caressing the skyscrapers at La Défense, while the right half begins with the same images in negative, suggesting the underbelly of capitalism. The right half is gradually taken over by footage from the poorer neighbourhoods in Paris, including the hotel where the film ends. At the same time the music (by Esbjörn Svensson Trio) slides from a harmonious acoustic piano theme to disharmonious keyboards.

Throughout the film, de Van refuses to couch Esther's pathology in a psychological discourse. Instead she simply shows the two tracks (high

capitalism and cutting), and leaves it to the spectator to establish the relation. This being said, the dichotomy is so clear-cut that it is difficult to avoid
a 'thermodynamic' reading of the story. In a capitalist logic of productivity
and efficiency, repressed life will erupt as self-harm. Or, to rephrase in terms
borrowed from Georges Bataille: when everything is about production and
homogeneity, then consumption and heterogeneity will find an outlet in the
form of (self-)destruction.

Again, my reason for drawing on Bataille's vocabulary is not simply to
explain that de Van's film thinks the pathological, bodily transgressions in
relation to the Bataillian distinction between heterogeneity and homogeneity,
but also to point to a *difference* between his thought and de Van's film. In *The
Accursed Share* (1949) and in the article on which this volume is based (*The
Notion of Expenditure* (1933)), Bataille indeed suggests that we cannot repress
our desire for 'unproductive expenditure' (Bataille 1967: 27). If we try, this
repression may lead to 'catastrophic consumption' such as war (Bataille 1967:
62–4). We will be suffering the desire for expenditure rather than living it in
positive ecstasies (that can be sexual, artistic or of other kinds). This seems
similar to *In My Skin*, only in de Van's film 'war' has been replaced by 'cutting'.
In other words, applying the Bataillian theorisation to *In My Skin* we have to
recognise that the outlet de Van shows us is much more private and 'narcissistic' (to use Quandt's term) than the one Bataille had in mind. It is therefore tempting to conclude that late capitalism leaves no space for a *collective*
response to the social repression of desire. The social catastrophe has been
replaced by a private, bodily catastrophe.

We have already seen that in *Twentynine Palms* the violence turned self-
destructive, and that in *Code Blue* the death–life dichotomy was internalised
in such a way as to produce a pathological subject. In the latter, I also found
a 'kind of sacrifice' – a transgressive (viewing) experience – which led
nowhere. We may wish to add that *In My Skin* suggests that at the turn of the
millennium, reification, the prioritisation of productivity and usefulness had
become so complete that members of society could only seek release through
experiences such as self-mutilation and self-sacrifice. As Best and Crowley
suggest (about a different but comparable corpus of recent French literature and film): 'Instead of the hope of climactic catharsis, current art tends
towards painful and anguished frustration' (Best and Crowley 2007: 135).

This is correct, but in the case of *In My Skin*, we also have to consider
how the film delivers this narcissistic implosion to the viewer. At the end of
the film, something happens. In her analysis Martine Beugnet (2007) briefly
remarks that the film becomes self-absorbed. I agree, but would add that in
the very last scenes, this narcissism becomes so rampant that the film turns
outwards. Esther is isolated in her hotel room, and she now goes further with

the cutting than she has ever done before. The extreme explicitness is accompanied by a shift in the relation to the spectator. De Van appears in almost every scene throughout the film, but so far we have either been looking *with her* (sharing her point of view), or *at her*, sharing the point of view of one of the secondary characters (not least her increasingly frustrated boyfriend). At the end of the film, the safety net created by the interposition of secondary characters is pulled away. Esther is alone (with a mirror and a camera) and she is engaged in a very narcissistic activity of documenting her bodily explorations. But de Van then allows the narrative to fall apart: we see Esther exit the hotel room, but immediately thereafter, she is back inside, lying on the bed, in a different shirt, looking straight into the camera. With this ellipsis we seem to leave the story world. The camera offers a close-up on her bruised face, and then pulls back in a slow spiralling movement; the movement is arrested and a dissolve takes us back to the close-up. This movement is repeated two times over and only at the third attempt does the camera pull back entirely, falling to rest in a still image of de Van as a bruised odalisque – a nature morte. It is impossible to know *when* these final shots take place.

It is crucial for the spectator's experience of this ending that the director and the main character are one and the same: this creates a very strong sense of unmediated spectacle. The ending is therefore experienced as a move away from fiction, towards a form of performance or body art (see also Tarr 2006: 85–6). At this point, we are face to face with someone who could be dead or alive, who looks like an object but seems to be fixating us as spectators. It might be Esther, it might be de Van. Her gaze (whoever 'she' is) interpellates the spectator 'directly'. Consequently this ending communicates a belief in art as address, as communication, as a means to change.

In this way, the film transgresses its frame by collapsing the distinction between extreme narcissism and direct spectatorial address. It is difficult to avoid considering the three spiralling pullbacks as a deliberate play with the most famous spirals in film history, those in Hitchcock's *Psycho*. After the murder of Marion Crane we first follow the water getting sucked down the drain (anticlockwise), before Hitchock pulls back from what has now become the eye of Marion in another slow, spiralling movement (clockwise). This is the experience of a descent into a formless universe and as we pull back we are on the other side, on the side of death, in a region where anything can happen. In de Van's final scene, on the other hand, we do not dive into the horror, but instead – with difficulty – find distance as Esther pulls away from us (anticlockwise). At the third attempt she ends up stabilised, well framed, lying on her right side (Marion is on her left), confrontationally arresting the viewer: 'this it is', the image seems to insists, 'deal with it!' This is both an extreme form of narcissism and an extreme spectatorial confrontation.

Figure 15   *Deal with it!* (In My Skin)

The ending thereby takes us towards oxymoric concepts like 'aggressive narcissism' and 'in-your-face passivity'. Once again, this is a film that goes fully into the dead-end of a self-destructive logic that seems at least partly to originate in a particular social structure. But de Van's film also opens a breach 'from below'. Whereas *Twentynine Palms* and *Code Blue* disappeared in the implosive finales, leaving the spectator shattered, *In My Skin*'s implosion is followed by a moment of desperation so confrontational that the film turns almost 'engagé'. In this respect, de Van's film feels like a more political and energetic film than the ones previously discussed in this chapter. As Steven Shaviro writes after the analysis of a very different set of films and music videos: 'When we are told that There is No Alternative . . . then perhaps there is some value in the exhaustive demonstration that what we actually have, right here, right now, is not a viable alternative either' (Shaviro 2010: 137). This is what de Van's ending so forcefully communicates. So even if de Van's film is far from offering a redemptive turn, this final address communicates to the viewer a sense that something must be done; it calls a social code blue. As Fredric Jameson writes in a different context, this form of negativity 'is very far from a liberal capitulation to the necessity of capitalism . . . it is quite the opposite, a rattling of the bars and an intense spiritual concentration and preparation for another stage which has not yet arrived' (Jameson 2005: 232–3).

Claire Denis's *Les Salauds*: nihilism as mental ecology?

My final example of a desperation film – perhaps the darkest – is Claire Denis's recent, dystopian offering *Les Salauds* (2013). This is a slow and highly aestheticised film with a particularly unpleasant plotline. Whereas the transgressions in the films of Dumont, Antoniak and de Van provoked the feeling that something *ought to* happen, Denis's desperation is both more insidious and more diffuse: this time the rattling of bars seems less audible.

The storyline is rather complex. At the dark heart of events stands the beautiful 16–17-year-old Justine (Lola Créton), whose parents cannot pay their debts to the wealthy businessman Laporte (Michel Subor). Laporte accepts this failure because Justine participates in a series of sexual sessions in a barn in the countryside. Darker still: Justine's father (Laurent Grevill) also takes part in the sessions, and in the serial abuse of his daughter who is being violated with a cob of corn (a reference to William Faulkner's *Sanctuary*). In an interview with *Cahiers du cinéma* (to which I shall return in some detail), Denis describes the incestuous relation between father and daughter as consensual, and notes that in the film's last scene the daughter invites the father to come to her (Denis 2013: 86). This is indeed true, but at that point we already know that after the father has answered this 'invitation', Justine will be taken to the hospital where the doctor (Alex Descas) discovers that her vagina needs surgical reconstruction.

None of this is clear from the beginning. Instead the film opens with the father committing suicide, and Justine walking naked through the Parisian streets at night, as if in a trance. Justine's mother (Julie Bataille) wants revenge over Laporte and she therefore calls upon her brother Marco (Vincent Lindon) who has spent most of his adult life at sea as the captain on a super tanker. He is our central character. We follow Marco's attempt at avenging his family, and we see how events gradually overpower him. Key to Marco's downfall is his seduction of Raphaëlle (Chiara Mastroanni), the mistress of Laporte. Laporte discovers the affair, and he immediately responds by signing his and Raphaëlle's 6–7 year old son, Joseph, up for a boarding school in Switzerland. The adultery culminates in a fight between Laporte and Marco that is cut short when Raphaëlle shoots Marco (no doubt in the hope of being able to keep her son in Paris). Before his death Marco discovers not only the secret about the orgies, but also that *his sister knew* about her husband's presence in the barn. The film ends with Justine's mother watching a piece of film footage that Marco has managed to retrieve from the orgies. At this point, Justine has already died in a car crash that she deliberately provoked.

This is Denis's darkest and most disturbing film to date (far darker, I would argue, than the notorious *Trouble Every Day* (2001)). Key to the darkness are the violence, the incest story and the fact that almost all characters exploit and deceive each other (and themselves). Of particular significance is the ending. On many levels it is confusing (morally, politically, aestetically), but in terms of action the scene is unambiguous. We watch the footage from the barn alongside the mother and the doctor, who has promised to support her in the process. On grainy CCTV-like images, the mother can see her naked husband. He touches his penis, the daughter reaches towards him, he places the cob of corn next to her face, lies on top of her, and then moves the corn down alongside her body; in other images, Laporte is watching. On the non-diegetic soundtrack the Tindersticks deliver an electronic reworking of a Hot Chocolate's (now particularly ominously titled) 1970s hit *Put Your Love In Me*. It is true that these images do not come unannounced – we have already seen the cob of corn, and we have witnessed Justine walking naked through the streets, blood down the inside of her thighs – but until this point they have not been made explicit. Now they are, and the film ends.[7]

The explicitness of the ending goes hand in hand with various forms of underdeterminacy, one of which is produced by the plot structure. Denis provides us with building blocks for a plot, but stops far short of providing a tightly woven narrative. The already mentioned scenes with the naked and bloody Justine are difficult to situate within the overall structure, and an early scene in which Marco imagines that he has killed Laporte and Raphaëlle's son in order to get revenge is pure fantasy. This confuses the spectator, who might now wonder if other scenes are imagined too.[8] As is customary in Denis's films, this loosening of the narrative structure appeals to the imagination of the spectator, inviting us to link the events, while also preventing us from gaining absolute certainty about their positioning.

It could therefore be said that the film works in accordance with the logic described by Sartre in my introduction: as an appeal to the imagination, the freedom, of the spectator. However, the key difference is that Denis invites the co-creation to take place in an area where few spectators are keen to go. For this kind of appeal to work – for the spectator to give up on her reluctance and follow the characters on their descent into darkness – the film therefore also needs to seduce. And it does so with a haunting, hallucinatory beauty. Denis aims to mesmerise the viewers, so that we follow (and help create) the story of Marco as he falls.

This seduction depends on the cinematography. In *Variety* Scott Foundas convincingly compared the cinematography of *Les Salauds* to Michael Mann's *Miami Vice* (2006). Elaborating on this insight, we might say that Denis shares with Mann the ability to create what Harmony Korine (speaking of *Miami Vice*) has described as a particularly 'liquid form of cinema'.[9] In *Les Salauds* the liquidity is thematic: from the opening close-ups of heavy rain running down windows, we are disorientated. It is difficult to tell what is up and what is down in the image; we are clearly watching a form of movement, but we cannot determine what kind (it could be a nightly close-up of a road shot from the front of a fast-moving car). But, as Foundas explains, the Mann-like liquidity primarily results from Denis's desire to use the digital camera to create 'a look that is distinctly non-filmic' (Foundas 2013). *Les Salauds* is Denis's first digital movie and in many scenes it has no depth, but only slippery, flat, texture-less surfaces in which the characters seem to have come unstuck. The spectator watches the beautiful images as if they were placed behind a glass pane. In this sense Denis successfully emulates her own experience of reading Faulkner: 'to read him is to fall' (Denis 2013: 87).

As in the films of Michael Mann, the seduction of Denis's spectator takes place in a particularly slick and stylised universe: most of the characters wear high-end clothes, drive expensive cars, and their bodies (whatever their age and gender) are well-kept and beautiful. All this beauty and luxury slowly tips into depravation, gloom and perversion. Furthermore, the seduction is represented on screen, in particular when Denis and Agnès Godard (her faithful director of photography) insist on the erotic attraction between Marco and Raphaëlle. Their first encounter is characteristic. To get close to Laporte, Marco has rented the apartment just above Raphaëlle. He finds himself going up to his apartment in a typically small Parisian elevator, in which Raphaëlle also rides. Denis films the scene without dialogue, using instead a conventional – but expertly performed – play with focus. Marco is in the foreground, in focus, looking down slightly, Raphaëlle is in the background, blurred. Her profile is to the left of the image, his to the right. She comes into focus (he becomes blurred), and a slight movement of her head now tells us that she is oriented towards him. Focus then shifts back on him. With these very subtle changes in focus, Denis manages to capture (or rather: create) an electric, erotic charge that fills the space between the characters. Bridging the short distance between the two is a pulse, and such pulsations will transport the characters – and their spectators – towards the darkest and most problematic regions of human desire.

The combination of seduction, underdeterminacy and horror produces an ambiguity that no political or ethical framing helps to stabilise. True, it is difficult to watch *Les Salauds* without being reminded of the Dominique Strauss-Kahn affair and other recent scandals of abuse of power. The figure of Laporte is in many ways a capitalist monster: he has ruined the familial shoe factory owned by Justine's parents, he abuses their daughter, and now he makes the cover of gossip magazines with his extravagant lifestyle, beautiful younger woman and dubious tax evasion schemes. He is used to treating people (women, in particular) as disposable belongings. Nevertheless, Denis largely refuses the political register. Even if Laporte, directly or indirectly, is the point of origin for the miseries of almost everyone else, he remains a slightly peripheral character: the spectator to a story of incest. In this way the political dimension slips into the background; it does not help to frame (and tame) the transgressive acts in the film.

Denis also refuses a moral relation to her characters. It is tempting to turn to the title (*Les Salauds*), which she has borrowed from the French translation of Akira Kurosawa's revenge drama *The Bad Sleep Well* (*Les Salauds dorment en paix* (1960); a much more political film).[10] Denis's title may suggest a condemnation of the characters – and Marco does not hesitate to call Laporte a 'salaud' on a number of occasions – but moralisation has never been her style. Indeed, as in *I Can't Sleep* the provocation of this film largely comes from its taking on controversial material without offering the moral framing one might expect. Denis herself goes far in this direction when she argues that 'There are no bastards in the film. Not really . . . They are "semi-bastards", perhaps' (Denis 2013: 86). And she continues: 'my intention never was to investigate the circles of power, or to make a film on incest. And I really like the character played by Michel Subor. It's an old man, he has a kid, it's Michel Subor' (Denis 2013: 86).

So how *are* we meant to relate to this feverish and unpleasant vision? If Denis does not offer a political or moral framing, from what position is she filming? The conclusion to the *Cahiers* interview provides some insight:

> CD: In *Le petit soldat* by Godard, Michel Subor first sentence is: 'I have no ideal, but I still have time to live'. This is a sentence that resonates with me. [. . .]. Perhaps I have expressed something that I cannot fully understand yet. I wanted to live through the situation of someone with no ideal. Perhaps that is a good thing after all. And perhaps the ideal will never come back. (Denis 2013: 88)

Denis thus seems to be filming from what we could call a nihilist position ('I have no ideal').[11] The quotation invites us to think that Denis continues, and radicalises, her variations on Subor's character from *Le Petit Soldat* (*The Little Soldier*) (1963). Already in Godard's film, Subor was a man without ideals – struggling to find a place between the Algerians and the French during the Algerian war of independence. In *Beau Travail* (1999), Subor kept the name Godard had given to him almost forty years earlier (Forrestier), and he was now adrift in northern Africa as a general in the French Foreign Legion. In this film Subor's character was the disenchanted representative of a former colonial power that had long since lost all legitimacy. In other words, his character remained politicised. In *The Intruder* and *White Material*, Subor no longer had the name given to him by Godard, but he continued to play characters

that allowed Denis to depict global inequalities and show post-colonial conflicts. These themes have not entirely disappeared in the recent film, but they
are no longer central: *Les Salauds* is arguably the least post-colonial of Denis's
film to date. Laporte's (and Denis's) nihilism can therefore haemorrhage
into the film without being kept in check by political critique. But maybe this
embrace of nihilism has its own value ('perhaps that is a good thing after all')?
What could be the value of embracing nihilism?

At this moment it is tempting to perform a redemptive turn. But as in
the analyses of *Twentynine Palms*, *Code Blue* and *In My Skin*, I shall resist this
temptation. We cannot transform the lack of an ideal, and the desperate, dystopian, transgressive narrative into a socially progressive act of filmmaking.
Neither the film, nor the interview with Denis, provides us with a justification
for a politically engaged or otherwise optimistic reading – we cannot even go
as far as the 'rattling of the bars' in Marina de Van's film. Perhaps the next
step into the darkness takes us to Adorno's characterisation of Beckett's plays
as 'being full of inaudible cries that things should be different' (Adorno 2007:
381) – but Denis adds to the inaudible a hypothetical dimension (*perhaps* there
is value – *perhaps*) that makes even Adorno's sentence seem too optimistic.
But what we do find in Denis's interview, in place of a redemptive turn, is the
insistence that film – and other arts – should be given licence to explore the
human psyche, freely:

> The realm of the imaginary, music, theatre, poetry, cinema, should allow us
> to go beyond the limits of the acceptable [sortir des limites de l'acceptable].
> In any case, these things are all part of us. I am woman, and I am not going
> to rape my daughter, but I can understand the father, just as I can understand
> Oedipus. That does not mean, I think it is a good thing. (Denis 2013: 88)

With this quotation we are back in the territory of the short Kristeva text that
I drew upon in my analysis of *Dogville*: the human psyche is rich and complex,
some of these complexities are antisocial and destructive; art is the proper
place to explore what escapes the norms of the acceptable. It is therefore
important to insist on the difference between life and art, only this will allow
art to have the 'ethical role' which consists in negotiating a relation to the
fullness of human experience.[12]

However, it might be relevant to introduce a slightly different way of
theorising this engagement with the antisocial: Guattari's notion of mental
ecology. In *The Three Ecologies* ([1989] 2008), Guattari proposes:

> Rather than tirelessly implementing procedures of censorship and conten-
> tion in the name of great moral principles we should learn how to promote
> a true ecology of the phantasm, one that works through the transference,
> translation and redeployment of their matters of expression. It is, of course,

legitimate to repress the 'acting out' of certain fantasies! But initially it is necessary for even negative and destructive phantasmagorias to acquire modes of expression – as in the treatment of psychosis – that allow them to be 'abreacted' in order to reanchor existential Territories that are drifting away. This sort of 'transversalization' of violence does not presuppose the need to deal with the existence of an intrapsychic death drive that constantly lies in wait, ready to ravage everything in its path as soon as the Territories of the Self lose their consistency and vigilance. Violence and negativity are the products of complex subjective assemblages; they are not intrinsically inscribed in the essence of the human species, but are constructed and maintained by multiple assemblages of enunciation. Sade and Céline both endeavoured, with more or less success, to turn their negative fantasies into quasi-baroque ones, and because of this they may be considered as key authors for a mental ecology. Any persistently intolerant and uninventive society that fails to 'imaginarize' the various manifestations of violence risks seeing this violence crystallized in the real. (Guattari [1989] 2008: 38, translation slightly modified)

Clearly, both Kristeva and Guattari are concerned with letting art and literature explore the phantasms that could threaten our mental health and crystallise in dangerous actions if left unattended. Kristeva, Guattari, von Trier and Denis all seem to agree that if we do not allow this work of 'image-forming' to take place in art, it might happen in the world; they are all wary of the dangers of denying the 'non-acceptable' its expression. But Kristeva theorises with the Freudian concept of the death drive, whereas Guattari is careful to distinguish himself from this concept which he finds too essentialist and tied up with an idea of subjectivity that is insufficiently ecological. Denis's 'liquid cinema', with its experience of falling, seems closer to Guattari's theorisations.

There are also important differences between von Trier's and Denis's dealings with that which lies beyond 'the acceptable'. In *Dogville*, von Trier could be said to deal with the non-acceptable in a 'master-ful' way, even if this mastery was also ironic. He manipulates the spectator, invites us to live through our antisocial desires, and aspires to make us confront them. In this process he also demonstrates – as do Sade, Céline and Denis – that the non-acceptable is a rich source for art. There is in *Dogville* a clarity and self-assuredness: Lars von Trier does *not* embrace a nihilist position, but is carefully producing *and staging* our confrontation with the inner bastard (his *Antichrist* seems to me altogether different). Denis's approach is not one of mastery: she is not entirely sure *what* she is communicating ('Perhaps I have expressed something that I cannot fully understand yet'), and she definitely does not want to treat incest as a *topic* ('I don't like the idea that one can make a film "about" incest'). She is not *using* the non-acceptable in a socially productive way, she is not even using the non-acceptable to warn us against our fascination for it. She is exploring nihilism without allowing the viewer to think that *Les Salauds* is a controlled exercise in provocation. The film *may* testify to a desire to move from nihilism to mental ecology, but we stumble upon the *perhaps* and therefore remain stuck between nihilism and mental ecology.

The pull of provocation (part II)

In this short engagement with *Les Salauds*, I have relied quite extensively upon the interview that Denis gave to *Cahiers du cinéma*. It is a remarkable interview, less for the quotations given here above than for those that will now follow. In the analysis of *Dogville*, I argued that this film pushed us to acknowledge the asymmetrical relation between ethics inside and outside the movie theatre. But I also added that von Trier himself failed to uphold this distinction at the press conference for *Melancholia* in Cannes: as he later admitted, he let himself 'be egged on by a provocation'. Denis's interview in *Cahiers du cinéma* is lower profile than von Trier's performance in front of the world press in Cannes (and she is sensible enough to not speak about Hitler), but in my opinion the interview nevertheless testifies to a comparable desire to provoke, and to the same confusion between intra- and extra-cinematic ethics.

Denis's observations are complex and provocative. On the one hand, she has a desire to state the obvious: incest exists, and it is in that sense part of human nature ('what is shown in the film is simply human'; Denis 2013: 86). Furthermore, she has (as already mentioned) the ambition to show without explaining: 'I did not have the impression that I was filming something disgraceful, but rather something indeed very violent that exceeds our understanding. I understand that such things can happen. There is humanity in incest. I acknowledge this [Il y a de l'humanité dans l'inceste. Je la reconnais]' (Denis 2013: 86). But just like von Trier, she takes these ideas further, and goes beyond the argument that 'incest happens, it is part of human nature.' Von Trier did this by introducing the ambiguous idea of 'sympathy', Denis shocks her interviewers with a number of complex sentences concerning the footage at the end of the film. The relevant passage begins when Denis, almost casually, notes that 'the fact that it is her father does not seem particularly shocking to me.' This clearly does shock Stéphane Delorme, and Denis therefore continues:

CD: But I have the impression you are looking at me with horror! I think
   what happens in the film is banal.
SD: No, what we see at the end is not banal.
CD: That's odd [curieux], I have the impression it's an almost baroque

image. It is inspired by Faulkner's *Sanctuary*, but in my film it is much less cruel, because at least it's her father [. . .].

SD: What do you mean by 'at least it's her father'?

CD: What I am trying to say is that she is not locked up in a barn, she consents. After all, you are allowed to love your father, I can't see what's wrong with that [on peut aimer son père, je ne vois pas où est le mal]. (Denis 2013: 83)

The insistence on the banality of incest here runs away with Denis as she lets herself be egged on by a provocation. The result is a hyperbolic performance of *not wanting to judge* ('I can't see what's wrong with that'), and I am therefore tempted, once again, to speak about a confusion between the cinematic and the extra-cinematic world. I suspect that for Denis it is the love of the actors and the other members of the crew that produces the slippage. When Denis (in a quotation given earlier) notes that there are no bastards in the film, not even Laporte – 'I really like the character played by Michel Subor. It's an old man, he has a kid, it's Michel Subor' – it seems that the love of the actor (Subor) blocks her view of the character. And Denis herself insists that this is a film that could work only with this particular cast – that she would not have liked to make it with other actors. It is as if the pleasure of working with all her regular actors (Subor, Lindon, Descas, Colin, Dogué), cinematographer (Godard), screen writer (Fargeau) and musicians (Tindersticks) not only allow this compelling and unpleasant exploration of the dark aspects of the human psyche – but also confuses Denis's moral compass in the interview.

The reason for citing the bewildering passage is not only, once again, to note the pull of provocation. Next to the insistence on banality, it is interest-

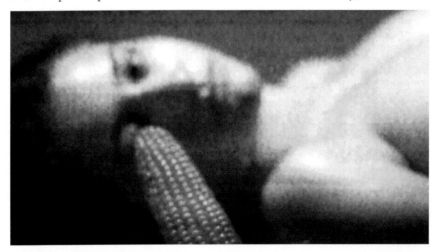

Figure 16   'At least it's her father . . .' (Les Salauds)

ing that Denis describes the last image as 'almost baroque'. We encountered the same adjective when Guattari explained how Sade and Céline were able to 'turn their negative fantasies into quasi-baroque ones'. This similarity is worth highlighting because it brings us back to the relation between fiction and reality (indexicality). It seems likely that the baroque images (and descriptions) are meant to pull away from the indexical. By going all the way – by going over the top – Denis tries to mark a distance from reality, rather than to drive home the referential (in the way, I argued, that de Palma tried to do). In *Les Salauds* this move towards the baroque depends on the cinematography: on the one hand, the final images have a grainy CCTV-quality and therefore come with a very high indexical value; on the other, the montage, framing, and camera movements are so stylised that the ending clearly cannot be seen as a form of raw footage (this is a 'CCTV camera' that moves around freely, experimenting with angles, framing and close-ups!). Furthermore, the sequence begins with the shot of a camera lens, followed by a shot in which Justine's father gazes directly at the spectator – typical instances of self-conscious modernist filmmaking. On the basis of this peculiar clash between CCTV aesthetics and modernist stylisation, it can be argued that this last scene takes a step towards the baroque. But exactly what does this mean?

One possible answer is to suggest that the final scene stands in a somewhat free relation to the (episodic) narrative: we are allowed to see the ending as an independent, but also exemplary scene. In other words the word 'baroque' can be used to justify a parallel with the extraordinary ending to *Beau Travail*. In terms of narrative, Galoup's (Denis Lavant) dance solo raises a high number of questions – Where in the narrative should this sequence be placed? Does Denis suggest that Galoup has died? – but at a more emotional level the ending makes perfect sense as a vignette illustrating the liberation of the energy the military man has worked so hard to repress. Likewise the final scene in *Les Salauds* challenges the narrative logic – Who is shooting these images? Why would any photographer film the camera lens? – but at an emotional level we can again consider the scene as a vignette presenting the dark pit from which the narrative has been emerging. However, this comparison with the cathartic ending to *Beau Travail* also demonstrates just how disheartening the ending of *Les Salauds* is: it is hardly surprising that critics have avoided the baroque reading.

A word on Catherine Breillat's *À ma sœur*

In the first chapter, I included an analysis of *Redacted* because its contrast with *Dogville* could help to clarify the arguments about a distinction between ethics inside and outside the movie theatre. At the end of this analysis of how the

different desperation films block the path from transgression to emancipation, a counterexample can once again help to clarify my argument. I will
therefore offer some brief (and slightly schematic) remarks about Catherine
Breillat's well-known *À ma sœur* (2001); an 'extreme' film that presents a very
different relation between transgression and emancipation.

À ma sœur tells the story of two sisters on summer vacation. Elena is 15 and
Anaïs a couple of years younger. Elena is slender, pretty and conventional:
she dreams of romantic love, marriage with her one and only, and a bourgeois life. Her younger sister Anaïs is mature and intelligent, overweight and
unconventional: she wants to lose her virginity, preferably with someone she
does not care about. She feels that only in this way can she avoid becoming
the 'achievement' of a man she loves. Despite (or perhaps because of) their
differences, the relation between the sisters is also tender and intimate.

The film includes two much debated rape scenes. The first is when Elena,
in an almost twenty-minute long and excruciatingly claustrophobic scene,
lets herself be talked into 'consensual' anal sex by a summer sweetheart who
argues that when the intercourse is anal, it does not count. It is not only the
argument, the inevitability of the outcome and the length of the scene that
disturbs the spectator,[13] but also the fact that the scene takes place in a room
where her younger sister is hearing everything (tears down her cheeks) while
pretending to have fallen asleep. Legally this may not be a rape, but as Breillat
makes very clear in the film (and in interviews), morally it is.

The other rape, that of Anaïs, mirrors that of her sister: legally it is a
rape, morally the situation is more complex. Driving home from summer
vacation in a state of familial dissolution following the mother's discovery
of Elena's misfortunes, the sisters and their mother pull over for the night.
As in *Dogville*, the film then suddenly turns 'bad taste', low genre. Von Trier
slips into vigilante mode (Bronson/Eastwood-style), Breillat's film turns
slasher. Almost out of nowhere jumps a man with an axe. He hammers the
axe through the front window of the car, into Elena's forehead, and then
strangles the mother.[14] Anaïs watches in a state of shock, urinating in her
pants. The killer sees this. Anaïs gets out of the car, the man pulls her into
the nearby woods, and begins to rape her. She does not fight back but instead
lies still; at the end of the act, we return to the art film as Anaïs embraces
her perpetrator in a gesture of absolution similar to that of Mouchette in the
rape scene of Bresson's eponymous film from 1967. *À ma sœur* then ends the
following morning as Anaïs is being taken out of the woods by policemen,
past the bodies of her sister and mother. She insists that she was not raped,
before looking straight into the camera in a final freeze-frame reminiscent of
Truffaut's *Les 400 coups* (*The 400 Blows*).[15]

The ending of Breillat's film has been widely debated and there is no doubt that 'the ambiguity of the scene, and the uncertainty over how it should be interpreted, is largely down to the way that it eschews dominant representational paradigms of rape and victimhood' (as Tanya Horeck writes about a (quasi-)rape scene in Breillat's *Romance*, in Russell 2012: 199[16]). This is not the place to offer an in-depth analysis of the film, but I will argue that Breillat's film does precisely the opposite of the desperation films I have been looking at here. As Trevor H. Maddock and Ivan Krisjansen (2003) have argued, Breillat's provocation is to present the final rape as a Georges Bataille-inspired experience of sovereignty. This does not mean that Breillat is condoning rape, but in the end sequence Anaïs reaches something like a complete ecstatic dissolution of her being: she is now, as Bataille would say, 'like water in water'. The film thereby not only suggests that the real rape is the one with Elena, it also suggests that the rape of Anaïs, as she says herself, is not a rape but something else. When Anaïs looks into the camera one last time, she is elsewhere. Obviously, Breillat very well knows that for most viewers 'her suggestion that to be raped is a potentially liberating experience stretches credibility, to say the least' (Vincendeau 2001: 18), but it is precisely this exercise of stretching our beliefs for which she is aiming. In that sense, Breillat offers a cathartic experience – while remaining acutely aware that most spectators will receive it as a slap in the face. The slap, Breillat seems to think, might just be what it takes to wake us up from our bourgeois slumber.

À ma sœur is not a desperation film; and the moment we understand that the shocking ending is meant to be liberating, it pulls away from the feel-bad register altogether. As mentioned, there is no doubt that Breillat knew the film could be seen differently than how she intended it, but on the other hand, any spectator familiar with her previous film *Romance* (1999) – where the heroine gives birth at the exact moment she blows her husband to pieces (having rigged a gas oven) – would suspect that *À ma sœur* is something very different from a story about the tragic summer vacation of a nuclear family. Breillat's film is not meant to leave the spectator shattered, it testifies to a continued belief in the link between transgression and emancipation.

3.3 THE AVANT-GARDE AS FARCE? KORINE'S *TRASH HUMPERS*

As will soon become evident, there is a gulf between the desperation films and Harmony Korine's *Trash Humpers* in terms of style, tone and cultural context. But Korine's film shares with the titles discussed so far in this chapter both a desire to provoke and a willingness to work on the relation between transgression and emancipation. Like all the films discussed in this chapter, *Trash Humpers* complicates this relation to the point where spectators disagree wildly on the question of how to understand it. But unlike the previous examples, Korine does this in a register that is largely farcical. Let us consider how the film operates.

Korine explains that he chose the title to make sure that no one could feel they entered the cinema under a false pretence. Similarly the opening shot removes all ambiguity: the film begins in daylight, with a shot of one of the male protagonists crouching, defecating in front of a carport. We are in a register that has little to do with the anguished tone of Dumont and Antoniak, the deadpan acting of de Van or the troubling explorations of Denis. In so far as *Trash Humpers* then has a plot, it follows a woman (Momma) and three men (Travis, Hervé and Buddy) roaming around Nashville. Without taking their clothes off, they spend a good deal of their time humping trash bins – at times they expand their repertoire to trees, fences, refrigerators and other objects. Each character wears a latex mask and a wig that make them look old and decrepit, but their body movements are youthful. This is basically 'white trash' humping trash bins. The soundtrack is dominated by their bizarre voices, high-pitched sound-spasms, often laughing or singing silly nursery rhymes about murder, in their heavy southern accents. The director's wife, Rachel Korine, plays Momma, and is assisted by Travis (Travis Nicholson) and Buddy (Brian Kotzur). Korine himself plays Hervé, and most of the time holds the camera.

In the fanzine that accompanies the DVD, Korine explains that *Trash Humpers* originates in a childhood experience. One night, as a boy growing up in Nashville, he saw from his window a group of old, drunken men and women pretending to hump trash bins. Thirty years later, still unable to get this scene out of his head, he made a film about four such trash humpers, the underbelly of American society.

It is a worrying film from the beginning – rich in vandalising and bizarre scenes of humping. But the action becomes outright disturbing after thirty-two minutes when we suddenly see a naked male corpse in a forest. He is lying face down, and the camera – held by a trash humper – carefully scrutinises him. We can only assume that this is the work of the trash humpers. In the rest of the film, the group spy on, humiliate and occasionally murder people in a series of incidents that give the film a very episodic structure. There are a lot of dirty and decaying settings and people – but because of the stylisation there is also a peculiar, haunting beauty in the film (as almost all reviews of the film acknowledged). This beauty holds the film together beyond the relative absence of a narrative and a psychological or indeed any other form of logic.

Trash Humpers relates to two different contexts: the first is popular culture phenomena such as *Jackass*, YouTube oddities, home videos, horror and zombie films. The film's episodic structure, the childish and destructive stunts, the disturbing rubber masks (which might recall Leatherface), and the fact that the humpers are doing the filming themselves – and performing for the camera – are just some of its affinities to these genres. The other context is a more high-art set of references including names from various avant-gardes and experimental video. Many of these avant-garde artists already draw on popular culture: we are, as Andreas Huyssen might say, 'after the great divide', beyond any distinction between high art and mass culture.

Trash Humpers as an avant-garde film

If we approach Harmony Korine's film from the question of how it relates to the avant-garde(s), it is important to say that *Trash Humpers* not only engages in the thematic exploration of the relation between transgression and eman-cipation, which I have associated with the avant-garde ethos, it also offers itself as an example of avant-garde art (rather than, for instance, a European art film). *Trash Humpers* is situated at the margins of the culture industry, and has many of the hallmarks of the avant-garde critique of 'the institution of art' (Bürger 1984).

For instance, *Trash Humpers* is a no-budget film. Korine explains that only six weeks elapsed from the conceptualisation of the project to the final cut being ready. The shooting was done over two weeks, on VHS and largely in the order of diegesis (since there is very little diegesis, this cannot have been the most challenging aspect of the project). The material was then edited on two VCRs largely with the same 'editing technique' one would use to copy VHS cassettes, and the result was finally transferred to 35 mm. The film high-lights its own no-budget status: at times the cassette is tracking, there is 'snow' on the images, most of which are shaky, underlit or overlit – the colours are unnaturalistic. It is these characteristics – the trash aesthetic – that help to give the film its particular haunting VCR beauty; a beauty particularly palpable in the scenes shot at night, under the strong streetlights.

The film premiered at the Toronto film festival, made it onto the festival circuit, but did not receive a general release. In her review of the film Amy Taubin insists on the status of *Trash Humpers* as a homeless 'post-movie' (Taubin 2010: 71). It does not fit the cinema-room, nor the YouTube plat-form that would be likely to destroy the monotony of the film by dividing it up into separate parts. Other critics have wondered if it perhaps rather fits the gallery space. This homelessness duplicates that of the trash humpers who sleep under bridges, squat houses and clearly have no fixed abode. Originally, Korine had considered a very different form of distribution: he thought about uploading the film to the web, uncredited, leaving it to be found by curious browsers as a kind of electronic message in a bottle from some obscure dis-aster zone. He also thought about simply leaving VHS copies in the streets for everyone to pick up. These plans speak to his desire to pull the film out of the traditional art (or film) market, and by that same gesture draw the spectator into a parallel world that History somehow managed to pass by. Even if Korine eventually dropped these plans for an alternative form of distribution ('I did not have the patience'), he has continued to speak about his film as a 'found object'. In this way, he could be said to align himself more thoroughly with the institutional critique that Peter Bürger associates with the avant-garde than the art films that have been my main case studies in this book (*Kindering* excepted).

At the same time, however, the film playfully partakes in the capitalist economy: it was produced in a limited edition VHS version (150 copies), each cassette 'individually vandalized by hand and signed by director Harmony Korine'; the soundtrack was released on EP and CD, again vandalised by the director, packaged in a brown paper bag and sold at the price of $15 – finally a very limited edition of three 35 mm prints was produced and packaged in cases hand-decorated by Korine, each sold for the price of $7,500.[17] This self-conscious and ironic play with the avant-garde and its relation to the culture industry – trash merchandise at truffle price – is one that can be found at almost every conceivable level at which it is possible to engage with the film.

There are many avant-garde works it could be logical to bring into the discussion of *Trash Humpers*. The opening scenes of defecation could be compared to some of Kurt Kren's actionist videos (for instance the 1967 video called *20 September*), and the masks of the protagonists also recall work by Kren and Viennese Actionists (as well as Ed Kienholz's installation piece *Five Car Stud* (1969–72)). But thematically and formally, the most obvious reference point is the American performance and installation artist Paul McCarthy. He is inspired by Kren and the Actionists and has also worked with rubber masks. It seems plausible that McCarthy's installation *The Garden* (1992) gets a nod in Korine's film. *The Garden* uses the set of a popular American western series called *Bonanza*, a piece of woodland: high trees, green grass, all in plastic. Walking around the set, the spectator discovers two life-like robots through the branches: an older man, whom McCarthy calls 'the father', can be seen humping a tree, while 'the son' is humping the ground. The installation and its very literal critique of US television culture (fuck *Bonanza*!) has elements of the grotesque, but the combination of the mechanical and the human, the vertical father and the horizontal son, the fact that these robots have no genitals, and the way in which the installation turns the spectators into voyeurs as we peak through the plastic branches, all disturb our desire to simply laugh off the installation. Korine's film contains several scenes of tree-humping (and fellatio on branches) which bring to mind McCarthy. Being filmed by the trash humpers themselves, and having made its way to the spectator as a form of found footage,[18] the film, again like *The Garden*, puts us in the position of being a voyeur: watching *Trash Humpers* is a bit like reading someone else's diary (see Kendall 2012: 54–5).

Other scenes in *Trash Humpers* can also be associated with McCarthy: in a lengthy scene, the humpers force the Siamese twins Mak and Plak, who are joined at the head by a peculiar form of umbilical chord, to eat a pile of pancakes soaked in washing up liquid. The combination of trash aesthetics, viscous materials, eating and the abject places Korine's scene in a universe similar to that explored by McCarthy in performances such as *Bossy Burger* (1991).[19] The similarities are hardly coincidental: even if Korine has not mentioned McCarthy in relation to *Trash Humpers*, he has talked about his admiration for McCarthy on other occasions. The two first met when Korine was in his early twenties (at the time of McCarthy's *The Garden* and *Bossy Burger*), and he was exhibiting his sellotape artwork in McCarthy's Los Angeles gallery. More recently they both participated in James Franco's appropriation art project *Rebel* (2012) alongside artists such as Ed Ruscha and Douglas Gordon – all delivering their (sometimes very free) take on Nicholas Ray's *Rebel Without a Cause* (1955). It is therefore logical to place *Trash Humpers* in relation to the intractable avant-garde – indeed, it is possible to regard the film as a very self-conscious engagement with the avant-garde.

This self-conscious relation to the avant-garde becomes very evident towards the end of the film, where we find a moment that draws particular attention to itself. The trash humpers are on a nightly ride, circling around Nashville, when Korine's figure, Hervé, embarks on a monologue from the driver's seat. The monologue is fairly long; in particular in the context of a film that generally uses voices to produce sound rather than meaningful dialogue (see Inouye 2012). Despite its slightly rambling nature, it is worth quoting extensively:

> This is important. You don't really understand the importance, but sometimes when I drive through these streets at night, I can smell the pain of all these people living in here. I can smell how all these people are just trapped in their lives – their day-to-day lives [. . .]. I can feel their pain, like coming from these trees and these houses. I can feel that pain and it hurts me to think that I live such a balanced life – all these people going to work . . ., going to pray on Sundays along with their children. And I never quite understand that; why anyone would choose to live that life. That's a stupid way to live. That's a stupid, stupid, stupid way to live.
>
> See what people don't understand is, we choose to live like free, free, free people. You know we choose to live like people should live. I don't follow no rules on Sunday, I don't eat no pies on Monday, I don't play no games on Tuesday, I don't cry myself to sleep on Wednesday.

> It's all just, I don't know . . ., one long game, I guess you could call it. One
> long, long game, you know. I expect we will win it, I expect that all these
> people will be dead and buried long, long before I even catch my second
> wind. I feel like a young boy.

With its critique of work, religion and the inanity of a bourgeois lifestyle,
with its insistence on youth and vitality, with its conception of life as a game,
Hervé's speech seems like an archetypical piece of avant-garde rhetoric.
When we add to this, that the monologue is one of the rare moments in the
film where a character makes sense (and that the sense-making is done by
Korine's own character, looking straight into the camera), it is tempting, as
Cameron Shaw has done, to read the monologue as delivering 'what we might
call the message of the film'. Shaw continues:

> It's a monologue about freedom and subversion, the dangers of conformity
> and the restorative power of anarchy. It is understood by that point that after
> our current conventions of success and stability die out, these characters will
> still be around to advocate for a new destruction, leading what they call the
> 'balanced life.' They'll live this way forever. (Shaw in Korine and Ackermann
> 2011: 76)

In emphasising the restorative power of anarchy, Shaw is pulling Korine's
film towards a progressive agenda, effectively presenting the protagonists as
a form of emancipatory heroes. *Trash Humpers* becomes a film that points to
a set of problems with the American dream and a bourgeois way of life; and
furthermore a film proposing that an anarchist energy could be a step in the
direction of solving these problems.

Korine's own comments about the film largely support this reading. In
various interviews and Q and A's he has described the trash humpers as
'mystics of mayhem' and talked about his 'deep love and admiration for
these characters. Not for what they do, but for the way they do it' (Korine
2009). From other interviews it seems clear that to Korine's mind, the trash
humpers do indeed embody a form of freedom. A typical interview quote
(from the online magazine *vulture*) offers this account:

> It's an ode to vandalism and the creativity of the destructive force. Sometimes
> there's a real beauty to blowing things up, to smashing and burning. It could
> be almost as enlightening as the building of an object. I wanted these char-
> acters to almost be like artists – artists of bad. Like they transcend vandalism
> and turn it into something creative, and they do it with such glee. There's no
> sense of morality in the film, they just do whatever they want.[20]

With this it should be clear that *Trash Humpers* can be put in an avant-garde
tradition – and more specifically in a tradition that has its roots in Dadaism.
This is the tradition we encountered in the first chapter, when I – via

Boris Groys – wrote about the Bakunian ('destruction is creation') and the iconoclastic dimension of avant-garde art; it is the avant-garde tradition that reappeared in a more aestheticised version in the slow-motion sequence of exploding consumer commodities at the end of *Zabriskie Point*.

Nevertheless, the question of what *Trash Humpers* does to this avant-garde tradition – how it relates to the intractable avant-garde – is still worth raising. Even if one believes the film tries to re-do the intractable avant-garde, the fact that it is *re*-doing would give to the transgressions a very different status from the one they had in the first instance (as indicated by the discussions referred to at the beginning of this chapter). In short, the film is more ambiguous than some of the quotations above invite us to think.

In my opinion Shaw's interpretation of Hervé's monologue – and of the film as a whole – is both too literal and too optimistic (and I also think that Shaw's quotation goes further than Korine's insistence on there being 'no sense of morality in the film'). Shaw neglects the deliberately exaggerated nature of Hervé's claim to 'a balanced life', and instead jumps at the chance to associate the transgressions of the trash humpers with emancipation. He does not consider the lethargic way in which Hervé delivers this monologue, or the fact that towards the end of the lecture Travis seems to have fallen asleep on the back seat of the car. Neither does he mention the many scenes in which the trash humpers seem far from embodying any restorative power. For instance, it is noteworthy that only two minutes after Hervé's monologue, Momma, empty bottle in hand, seems to be suffering an existential crisis, imploring God for help ('I don't mean to do wrong Lord. Why don't you guide me? I don't know which way I am going'). The point of this quick move from a monologue about the freedom and happiness of trash humping to Momma's existential crisis is not to suggest that truth lies in the experience of crisis. Rather the point is that these moments counterbalance each other, and thereby invite the viewer to think twice before accepting Hervé's (and to some extent Korine's) claim that the trash humpers embody vitality and freedom.[21]

My reading of *Trash Humpers* therefore comes closer to the one Benjamin Halligan offers of Korine's earlier film *Gummo* (1997) when he writes that 'Korine invites and then rejects any liberal agenda' (Halligan 2012: 154). In *Trash Humpers* the same applies: there is again a (pleasurable) transgression of the norms of the bourgeois society, but also a destabilisation of any ideals about the political progressiveness of transgression. It is true that Korine's film aligns itself with the anti-bourgeois position of the trash humpers, but contrary to what Shaw suggests, it is not easy to turn these largely lethargic – racist and murderous – trash humpers into agents of revolution and social revitalisation. In other words: *Trash Humpers* does not fully embrace

Figure 17   *Travis, Momma and Buddy: emancipatory heroes? (*Trash Humpers*)*

first-generation avant-garde, nor does it simply mock or undermine it. Like *Twentynine Palms* (but in a very different register), it transgresses bourgeois norms *and* deliberately disappoints progressive expectations.

Korine and Dumont are obviously far from being the first directors to perform this double transgression, creating films that some viewers find ideologically ambiguous, and others outright conservative ('a grandiose form of passivity' as Quandt wrote). Something comparable can be said about two of the films with which *Trash Humpers* has most often been associated, Werner Herzog's *Even Dwarfs Started Small* (1970) and Lars von Trier's *The Idiots* (1998).[22] A short engagement with these films will help to further situate Korine's provocations.

Dwarfs

Herzog's film is set in what appears to be a correction house situated in the lunar landscapes on the island of Lanzarote (the German word used for the institution ('Anstalt') can – appropriately – refer to anything from a mental hospital and a prison, to an educational institution). The film is shot in black and white, in what already at the time was a dated 1:37 ratio. This gives the film a deliberately anachronistic character: as with the VCR-aesthetics of *Trash Humpers* we seem to be in the past, or perhaps even outside time. The inhabitants of the institution are rioting against the authorities, here represented by a vice-principal of the institution (Paul Glauer). This vice-principal has taken one of the inmates hostage, and has barricaded himself in his office; outside, chaos reigns.

All roles are played by dwarfs, and they are (at least) as nasty and destructive as other actors who more frequently appear on film. It is not that the film is set in an institution for dwarfs – it is rather that the world in which it takes place only holds dwarfs, as if the human race had shrunk. Most of the characters vandalise the institution and many treat each other with cruelty. A large group of seeing dwarfs harass a couple of blind dwarfs, they engage in food fights, set fire to potted plants, and at a certain point they form a long procession, the first in the line carrying a crucified monkey, which the seeing dwarfs have abducted from the blind dwarfs. These activities are interspersed with (other) images of cruelty towards – and by – animals: chickens are shown to 'cannibalise' other chickens (we see a live chicken pecking on a dead chicken, but we also see a healthy chicken pecking at one that is simply limping); in another scene the dwarfs kill a sow that has small piglets, and the piglets later return to suckle at the teat of the dead mother. At the end of the film, the vice-president has escaped from the office (after some obscure act of torture to his hostage, we are led to believe) and now he has completely lost his mind: he is talking to a dead tree, claiming that he can point a finger at the tree for longer than it can point a branch at him. Meanwhile the protagonist, Hombre (Helmut Döring), is next to a dromedary, the animal is on its knees, and Hombre is laughing in his characteristic, high-pitched voice. This laughing continues for several minutes until it becomes unclear whether Hombre is laughing or choking, and we fear that he will literally laugh himself to death. The madness – and the maddening effect – of the film is heightened by its sound: not only is Hombre's voice bizarre, high-pitched and grating (seemingly without any relation to his body), the music during the film is a combination of ritual music from Africa (recorded for the film Herzog had just shot, *Fata Morgana* (1971)), and a folk song from Lanzarote, sung – almost shouted – specifically for the film by an 11-year-old girl who was placed in a grotto and instructed to sing her soul out.

In many scenes we find circular movements, such as the repeated scenes with a driverless car going round in circles, the dwarfs chasing it. These scenes seem to sum up the absence of narrative progression that characterises the film as whole. The film is told in an incomplete flashback: it opens in a room that appears to be located at the police station; the dwarfs have all been taken in for interrogation, the rebellion has failed, and Hombre is insisting that he will not give the others away (but they are already waiting for their turn outside the door). We then watch the vandalising in a flashback, but never return to the frame. Given all these characteristics, it is hardly surprising that Korine described his first experience of watching *Even Dwarfs Started Small*, one of his favourite films, as that of a 'cinematic abduction by UFO' (in Halligan 2002: 153).

Released in 1969, the film was immediately associated with the events of May '68. It is well known that Herzog was sceptical (to put it mildly) about the efforts of the rebelling youth, and that he has never considered himself to be a political filmmaker ('because I have never been into using the medium of film as a political tool, my attitude really put me apart from most other filmmakers'; Herzog 2002: 56).[23] On the relation between *Even Dwarfs Started Small* and '68, he has been contradictory. Often, he has denied the film was satirising the rebelling youth by intimating that the ideologues of '68 were intellectual dwarfs; occasionally, he has suggested that critics were right to link the film to its specific historical context. Either way, the film is clearly engaged in a double negation: it disturbs bourgeois norms and political respectability by having a group of dwarfs engage in various forms of destructive and transgressive activities; but it also disturbs liberal viewers by refusing to establish any obvious link between these transgressions and a progressive political agenda. As a result many critics have tended either to condemn the film as a gratuitous provocation, a fetishisation of dwarfs engaged in blind destruction, or to defend it by forcing it through a progressive reading. In the most optimistic of such progressive readings, the dwarfs might even be recast as transgressive heroes fighting their way to freedom.

An example of this optimism can be found in a recent article by William Verrone, 'Transgression and Transcendence in the Films of Werner Herzog'. He finds in *Even Dwarfs Started Small* 'a positive vision of human emancipation' (Verrone 2011: 185); even if (as I believe the following quotation from his article also demonstrates) the film resists such a univocally positive portrayal of the ravaging dwarfs:

> The central characters of the narrative, which are all played by dwarfs, overthrow the leaders of the asylum/school where they have been held, humiliated, and subjugated to rituals that do not allow them any freedom. In order to transgress these boundaries, they must resort to chaos and violence; there is no alternative. Their struggle is a struggle for dignity. Essentially, when the characters become in control of the prison-house where they have been entrapped, they become spiritually free from certain laws. Herzog does indeed show them as quite mad (there is no explanation for their rebellion, nor do they actually 'succeed' or gain anything in overthrowing their 'masters'), but the overall point seems to indicate that with transgression comes transcendence – here a collective sense of freedom from authority. (Verrone 2011: 197–8)

With this reading we obviously get close to Shaw's interpretation of *Trash Humpers*. However, before comparing *Even Dwarfs Started Small* and Korine's film, let us also consider von Trier's *The Idiots*. It should be noted from the outset that this film can only partly be described as a feel-bad film in the sense

I have given to the term; in important respects it is closer to Breillat's *À ma sœur*.

Idiots

In terms of psychology, sociology and plot development Lars von Trier gives the viewer much more to work with than Herzog, but his film nevertheless remains ambiguous. We follow a group of middle-class friends in their late twenties pretending to be idiots – 'spassing', as the film puts it – in public settings.[24] The most vocal group members consider the activity as a form of revolutionary activity. They see themselves provoking the doxas of Danish society, presenting the spassing as an emancipatory activity for both body and mind (but at night they happily return to the big villa of a rich uncle, where they have taken refuge). When the leader of the group, Stoffer (Jens Albinus), suggests that they must raise the stakes by moving the spassing to a setting that matters for them personally, they prove unable to do so, the group dissolves, and they return to their bourgeois lives as teachers and advertising agents.

At this level, *The Idiots* comes across as a satire of romantic, anti-bourgeois aspirations (not unlike Paul Nizan's novel *La Conspiration* (1938) which inspired Godard's *La Chinoise* (1967)). However, certain scenes complicate this reading, and suggest that the spassing exercise has a power that cannot be reduced to the simplistic political agenda that some of the group members promote. For instance, we see how the fragile Josephine (Louise Mieritz), who is suffering from some unspecified psychological illness, falls in love with Jeppe (Nikolaj Lie Kaas), and spasses her way to a condition where she no longer needs her medication (until her father shows up, bringing back the 'law'). We also see how one of Stoffer's scenes of spassing produces a psychological instability that is real, rather than simulated. But first of all, the ending complicates the film, pulling *The Idiots* away from its otherwise largely satirical register and closer to a belief in the emancipatory potential of transgression.

At the end Karen (Bodil Jørgensen), the outsider of the group, goes back to her family to see if she can pass the spassing test. As her moment of spassing approaches, we learn that just before the beginning of the film her newborn baby had tragically died. She could not cope with the trauma, so instead of going to the funeral, she ran away without telling neither her husband nor anyone else. She ended up in the group of idiots where no questions were asked. Now she is back, accompanied by her chosen witness Susanne (Anne Louise Hassing). The family is shocked to see her – and shocked when she spasses. Her husband slaps her in the face, Karen cries, and then she and Susanne leave. We are invited to think that the spassing exercise has liberated her, that she can now begin to work her way through the trauma of losing her child.[25] This ending brings *The Idiots* close to the more cathartic register we also found in *À ma sœur.*

In summary, von Trier's film seems to invite a distinction between a socio-political transgression that has little efficiency, and a more existential and spiritual transgression which is given emancipatory potential. It is tempting to consider this as a depoliticised version of the avant-garde: at the psychological level von Trier's film maintains a belief in the transgression, at a political level no such belief is expressed. It is not that the film is uninterested in the political, it is rather that von Trier mocks the hypocritical anti-bourgeois discourse of Stoffer and Axel. This does not exclude the possibility that von Trier would look more sympathetically at other, less superficial forms of political revolt, but there is little doubt that the provocation of *The Idiots* not only comes from the scenes of unsimulated sex (the famous gang-bang scene) and the use of actors with Down's syndrome, but also from its refusal to promote a politics of transgression.

Trash humpers, dwarfs and idiots

With these very brief descriptions of Herzog's and von Trier's films, let us now return to *Trash Humpers.* First it can be said that all three films play with a new form of feel-bad that we could call the *feel-bad farce.* In each case the directors stimulate a desire to laugh, but the spectator will feel uncomfortable giving in to this desire: is it appropriate to laugh at films that depict insurrectionist, vandalising dwarfs, pseudo-revolutionary pseudo-idiots (next to actors with Down's syndrome), and idiotic murderers who spend much of their time humping inanimate objects? We wonder if we would be laughing *at* these characters or *with* them; and because we wonder, we are deprived of the release the laughter could give. In the case of these dark comedies – 'it's the darkest comedy you can imagine', says Herzog about *Even Dwarfs Started Small* – the cathartic emotion that is being called forth, and halted, is therefore laughter. The films also stimulate a range of other emotions (the ending of *The Idiots*, for instance, will probably not make spectators laugh), but they add to the general unpleasantness an ambiguous (and necessarily unfulfilled) desire to laugh away the events depicted.

The main reason for bringing in Herzog and von Trier was that these film-makers also perform a double transgression. But as indicated by the remarks above, their films differ on the relation between transgression and emancipation. *Even Dwarfs Started Small* is concerned with destruction and madness; many critics have been good at bringing out a more 'noble' and 'progressive' dimension in the dwarfs' rebellion, but I find it difficult to give an optimistic reading of this bewildering film. Von Trier's film, on the other hand, adds to the destruction and rebellion a more romantic belief in the existential, transcendental dimension of transgression. This becomes particularly clear at the end of the film when Karen's spassing is given a spiritual dimension largely absent from the more dadaist spassing that we have hitherto been witnessing.[26] It is not that Herzog is blind to such 'ecstatic truths' (to use his own expression), but unlike William Verrone for instance I do not think that the 'ecstatic truths' in *Even Dwarfs Started Small* give grounds for optimism. In this film, Herzog is at his most defiantly nightmarish, and the film is therefore more monotonous and less plot-driven than von Trier's. We begin with the ending in the police station and then watch in flashback; this effectively undermines the possibility of a redemptive ending. The last images of the film drive this negativity home: as mentioned, Hombre and the vice-president are now both mad, locked into two completely meaningless and exhausting activities, fighting battles against a tree and a dromedary, slipping away from any recognisable form of humanity. Hombre's interminable laughter at the end of *Even Dwarfs Started Small* can be seen as the perfect expression of this non-redemptive stance: we listen to a throat that strangles itself by desperately seeking the cathartic dimension of laughter.[27] But how about *Trash Humpers*? Where does it stand in relation to the question of transgression and emancipation? Does it lean towards the potentially more optimistic ending of von Trier, or is it as mad as Herzog's film?

Korine's film shares Herzog's stasis and repetition. This is a film in which transgression – for instance the dry-humping of trash bins – is repeated over and over again. We quickly get to the point where seeing grown-ups in rubber masks doing infantile things becomes tiresome and drains away the drama. Consequently, the most radical moments of transgression – the killings – almost sneak through the back door. They produce a curiously self-reflexive range of emotions in the spectator that may remind us of the meta-emotions that *Elephant* generated by 'disappointing' our desire for drama. Instead of being shocked, the spectator of *Trash Humpers* will be disturbed by watching a bloody corpse with a certain amount of disinterest. This results from the carefully orchestrated play with repetition. At the level of sound, the repetition is produced by the return of the nursery rhymes, the laughter and the bizarre sound-spasms of the trash humpers (these point back to *Even Dwarfs Started Small* – few films sound like these two); at a spatial level, repetitions can be found in the many circular movements such as those of the humpers driving and cycling around in circles (this also points back to Herzog's film). Largely due to these repetitions, the emancipatory energy – what Shaw called 'the restorative power of anarchy' – is undercut by boredom. It is true that the trash humpers do have energetic outbursts – tap dancing on debris, smashing old television sets – but mostly they are lethargic. They look old, they carry crutches, they take turns at sitting in a wheelchair, and as the film progresses they are often shown lying down, semi-dead with empty bottles at their side. The overall result is the invention of what could be called 'the lethargic transgression'.

It is interesting to briefly compare with Korine's subsequent film: *Spring Breakers* (2012), another film largely built on repetitions. We follow four high school girls going off to Miami on a spring break.[28] A thin plotline with crime elements forms the basis on which we see the girls in fluorescent bikinis, repeating the same lines over and over ('spring break for ever!'). Korine offers images that in themselves are the kind of MTV-party stock images we are familiar with from advertisements, magazines and television. The very deliberate repetition of these clichés exhausts the viewer, producing an effect (that I imagine is) comparable to watching music videos with Nicki Minaj (*Starships*) on a loop (Minaj's music is used in the film). The editing enhances this repetition: Korine returns to the same images again and again, including numerous slow-motion dance sequences, flooding us with an incessant movement that goes nowhere. We can consider *Spring Breakers* a piece of pop art: because Korine repeats, he subverts the girls' fetishisation of the unique moment. But *Spring Breakers* does at least three things at the same time: fundamentally, it is a critical project aiming to expose the vacuity of the young girls' (and boys') hedonism. But this exposure goes hand in hand with an ambiguous recycling of both sexual and racial stereotypes: it *relies on* the repetition of these clichés. Additionally, the film is a vehicle for delivering some astonishing shots of fluorescent colours in the dark night, including a particularly beautiful final shot with two of the girls walking off the screen, in an image that has been tilted almost 180 degrees. Now the liquid feeling of the film is taken to a logical climax as all spatial constraints are abolished, weightlessness takes over, and we enter a sphere that recalls the one Steven Shaviro analyses in *Post-Cinematic Affect*: 'a kind of ambient, free-floating sensibility that permeates our society today, although it cannot be attributed to any subject in particular' (Shaviro 2010: 2). Due to the tensions between social critique, the repetition of offensive clichés and the fascination for a particularly liquid form of cinematography (including pixilation of the images), the film disorients its spectators.

If *Spring Breakers* offers both a critical and fascinated take on a vacuous youth culture, can we then see *Trash Humpers* as a critical and fascinated pastiche of a transgressive avant-garde group – and *their* cult of the unique and particularly meaningful moment? No. Even if the two films are more related than would at first seem to be the case, it cannot be said that the four trash humpers and the four spring breakers receive the same treatment. It is important to stress that *Trash Humpers* does not fully undermine the transgressive energy, but remains a provocative and occasionally very unpleasant film. Both films exhaust the spectators with repetitions that contrast the transgressions, but Korine seems more sympathetic to the trash humpers than he does to the society that produced the spring breakers. This is particularly clear in the last scene of *Trash Humpers* where Korine outbids the complexity of the ending to *Julian Donkey-Boy* (1999) (which famously includes the protagonist's voyage on a bus with a dead baby), producing a series of surprisingly contradictory emotions. This gives the film a 'richness' that brings it one step closer to the romanticism of *The Idiots*, suggesting a 'meaning-fulness' that was not present in *Even Dwarfs Started Small*.

Late at night the female trash humper goes into a house and steals a sleeping baby. The last images show Momma under the streetlights, singing to the baby, pushing a buggy back and forth. Some viewers find these images particularly unsettling. The helpless baby has been kidnapped, and Momma is ad-libbing to the tune of a childlike song that we have come to associate with violence and murder. Throughout the film we have seen the trash humpers (and the characters they encounter) smashing dolls with hammers, wrapping them in cling film, or tying them with string to their BMXs, dragging them over the gravel and grass as they bike around in circles. We may now fear that the kidnapped baby will get a similar treatment (see Inouye 2012: 48).

But there are other ways to understand the final scene. We may be tempted to push towards a more redemptive interpretation. Could it be that the baby should be seen as the possibility for a new beginning – not least for the trash humpers? With her gentle singing Momma calms the crying baby. At the end, she does become a 'momma'; there is an element of fulfilment. The camera moves gently around her, the scene is intimate, almost everything but the child and Momma is in the dark. Furthermore, it is tempting to speculate and suggest that this scene is transcended by extra-diegetic circumstances: it is shot by Korine himself, his wife Rachel plays Momma, and at the time of shooting they had just had their first daughter (it is possible that she is the baby in the film).[29] In this way the film ends with (something like) a tender, sentimental family scene; Korine, once again undercutting our expectations about what this provocative (avant-garde) film should be like.

To sum up the *Trash Humpers* experience, we therefore have to say that the film challenges social norms – embracing transgression, childishness, sexual perversions and violence. At the same time it provokes the liberal viewer, confusingly playing with an emancipatory rhetoric without delivering any substantive grounds for optimism: even if Shaw disagrees, it is difficult to turn these (racist and murderous) trash humpers into revolutionary heroes. In all these respects *Trash Humpers* seems comparable to Herzog's *Even Dwarfs*

Started Small. Furthermore, by repeating the transgressive actions again and again, the film undercuts any cathartic release, any Nietzschean energy, and introduces instead an element of boredom and melancholia (not unlike what would later happen in *Spring Breakers*). Towards the end, we are therefore not far from what Sianne Ngai terms 'stuplimity' – a combination of shock and boredom that pulls the reader (or here: the spectator) into a form of lower-level consciousness where there is little intentionality, no clear distinction between subjects and objects (Ngai 2007). Finally, however, within this bored-transgressive world, the film invites the viewer to be sensitive to a certain form of beauty and tenderness. This beauty culminates in the last affectionate and provocatory scene, where Korine takes a step (just one) in the direction of von Trier's more meaning-ful and multi-layered conclusion in *The Idiots*. Korine here holds out 'the family' – this, the most bourgeois of bourgeois institutions! – as an ambiguous ideal. All these emotions co-exist as the spectator drifts between moments of transgression, boredom, laughter, repulsion, melancholia and beauty. The result is haunting and profoundly anti-cathartic.

James Quandt's text implied that the new French extremity was the avant-garde as farce. In the first two sections of this third chapter I disagreed, and described Dumont's film as a passionate expression of the severance of transgression from emancipation, and next we followed Antoniak, de Van and Denis on other desperate one-way trips into the dead-end. When it comes to Korine, however, the response most 'true to the spirit' of *Trash Humpers* – and certainly the shortest – seems to me different: 'yes, *Trash Humpers* is the avant-garde as farce.' It is so partly in the Marxian sense of a simulacrum, a travesty, a hollowing out of the avant-garde, and partly in the more Alfred Jarry-esque sense, in the *Ubu Roi* vein. It begins with a man defecating in front of a carport – 'Merdre!' – and goes downhill from there (claiming a couple of casualties on the way). Like many good farces *Trash Humpers* brings together moments of tenderness, melancholia and provocation, and like many good farces it works with what is already there (avant-garde figures and popular culture), twisting and turning these figures, deliberately creating expectations it will not meet, throwing the figures back in our faces. The difference between *Ubu Roi* and *Trash Humpers*, however, has to do with the level of energy. The king was not tired whereas the trash humpers are; but this also makes them oddly touching.

Resisting redemption

Why then are the films in this third chapter disturbing? The conventional answer has been: because they confront the spectator with strong images of sex and violence. Perhaps. But my point has been that a complementary, and also more intense, form of disturbance comes from the creation of the non-cathartic viewing position. It is the ambiguity of the films that provokes; an ambiguity that seems particularly palpable in the moments when transgression reveals itself as a dead-end or a repetition, an ambiguity that makes these films particularly resistant to our desire to relate them to a progressive agenda – politically or ethically (I shall return to this point in my conclusion).

This comes close to Quandt's diagnosis, and as already noted I understand why he writes that the 'authentic liberating outrage' is arrested (Quandt 2011: 25), and why he has a hard time finding a positive political project in these films. However, where I part ways with Quandt is on the question of how to read this ambiguity. I do not see these films as a form of passivity. It is more accurate to say that they explore a series of social, cultural and personal dead-ends. This is the work of a group of directors who have the sensitivity to register an impasse, but not the optimism (or naivety) to think they can push through it. The fact, that they do not have a group identity (in the way the dadaists and the surrealists had) undoubtedly plays in; but it is more important to remember that the emancipatory discourses that surrounded the dadaists and surrealists – communism, socialism, anarchism – no longer feed into general cultural production. As indicated by some of the quotations I have given throughout this chapter (from texts by Adorno, Jameson and Shaviro), I am not sure that it is a bad thing when a film enters a dead-end. Again, it seems to me a question of maintaining a distinction between art and life, and more specifically, of thinking the asymmetrical relation between politics and aesthetics. Politically, the strategy of going into the dead-end is problematic and counter-productive; aesthetically, perhaps not.

What can we reasonably demand of these directors? What can we reasonably demand of art? Leo Bersani confronts this vast problem in *The Culture of Redemption* (1990), where he criticises the widespread idea that 'art has the authority to master the presumed raw material of experience in a manner that uniquely gives value to, and perhaps even redeems, that material' (Bersani 1990: 1). Bersani associates this idea with what he calls 'the aesthetics of redemption'. In this aesthetic, art is supposed not only to confront the injustices and catastrophes of life and history, but also, via these confrontations, to repair, correct and possibly even redeem such catastrophes. In the redemptive aesthetic the motto is: 'Experience destroys, art restores' (Bersani 1990: 14). The problem with such a view of art is not only that artists cannot be expected to repair and correct the catastrophes of life and history. Art, one hopes, can stimulate productive ideas, but the more 'transitive' (to use de Duve's word) and redemptive the ambition of the artist is, the greater the risk of denying the complexity of the experiences with which the artist reckons. Bersani therefore also makes the point that the culture of redemption can very quickly become a culture of sublimation – and ultimately 'a culture of death' (Bersani 1997: 5). The ordering of the problematic and painful reality, the stubborn desire to make sense of the world in such a way as to soothe or redeem, will invite us to forget the problems, and thereby result in an art that effectively embalms the situations it is dealing with. This argument is related to the point I made when dealing with the un-framing of Columbine in *Elephant*. *Elephant* does not offer a narrative that makes sense of high school shootings, it does not allow us to get past these events. It gives a number of elements to think with, but it disappoints viewers who seek a quick move from 'representation' to 'redemption'. The films I have discussed since *Elephant* (*Innocence*, *Kindering* and those in the present chapter) do not engage with history as clearly as the interventionist films did. They therefore seem so alien to the culture of redemption that many viewers wonder *what* they are concerned with. However, as I have attempted to argue throughout this and the previous chapters they do engage with very timely questions – for instance, about the status of transgression and liberation in contemporary culture – and with the exception of *À ma sœur* and *The Idiots* they do so in distinctively non-redemptive ways.

NOTES

1. In response to the critics who suggest that the extreme films are particularly 'marketable', it may be worth noting that this was not always the case. The example that will concern us here, Bruno Dumont's *Twentynine Palms*, did not prove particularly successful, critically or commercially. It is revealing that on the English DVD-cover of Dumont's following film, *Flandres* (2006), he was presented as 'the award-winning director of *La Vie de Jésus* (*The Life of Jesus*) and *L'humanité* – *Twentynine Palms* was passed over in silence.

2. The distinction between an anarchic, romantic avant-garde from the interwar period, and a more minimalist and reflexive avant-garde from the post-war period is obviously a reductive one. It seems more sensible to give up on this narrative of development (or degeneration) and think of these different traditions as existing side by side. Dada and surrealism alongside De Stijl and Bauhaus, Viennese actionism and situationism alongside minimalism and pop art. In this chapter, the focus will be on the intractable avant-garde, a tradition with which both Dumont and Korine have affinities.

3. Katia Golubeva is the Yekatarina Golubeva who played the lead in Claire Denis's *I Can't Sleep*. In Dumont's film she is now credited using the abbreviated version of her first name.

4. As Lisa Coulthard writes, this piece of the dialogue further serves to reduce the distance between the characters (here Katia) and the (dry) desert (Coulthard in Russell 2012: 177).

5. When asked about how the final scene in *Flandres* allows the shift from sex to love, Dumont explained: 'That was the general idea I had at the start. There had to be love at the end . . . There had to be a line keeping the script on course so that I could go deep into the violence, knowing that there would be a way out' (Henric and Millet 2006: 33). It is precisely this way out which we do not find in *Twentynine Palms*. I would argue that Dumont's most recent (and in my opinion, best) film – *Camille Claudel, 1915* – is the only other example of a decidedly non-redemptive film in his filmography. It ends with a title-card explaining that Camille Claudel would live the remaining twenty-eight years of her life in the asylum. Although it is non-redemptive, this film does not aim for the provocative disturbance of the spectator that we find in *Twentynine Palms* and many of the other Dumont films.

6. It should be added that after the suicide and after the screen has gone black, Marian reappears – in super-slow images, naked, water falling down from beyond the frame of the image, again to the soundtrack of Hildegard von Bingen. This is a spiritual moment extracted from the narrative; a cleansing of body and soul. It points back to the images that opened the film (before the dying woman) – here we saw the same 'shower', but Marian was not yet there. Although these scenes embed the film in a sacred universe, they also give to the film a cyclical nature that makes it difficult to read the ending as cathartic (as mentioned, in the interview on the DVD Antoniak explains that she wanted to leave the spectator shattered).

7. Denis was heavily criticised for this ending. In *Cahiers du cinéma*, Nicolas Azalbert, for instance, described it as 'completely superfluous' (Azalbert 2013: 54).

8. In Cannes the film was shown in a cut that included two fantasy scenes. Many interviews relate to this cut, and many early reviews underline how difficult it is to follow the plotline. The DVD cut is leaner.

9. Korine has used this expression on several occasions, for instance on the commentary track for *Spring Breakers*. Denis notes that the soundtrack for *Les Salauds* is inspired by the soundtrack Tangerine Dream made for Mann's *The Thief* (1981).

10. It is tempting also to associate *Les Salauds* with the homonymous *Salò*. In the interview with *Cahiers du cinéma* the Pasolini reference comes up in relation to a discussion of whether *Les Salauds* shows ignominy. Denis insists that her film does not, and she strongly associates the ignominious in Pasolini's film with the fact that the film depicts a political *system*.

11. It may be true, as Jean-Pierre Faye has argued, that 'nihilism is a variable', that there are only specific uses for the term (Faye in Weller 2011: 9). But it is also true that once such specific use is precisely the definition of nihilism as 'being without ideal'.

12. Denis does indeed distinguish between a moral relation to the characters and the plot, and a moral role for art:

J.-S. C.: Are you trying not to have a moral view on the story?

CD: Of course, I have a moral view of the film I am making. But I have no desire to have a moral view on a girl who lets herself be done by her father, or a father who would do this to his daughter. Those things do not interest me. And what would I know about that? That form of morality is no more relevant to me than when you have certain erotic dreams in which you imagine something very powerful. Morality is something else [La morale c'est autre chose].

13. This rape, given largely in a series of static shots, is an excruciating scene that may remind the viewer of Mr Bebe's rape of Găbiţa and Otilia in Christian Mungiu's *4 months, 3 weeks and 2 days* (2007).

14. It can be argued that this entire ending, from the hazardous drive on the motorway onwards, moves the film into a semi-phantasmagorical sphere – to reuse Guattari and Denis's term: the ending is deliberately 'baroque'. Among the many strange aspects is the fact that the mother does not appear to wake up with the smashing of the window (see Brinkema 2006: 159–60).

15. In the UK the film was cut, and the censored version makes little sense: we only see the beginning of attack, and we do not see the absolution. In this context Anaïs's final words – which we are meant to understand literally – can only be taken as an expression of her denying what actually happened.

16. I realise that the expression '(quasi-)rape' makes for uncomfortable reading; however, I believe that it is precisely such unpleasant regions that Breillat (and some of the other directors studied here) force us to visit.

17. These prices are taken from ultraculture.co.uk. *Trash Humpers* also inspired a joint exhibition between Korine and Rita Ackerman at the Swiss Institute of Modern Art (New York): *Shadowfux*. Here Ackerman created a series of large mixed media works on the basis of still images from Korine's film.

18. Korine suggests the film could have been found in an attic, or buried in some ditch. This recalls Godard's *Weekend* (1967) in which one of his characteristic, animated title-cards states that the film has been 'found in a scrapyard'.

19. In *Bossy Burger* McCarthy wore an Alfred E. Newman mask, and had his character 'cook' (or rather 'mess with' ketchup, milk, mayonnaise and other things), make sexual drawings, and perform to the camera in a both threatening, infantile and humorous way. The one-hour long performance was made for camera, and the public then watched the film on the set where the performance had taken place.

20. www.vulture.com/2009/10/harmony_korine_on.html (last accessed 10 June 2014).

21. The sudden shifts in mood (between horror, comedy, tragedy and melodrama), the odd names such as Mak and Plak, the vaudeville episodes of bodily slapstick (including Hervé's/Korine's bravura act as a tap-dancer in a Confederate t-shirt), the non-sequitur dialogue, and the post-apocalyptic setting and ambiance are just some of the many elements in Korine's film that recall Samuel Beckett's plays.

22. The references to Herzog and von Trier are logical; also because they can be

motivated biographically. Herzog has appeared in several of Korine's films (*Julian Donkey-Boy* and *Mister Lonely*), and Korine was one of the best-known directors to adopt Lars von Trier and Thomas Vinterberg's *Dogma 95* concept (for *Julian Donkey-Boy*). Korine, however, notes that he did not have either in mind when making *Trash Humpers*, nor did he have in mind *The Texas Chainsaw Massacre* or any of the zombie films that have occasionally been mentioned in various review articles. The only film he mentions as a source of inspiration is William Eggleston's *Stranded in Canton* (1973). This beautiful, black and white documentary does indeed have clear links to *Trash Humpers*. *Stranded in Canton* is 'not about anything', but simply shows 'another side of the world' (Eggleston). We follow a group of low-life characters in the southern states; they are often drunk, and towards the end of the film they gravitate towards more and more radical transgressions, often playing up to the camera. We watch a man biting heads of live chicken; another man drinks beer, puts the bottle up his anus, then drinks again; and we also have a scene of Russian roulette accompanied by a very noisy electric guitar (a noisy guitar also dominates a scene in *Trash Humpers*). This similarity of tone obviously must not make us forget that Korine's film can in no way be called a documentary.

23. In an article titled 'Against the image' Paul Sheehan gives this quotation, and continues: 'The position Herzog has consistently adopted since he started making films has been that of the counter-revolutionary. His concern is not so much with systems of injustice or oppression as with the suffering, isolated individual, whose alienation is existential rather than political, and for whom the only "cure" is ecstatic release or visionary excess rather than a reconfiguring of social relations. Too pessimistic for genuine social critique, Herzog's films depict situations in which myth displaces politics, and the irrational takes precedence over the analytical' (Sheehan 2008: 118). The word 'counter-revolutionary' seems to me too strong and indicative of a widespread tendency to demand that filmmakers be explicitly political (or perhaps: political in a conventional way); on the other hand, the push from politics to myths (and nightmares, we might add) is certainly relevant to *Even Dwarfs Started Small*.

24. The film can be seen as an engagement with ideas about the liberation of the body and hence spirit that can be found in the theatre writings of Artaud, later developed by Jerzy Grotowski in his writings *Towards a Poor Theatre* (1975).

25. The ending is ambiguous, and it is possible to read it differently. A thought-provoking (and to non-Danish readers probably unknown) interpretation can be found in Christian Braad Thomsen's *Film med håndskrift* ([*Handwritten Film*] 2011). Braad Thomsen argues that rather than becoming liberated, Karen slips into psychosis. She now fully identifies with her lost object (the baby), turns into a baby herself, and in her scene of spassing is eating like a baby. Therefore, the ending is Karen's Norman Bates moment. Norman becomes his own mother, Karen becomes her own baby, both end up lost. (Braad Thomsen notes that he has presented this analysis to von Trier, and that the director sees the ending as

liberating – however, Braad Thomsen's interpretation of the ending cannot be discarded.)

26. This shift from dadaist satire to a more 'serious' exploration of the potential of the spassing exercise is accompanied by a shift in cinematography. At the end, von Trier no longer participates in the spassing with shaken handheld images, and rapid cuts, but instead settles down, opting for more stable images and longer takes, allowing the actors to perform.

27. This is not meant as a normative statement. A film that introduces an element of 'hope' at the end, such as *The Idiots*, is not necessarily better or worse than a film that does not.

28. A lot of the reception and marketing of the film focused on the casting of Disney Channel actresses Selena Gomez, Vanessa Hudgens and Ashley Benson in this supposedly daring film. And there is little doubt that with this casting, Korine was aiming for a subversive gesture not unlike McCarthy's treatment of *Bonanza* (in *The Garden*) or Paul Verhoeven's casting of television actors in *Starship Troopers* (1997). Compared with McCarthy and Verhoeven, however, Korine seems slightly more sympathetic to the pop culture world that he is drawing on.

29. In an article in the *LA Times*, Korine was asked whether the baby was his (and whether his film was a response to the anxieties of becoming a father). Not surprisingly, given the slightly pathologising approach to the film and its director, Korine avoided an answer: "'I think it's best for me not to say,' he said. 'I really couldn't tell you, or I really wouldn't want to say just because I feel like certain things are just best left unsaid, just watched and felt.'" (http://articles.latimes.com/2010/may/14/entertainment/la-et-trashhumpers-20100514).

Conclusion

HUMANISM XL

In the introduction, I briefly presented Sartre's ideas about how literature and art can help to realise the Hegelian ideal of mutual recognition. Sartre argued that when reading a book (or looking at a painting), the minds of the reader and author collaborate on the creation of the work in such a way that both use their imagination (their freedom), and both find their imagination stimulated by that of the other. The result of Sartre's analysis was an understanding of art as an 'exercise in generosity' and the propagation of freedom. This activity, Sartre furthermore suggested, also has political repercussions.

The different films discussed in this book all seem to challenge the Hegelian set-up. They do not engage the imagination of the spectator in such a way that we feel compelled to talk about the artistic exchange as an act of collaboration, a harmonious dialogue and a joyful 'spinning top'. The films in the first chapter instead come across as assaultive. *Dogville*, *Daisy Diamond*, *Funny Games* and *Redacted* lock the spectators into a very unpleasant position. The experience of watching such films is not one of freedom and recognition, but rather one of being humiliated and harassed. The directors achieve this by asking us to produce the images while at the same cheating us (hiding the true identity of Grace), confusing us via an aggressive play between fiction and (intra-diegetic) reality (*Daisy Diamond*), addressing the spectator in a direct and sadistic way (*Funny Games*), throwing us between various image-sources, shaking our epistemological apparatus (*Redacted*), and, more generally, by addressing the spectator in a manner that postulates that they know more about us than we do about ourselves – and that what 'extra' they know about us is unpleasant. It is not surprising that many spectators have responded to these films with strong negative emotions.

The films studied in Chapter 2 were very different, but they could still be understood as challenges to the Hegelian dialectic of recognition. In these films the spectator was no longer forced into the position of the 'slave', but she remained in an unpleasant position that can be associated with inferiority. Now, it was as if the dialectic framework was crumbling away. We were not sure exactly how we were being addressed, what we were watching, and what the director's intentions were. In this position of 'not knowing', it was difficult to evaluate, to act and to do the things generally associated with being a responsible individual. The unpleasantness of the experience was intensified by the fact that the suspension of judgement took place in an environment where we would feel particularly compelled to judge and act. Many of the films in Chapter 2 were dealing with political and social affairs to which we want to respond (*Elephant*, *I Can't Sleep*, *Hidden* and also the coda on *Play*). Something comparable could be said about the other films in this second chapter. They concerned children (and education) – a topic associated with the idea of subject *formation*, and therefore another area in which the ungrounding of the spectator is likely to produce a particularly intense feeling of unease.

In the last chapter, I changed approach slightly, and tried to situate the feel-bad corpus historically, intellectually. This was done via a discussion of how the films negotiate the relation between transgression and emancipation. However, we still encountered a series of feel-bad logics that violate the dialectic of recognition. The 'desperation films' (Dumont, Antoniak, de Van and Denis) depicted extremely bleak situations, and furthermore sought to 'transmit' their despair to the viewer. Like the films in Chapter 1, they stimulated a very strong desire for release in the spectator; to a large extent this was done by playing with avant-garde logics that invite us to think that 'transgressions' will lead to 'emancipation' and (secular) 'redemption', but here the realisation of such ideals was ultimately refused, and instead the spectator was left shattered. My argument was that the disappointment of an emancipatory desire could be found in many contemporary art films. Are these films nihilistic, or should they rather be seen as uncompromising denunciations of a nihilism the directors find in our society, an attempt to provoke a spectatorial response? Denis herself introduced this question of nihilism in relation to *Les Salauds* and neither the film nor Denis's comments allow us to move beyond this possibility.[1] On the other hand, Dumont, Antoniak and, in particular, de Van transfer their despair to the spectator with such a noisy 'rattling of the bars' that it seems more appropriate to consider the films as an attempt to provoke anger in the spectator. All films, however, refuse to contribute to the culture of redemption; they stay feel-bad.

Harmony Korine's feel-bad farce *Trash Humpers* was another troubling film, featuring a group of 'artists of bad' (Korine) that did not refrain from, occasionally, killing the other marginal characters they encountered. Here the feel-bad emotion partly stemmed from the film's provocation to laughter. It is tempting to laugh in order to escape the situation that we have been put in, but we hold back. Again, it is difficult to establish a position in relation to the film. We do not really know *what* we would be laughing at, and we do not know if we would be laughing *at* or *with* the trash humpers. It was this indeterminacy that led me to compare Korine's film with Herzog's dwarfs and von Trier's idiots; the indeterminacy undercuts the possibility of the cathartic release that the laughter would have provided us.

The Hegelian framework is thus being destabilised in various ways by these films. But if the feel-bad films violate these good ideals about recognition, *Bildung* and democracy, why then write about them? Why watch them? Why teach them? This book has offered a number of answers to these questions. I have attempted to show that the feel-bad corpus is not anti-democratic, anti-enlightened or unethical, but instead contributes to political and ethical debates. The feel-bad corpus might not be the first place that humanistic scholars go to corroborate their ideas about the civic virtue of the experience of art, but I believe it is one of the places we should go.

Dogville fits perfectly into a contemporary humanistic education: it can be used as a springboard for the discussion of what we might call the ethics of a human subject who only partly understands herself. As argued via Julia Kristeva's small text about 9/11, it is important to acknowledge that in the wrong circumstances we are all capable of acting in ways that are anathema to our ideals. This is what von Trier communicates via the story of Grace. But the specificity of the feel-bad film is that he does not simply tell a well-intentioned story about how we may betray our ideals, he transforms the movie theatre into an experiential venue, manipulating heavily in order to make us undergo the dangerous experience. This is the Artaudian dimension of going via the body of the spectator to her metaphysics – the operation may not be pleasant, but the patient will survive. It is also a form of exploration that art has always excelled at, not least sacred art. As Kristeva reminded us: traditionally religion has been one of the places where evil and transgression could be felt, thought and explored. With the diminishing influence of religious cultures in the Western world, we now seem to be losing the ability to relate to the fantasies we encounter on petroglyphs, in Greek dramas, in Dante, Bosch, Sade, Céline – everywhere in the history of the arts, religious or not. The feel-bad films partake in the resistance against the reduction of the cultural field. However, in order for this experimental approach of the feel-bad logic to be acceptable, we must – as I have argued repeatedly over these pages – allow for an asymmetrical relation between the ethical standards inside the cinema and those outside. This does not mean that everything is allowed, but we cannot restrict ourselves to the relatively direct model that Sartre and Bourriaud proposed (a model in which relations in art should provide us with a model for relations in society) without, dangerously, robbing ourselves of a possibility to think the human psyche in all its complexities.

Other films similarly take advantage of the exceptionality of the movie theatre. For instance, I argued that the subtle pulling apart of the Hegelian set-up that we find in films of unease such as *Elephant*, *Hidden* and *I Can't Sleep* (and one could add *Muriel*, which I didn't find space to engage with) was driven by ethical considerations, and more specifically by a belief in the ethical and political potential of extending the distance between observation (or rather, experience) and judgement. These films sought to open a space where we could accompany the floating bodies on the screen; in my opinion this did not mean that they were politically conservative or eager to 'set aside the burden of interpretation' (as some critics argued), rather that they reminded us of the difficulties of judging, and of the necessity of acknowledging that judgements must be based on the recognition that we do not fully know the situation we will be judging.

As such, these feel-bad films do not oppose a tradition of *Bildung* and education. On the contrary, they help to develop a 'humanism XL' – a form of humanism that takes into account the fact that we cannot fully know ourselves, that the human psyche is a much richer (and also more problematic) field than we may sometimes be inclined to believe when we read about art as an exercise in democracy, empathy, and so on. I should add that this would be a humanism that considers the complexity of the human psyche not only as the potential source of serious problems, but also as a field rich in potential – both ethically and aesthetically. With these arguments, I am in line with other critics who have written about these transgressive films arguing that – despite appearances – these films can find a place within an Enlightenment tradition; that they can in fact add to this Enlightenment tradition by forcing us to consider the question of its limits.[2]

At this point, it is fair to return to Sartre's 'Why Write?' (discussed in the introduction above) in order to note that this is a more complex text than my previous remarks have suggested. Conventionally, Sartre's text is read as an argument about how author and reader come together in perfect harmony, how they confirm (and fully conform to) each other. But the view that 'Why Write?' puts forth an 'optimistic humanism bordering on the comic', as Denis Hollier put it, is reductive (Hollier 1986: 95). If we look more closely at the essay, we will notice that Sartre writes that the author is wrestling with something that she does not entirely know ('a silence'), and the reader is receiving something that can never fully be accessed (again Sartre speaks of 'silence' – but this second silence is distinct from the first). In this manner, which I have written about elsewhere (Lübecker 2009), the exchange between writer and reader is shot through with silence. The silence not only complicates the idea of art as the site for a seamless intersubjective understanding, instead allowing us to see that for Sartre too full self-consciousness is unrealisable;

it also guarantees that reading becomes an exercise in freedom, instead of simply being an exercise in filling in the blanks, picking up on salient points, patiently reconstructing what the author put into the text – as if art were a crossword puzzle. There is much more to say about this, but the point in this specific context is that Sartre's exchange depends upon an element (silence) that goes beyond any idea of communication as a straightforward exchange. His subjects (both writer and reader) are also ungrounded.

In a somewhat comparable way, contemporary readings of Hegel have emphasised that rather than being a model for how to achieve full self-understanding, the master–slave passage can be read as an account of how we are compelled to put ourselves at risk (see Butler 2005, and Butler and Malabou 2010). To become what we are (a goal that we will never achieve), we want to put ourselves at risk; we want to confront that which ungrounds us. In such 'ecstatic' readings of Hegel (Butler 2005: 27), the master–slave passage is therefore not an argument about the imperialist desire for full self-consciousness; it is rather the story of our stubborn desire to be ungrounded by that which exceeds us (see also Nancy 1997). Hegel – and his dialectic of recognition – can thus be read in accord with what I called the 'humanism XL'. Surely, we step into the darkness of the movie theatre first of all to be ungrounded?[3]

Unpleasure is one of the things that make it reasonable to give the feel-bad films the freedom they need to explore a number questions that would be seen as problematic outside the cinema. The fact that these films produce unpleasure not only provokes us and makes us reluctant to trust the directors (sharpening our critical apparatus), it also helps to maintain a distance between the world and the movie theatre. It is difficult to imagine that a film such as *Funny Games* would inspire any form of unethical, perverse behaviour.[4] It is almost as if the film monopolises perversion, and the spectator can now only respond with ethical reflections. Indeed, when Haneke aims to radically separate violence from pleasure (and sexuality) – putting in place instead a terror machine of a film – it is because he believes that with regard to the place of violence in contemporary visual culture, the danger lies with pleasure. This is a well-known argument. For instance, it is the argument that pulled a (cut) version of Pasolini's *Salò* (1975) through the British Board of Film Censors (BBFC). And five years later when the film was under renewed scrutiny, the BBFC argued that *Salò* showed violence and perversions in such a disturbing and unpleasant way that no one could doubt that the director was condemning the torture he depicted: 'this is a turn-off film and not a turn-on' (Ferman [1979] 2009: 16). Thus unpleasure keeps the spectator from wanting to 'import' the transgressions into everyday life. In my vocabulary: Pasolini used feel-bad emotions to maintain a distinction between transgression inside and outside the cinema.

Therefore it is necessary to provide a clarification on the relation to the avant-garde. As mentioned, Bürger argued that one of the defining characteristics of the avant-garde was the ambition to do away with a distinction between art and life. There are many good arguments for such a reading, and it is easy to see how this ambition can be found in twentieth-century art and culture – all the way up to the ideals that Nicholas Bourriaud puts forth and the artworks he writes about. Bürger notes that the historical avant-garde failed in this ambition to integrate art into life praxis – but he adds that the failure was of such a kind that it helped to make visible the various ideological structures that dominate (and police) the field of art. When it comes to the feel-bad films, however, the desire to do away with the distinction between art and life does not strike me as a primary concern. There is no desire to abolish the distinction between life and art because the works of art do not come with the utopian dimension they often had for previous generations. They do not 'embody' a social ideal, but more often the painful distance to such an ideal: they try to force a way from transgression to emancipation, but often fail in this endeavour. The transgressive moments therefore have a greater 'density' than was the case in those optimistic and utopian fractions of the historical avant-gardes where transgression had a transitory role, opening towards a new world. With the reduced transitivity comes a greater ambiguity and a set of contradictory emotions (as in *Les Salauds*, *The Idiots*, *Trash Humpers* and *Even Dwarfs Started Small*). One may regret this ambiguity and long for the more explicitly political works, but the strong-minded (strong-stomached?) spectator may also listen to the ambiguities of the experience of the social impasse that these contemporary directors communicate.

EXTRA-ETHICAL CINEMA?

It would be easy to end there. In that way, we would effectively have a positive answer to one of the last questions that was raised in the introduction. The introduction differentiated between different uses of the word 'catharsis' and we saw how Haneke presented *The Seventh Continent*, and more generally his ideal of cinema, as cathartic; then, I asked whether the feel-bad films, with their deadlock on spectatorial catharsis, all produce emotions that – after discussions and debate – feed into the more general idea of cinema as social catharsis. On the basis of *Dogville*, *Funny Games*, *Elephant*, *Hidden*, *I Can't Sleep* and many of the other films discussed, the answer now seems to be a resounding 'yes'. Yes, these provocations are indeed meant to stimulate ethical and political thought, and the films therefore fit a humanistic framework by allowing us to negotiate our relation to the elements that produce pity and fear.

In *Spectatorship: The Power of Looking on* (2007), Michele Aaron presents a theory of spectatorship along such lines. Aaron first establishes a distinction between ethics and morality, and then she goes on to prioritise the first at the expense of the latter. This is how the distinction is presented:

> This distinction becomes fundamental here for within it lies the all important prioritisation of (ethical) recognition, realisation, reflection – the stuff of agency – over (moral) prescription, proclamation and punishment – the stuff of ideology. In other words ethics . . . is all about thinking through one's relationship to morality rather than just adhering to it. It is about our personal powers of reasoning and choice when faced with, say, social custom, rather than our complete and immediate accord. (Aaron 2007: 108–9)

Because she establishes the distinction between ethics and morality in such an unambiguous and normative manner, Aaron can then define ethical spectatorship with great clarity (this is one of the strengths of her theory). Ethical films are those that provoke us to consider our moral frameworks – films that nurture reflection. Her examples include Dogma 95 films such as *The Idiots* (von Trier) and *Festen* (Vinterberg), Haneke's *Funny Games*, but also more mainstream films such as *Basic Instinct* (Verhoeven), and self-reflexive films like *Peeping Tom* (Powell) and *Strange Days* (Bigelow). A counterexample is Steven Spielberg's *Saving Private Ryan*. It moves us, but it does not make us think about our moral frameworks; it mesmerises and pacifies.

A consequence of the way Aaron presents her dichotomy is 'that for a film to be immoral is near impossible' (Aaron 2007: 118). By this she means that the question of how a film relates to the existing moral frameworks will always be part of the horizon of expectation for the viewer. Films necessarily relate to the existing social customs. On the other hand, a film can be amoral, or anti-moral. It can be against morality, it can provoke the moral codex that dominates society. But that will precisely tend to make the film ethical – it will stimulate a reflection on the moral system the film engages. Using the Danish spelling of Dogma, Aaron writes:

> Dogme is, in many ways, amoral cinema, and it is ethical because of it: it renders morality irrelevant in its ethical emphases. Indeed amorality – as the absence of interest in or deference to morality – could be seen as an essential ingredient to ethical cinema. (Aaron 2007: 117)

As we have now seen, many of the films discussed in this book inspired me to make similar arguments. However, some of them also resisted this recuperative move – and I would like to end by emphasising this resistance. Films such as *Innocence*, *Kindering* and *Les Salauds* challenge existing moral frameworks, but in these particular films I am not sure that the amorality can be retrieved as ethics quite as smoothly as Aaron's quotation suggests. And if we consider *Trash Humpers* and *Even Dwarfs Started Small*, they certainly challenge and provoke with their amorality, but I doubt that Korine and Herzog made these films to stimulate ethical thought. At the very least, we have to acknowledge that it is much more difficult to retrieve the amorality of *Trash Humpers* and *Even Dwarfs Started Small* at the ethical level, than it is to perform a similar operation on *The Idiots*, *Funny Games* and *Elephant*, for instance. At a more general level we may even wonder if the most appropriate response to these films is to think about the ways in which they provoke the existing moral frameworks.

In other words, confronted with these films I get the sense that to some extent an ethical framing distorts. This is not to deny that these films can stimulate ethical reflection – we have seen they can. However, I would argue that the disturbance generated by these films also comes from their ability to interrupt such ethical readings. In that moment of suspending the move from amorality to ethics, they instead offer to the spectator a unique dreamlike (or nightmarish) experience. Watching *Even Dwarfs Started Small* or *Trash Humpers* is an experience of radical deframing that challenges our desire to regard the films as ethically or politically productive. It can be argued that the directors themselves are the first to experience this challenge: Herzog describes *Even Dwarfs Started Small* as a nightmare, 'a crazy film, a sick film', almost as if he did not direct it. Brakhage's introductory remarks to *Kindering* suggested he was uncertain about what kind of film he has made, and Denis explicitly states that *Les Salauds* escapes her. Korine's insistence on *Trash Humpers* as a found object not only brings the film into an avant-garde tradition, it also serves to extend the distance between director and film.

So even if it is true that cinema can be an excellent partner when we seek to make sense of the world (an excellent partner also because no 'answer' it gives will be definitive), it is equally true that cinema can help to make life opaque and strange. Some provocative films might challenge our view of politics, ethics and ourselves, some films challenge us in such a way that we begin to wonder about the frameworks we use when we approach a film. Most of these particularly challenging films will eventually find their frames, but it is also possible that some of them will continue to confuse our attempts to use film as a way to make sense of the world.

NOTES

1. I distinguish between nihilism (there is no meaning) and cynicism (which reintroduces the question of meaning, but only from an egotistical point of view). The term cynicism has no relevance for a discussion of Denis (but it is very relevant for discussion of many other aspects of contemporary film and television culture).

2. However, as we shall see, my corpus of films does not inspire me to go quite as far as Asbjørn Grønstad does: 'It is my contention that most, if not all, of the films previously alluded to are really preoccupied with deeply humanist issues even as they at times seem ostensibly misanthropic' (Grønstad 2012: 10).

3. This is not to suggest that only feel-bad experiences unground. As Elaine Scarry writes in a wonderful passage from *Beauty and Being Just*: 'When we come upon beautiful things . . . [it] is not that we cease to stand at the center of the world, for we never stood there. It is that we cease to stand even at the center of our own world. We willingly cede our ground to the thing that stands before us' (cited in Sobchack 2004: 298–9).

4. Difficult, but obviously not impossible. There may be pathological individuals for whom the film functions in unintended ways – we know that the Oslo terrorist Anders Breivik had *Dogville* on his Facebook list of favourite films (alongside Ridley Scott's *Gladiator* (2000) and Zack Snyder's *300* (2007)).

Bibliography

Aaron, Michele (2007) *Spectatorship. The Power of Looking On.* London: Wallflower.

Abella, Adela and Zilkha, Nathalie (2004) 'Dogville: A Parable on Perversion', *International Journal of Psychoanalysis*, 85, pp. 1519–26.

Adorno, Theodor (2007) *Negative Dialectics.* London: Continuum.

Ambrose, Darren (2013) *Film, Nihilism and the Restoration of Belief.* Winchester: Zero Books.

Aristotle (1965) *Poetics*, in *Classical Literary Criticism: Aristotle 'On the Art of Poetry', Horace 'On the Art of Poetry', Longinus 'On the Sublime'*, trans. T. S. Dorsch. Harmondsworth: Penguin.

Artaud, Antonin ([1938] 1970) *The Theatre and its Double*, trans. Victor Corti. London: Calder and Boyars.

Azalbert, Nicolas (2013) 'En eaux troubles – *Les Salauds* de Claire Denis', *Cahiers du cinéma*, 691, p. 54.

Backman Rogers, Anna (2012) 'Ephemeral Bodies and Threshold Creatures: The Crisis of the Adolescent Rite of Passage in Sofia Coppola's *The Virgin Suicides* (1999) and Gus Van Sant's *Elephant* (2003)', *NECSus Journal*: online at http://necsus-ejms.org/ephemeral-bodies-and-threshold-creatures-the-crisis-of-the-adolescent-rite-of-passage-in-sofia-coppolas-the-virgin-suicides-and-gus-van-sants-elephant-by-anna-backman-rogers/.

Backman Rogers, Anna (2013) 'Realism and Gus Van Sant's *Elephant*', in Cecília Mello and Lúcia Nagib (eds.), *Realism and the Audiovisual Media*. Basingstoke: Palgrave Press, pp. 85–95.

Badley, Linda (2010) *Lars von Trier.* Urbana: University of Illinois Press.

Bainbridge, Caroline (2007) *The Cinema of Lars von Trier: Authenticity and Artifice.* London: Wallflower.

Barker, Jennifer (2009) *The Tactile Eye: Touch and the Cinematic Experience.* Berkeley: University of California Press.

Barthes, Roland ([1980] 1981) *Camera Lucida: Reflections on Photography*, trans. Richard Howard. London: Cape.

Barthes, Roland ([1957] 1990) *Mythologies.* Paris: Points Seuil.

Bataille, Georges ([1949/1933] 1967) *'La Part maudite', précédé de 'La notion de dépense'* [*'The Accursed Share' preceded by 'The Notion of Expenditure'*]. Paris: Les Éditions de minuit.

Bataille, Georges (1973a) *Théorie de la religion.* Paris: Gallimard-Tel.

Bataille, Georges (1973b) *Oeuvres complètes*, vol. 5. Paris: Gallimard.

Bataille, Georges ([1955] 1983) *Manet.* Genève: Skira.

Baudrillard, Jean (1988) *L'Amérique.* Paris: Le Livre de poche.

Bazin, André (1987) *Le Cinéma de la cruauté.* Paris: Flammarion.

Bergdahl, Gunnar (2010) 'Gestaltning och Authenticitet – et seminarium: Roy Andersson och Ruben Östlund', *ArtMonitor*, 9, pp. 8–24.

Bersani, Leo (1997) 'A Conversation with Leo Bersani, Tim Dean, Hal Foster, Kaja Silverman and Leo Bersani', *October*, 82, pp. 3–16.

Bersani, Leo (1990) *The Culture of Redemption*. Cambridge, MA: Harvard University Press.

Best, Victoria and Crowley, Martin (2007) *The New Pornographies: Explicit Sex in Recent French Fiction and Film*. Manchester: Manchester University Press.

Bettinson, Gary and Rushton, Richard (2010) *What is Film Theory? An Introduction to Contemporary Debates*. Maidenhead: The Open University Press.

Beugnet, Martine (2004) *Claire Denis*. Manchester: Manchester University Press.

Beugnet, Martine (2007) *Cinema and Sensation: French Film and the Art of Transgression*. Edinburgh: Edinburgh University Press.

Bishop, Claire (2012) *Artificial Hells: Participatory Art and the Politics of Spectatorship*. London: Verso.

Boillat, Alain (2011) 'L'œil d'*Elephant*: l'espace d'un regard', *Décadrages*, 19, pp. 48–69.

Bordwell, David (1999) 'The Art Cinema as a Mode of Film Practice', in Leo Braudy and Marshall Cohen (eds.), *Film Theory and Criticism*. Oxford: Oxford University Press, pp. 716–24.

Bordwell, David (2006) *The Way Hollywood Tells It*. Berkeley: The University of California Press.

Bouquet, Stéphene and Lalanne, Jean-Marc (2009) *Gus Van Sant*. Paris: Cahiers du cinéma.

Bourriaud, Nicolas (2002) *Relational Aesthetics*, trans. Simon Pleasance and Fronza Woods with Mathieu Copeland. Dijon: Les Presses du réel.

Braad Thomsen, Christian (2011) *Film med håndskrift*. Copenhagen: Tiderne Skifter.

Brakhage, Stan (2011) *Essential Brakhage: Selected Writings on Filmmaking by Stan Brakhage*. New York: Documentext.

Brand, Roy (2008) 'Witnessing Trauma on Film', in Paul Frosh and Amit Pinchevski (eds.), *Media Witnessing: Testimony in the Age of Mass Communication*. Basingstoke: Palgrave Macmillan, pp. 198–215.

Brecht, Bertolt ([1948] 1960) *Kleines Organon für das Theater* [*A Short Organum for the Theatre*]. Frankfurt am Main: Suhrkamp.

Brecht, Bertolt (1978) *Brecht on Theatre*, translated by John Willett. London: Methuen.

Brecht, Bertolt ([1955] 2008) *Kriegsfibel*. Berlin: Eulenspiegel Verlag.

Brinkema, Eugenie (2006) 'Celluloid is Sticky: Sex, Death, Materiality, Metaphysics (in Some Films by Catherine Breillat)', *Women: A Cultural Review*, 17, 2, pp. 147–70.

Brinkema, Eugenie (2014) *The Forms of the Affects*. Durham, NC: Duke University Press.

Brown, William (2013) 'Violence in Extreme Cinema and the Ethics of Spectatorship', *Projections*, 7, 1, pp. 25–42.

Bukatman, Scott (2009) 'Vivian Sobchack in Conversation with Scott Bukatman', *The Journal of e-Media Studies*, 2, 1.

Burdeau, Emmanuel (2008) 'Là' and 'En ligne avec Brian de Palma', *Cahiers du cinéma*, 631, pp. 10–11 and pp. 12–16.

Bürger, Peter ([1974] 1984) *Theory of the Avant-Garde*, trans. Michael Shaw. Minneapolis: University of Minnesota Press.

Butler, Judith (2004) *Precarious Life*. London: Verso.

Butler, Judith (2005) *Giving an Account of Oneself*. New York: Fordham University Press.

Butler, Judith (2009) *Frames of War*. London: Verso.

Butler, Judith and Malabou, Catherine (2010) *Sois mon corps: une lecture contemporaine de la domination et de la servitude chez Hegel*. Paris: Éditions Bayard.

Cartwright, Lisa (2008) *Moral Spectatorship*. Durham, NC: Duke University Press.

Caruth, Cathy (1996) *Unclaimed Experience: Trauma, Narrative, and History*. Baltimore: Johns Hopkins University Press.

Chapman, James (2008) *War and Film*. London: Reaktion.

Chiesa, Lorenzo (2007) 'What is the Gift of Grace? On *Dogville*', *Film-Philosophy*, 11, 3, pp. 1–21.

Clark, Tim (2006) 'Bruno Dumont: The Sacred and our Experience of Violence', *Parachute*, 123, pp. 94–119.

Clover, Carol (1987) 'Her Body, Himself: Gender in the Slasher Film', *Representations*, 20, pp. 187–228.

Coumoul, Sylvain (2005) 'Innocence de Lucile Hadzihalilovic', *Cahiers du cinéma*, 597, p. 53.

Courcoux, Charles-Antoine (2011) '*Elephant Men*: la dialectique du pachyderme. Pour une visibilité du genre', *Décadrages*, 19, pp. 85–100.

Danto, Arthur (2003) *The Abuse of Beauty*. Chicago: Open Court.

De Duve, Thierry (1996) *Kant After Duchamp*. Cambridge, MA: MIT Press.

DeLillo, Don (1991) *Mao II*. New York: Viking Press.

Denis, Claire (2013) 'L'irrémédiable: dialogue avec Claire Denis, entretien réalisé par Jean-Sébastian Chauvin et Stéphane Delorme', *Cahiers du cinéma*, 691, pp. 82–8.

Didi-Huberman, Georges (2009) *Quand les images prennent position*. Paris: Les Éditions de minuit.

Downing, Lisa and Saxton, Libby (2010) *Film and Ethics: Foreclosed Encounters*. London: Routledge.

Dumas, Chris (2012) *Un-American Psycho: Brian de Palma and the Political Invisible*. Bristol: Intellect.

Ebert, Roger (2007) *Redacted*. http://www.rogerebert.com/reviews/redacted-2007 (last accessed 10 June 2014).

Elsaesser, Thomas and Hagener, Malte (2010) *Film Theory: An Introduction through the Senses*. London: Routledge.

Erickson, Steve (1994) 'Review of *I Can't Sleep*, Claire Denis', *Cinéaste*, June, p. 64.

Ferman, James ([1979] 2009) 'Letter to the director of Public Prosecutions'. Reprinted in DVD/Blu-Ray booklet for Pier Paolo Pasolini *Salò* (BFI collection).

Fibiger, Bo (2003) 'A Dog Not Yet Buried – Or *Dogville* as Political Manifesto', *P.O.V.* 16 (December) <http://pov.imv.au.dk/Issue_16/section_1/artc7A.html>.

Foster, Hal (1996) *The Return of the Real: Avant-Garde at the End of the Century*. Cambridge, MA: MIT Press.

Foundas, Scott (2013) 'Film Review: *Bastards*', http://variety.com/2013/film/reviews/cannes-film-review-bastards-1200489090/ (last accessed 10 June 2014).

Fox, Dominic (2009) *Cold World: The Aesthetics of Dejection and the Politics of Militant Dysphoria*. Winchester: Zero Books.

Frey, Mattias (2012) 'Tuning Out, Turning In, and Walking Off: The Film Spectator in Pain', in Asbjørn Grønstad and Henrik Gustafsson (eds.), *Ethics and Images of Pain*. London: Routledge, pp. 99–111.

Gallese, Vittorio and Guerra, Michele (2012) 'Embodying Movies', *Cinema: Journal of Philosophy and the Moving Image*, 3, pp. 183–210.

Geil, Abraham (2013) 'The Spectator without Qualities', in Paul Bowman (ed.), *Rancière and Film*. Edinburgh: Edinburgh University Press, pp. 53–82.

Gilroy, Paul (2007) 'Shooting Crabs in a Barrel', *Screen*, 48, 2, pp. 233–5.

Grodal, Torben Kragh (2009) *Embodied Visions: Evolution, Emotion, Culture and Film*. Oxford: Oxford University Press.

Grotowski, Jerzy (1975) *Towards a Poor Theatre*. London: Methuen.

Groys, Boris (2008) *Art Power*. Cambridge, MA: MIT Press.

Grønstad, Asbjørn (2012) *Screening the Unwatchable: Spaces of Negation in Post-Millennial Art Cinema*. Basingstoke: Palgrave Macmillan.

Grundmann, Roy (ed.) (2010) *A Companion to Michael Haneke*. Oxford: Wiley-Blackwell.

Guattari, Félix (2008) *The Three Ecologies*. London: Continuum.

Guerlac, Suzanne (1997) *Literary Polemics: Bataille, Sartre, Valéry, Breton.* Stanford: Stanford University Press.

Hagman, Hampus (2007) '"Every Cannes Needs its Scandal": Between Art and Exploitation in Contemporary French Film', *Film International*, 5, pp. 32–41.

Halligan, Benjamin (2002) 'What is Neo-Underground and What Isn't: A First Consideration on Harmony Korine', in Xavier Mendik and Steven Jay Schneider (eds.), *Underground U.S.A.: Filmmaking Beyond the Hollywood Canon.* New York: Wallflower, pp. 150–60.

Halliwell, Stephen (2002) *The Aesthetics of Mimesis.* Princeton: Princeton University Press.

Haneke, Michael (1992) 'Film als Katharsis', in Francesco Bono (ed.), *Austria (in)felix: Zum österreichischen Film der 80er Jahre.* Graz: Edition Blimp, p. 89.

Henric, Jacques and Millet, Catherine (2006) 'Bruno Dumont – droit dans le réel', *Art Press*, 326, pp. 28–35.

Herzog, Werner (2002) *Herzog on Herzog*, ed. Paul Cronin. London: Faber and Faber.

Holdt, Jacob (2011) *Amerikanske billeder [American Pictures].* Copenhagen: Per Kofods Forlag.

Hollier, Denis (1986) *The Politics of Prose: Essay on Sartre.* Minneapolis: University of Minnesota Press.

Horeck, Tanya and Kendall, Tina (eds.) (2011) *The New Extremism in Cinema: From France to Europe.* Edinburgh: Edinburgh University Press

Horsley, Jake (2005) *Dogville vs. Hollywood.* London: Marion Boyars.

Huyssen, Andreas (1987) *After the Great Divide.* Bloomington: Indiana University Press.

Inouye, Shaun (2012) 'Debasing the Voice: Subversive Vocality in Harmony Korine's *Trash Humpers*', *The Soundtrack*, 5, 1, pp. 37–49.

Iversen, Gunnar (1987) *Den indre svinehund: Essays om fred og fordragelighed.* Copenhagen: Nyt Nordisk Forlag.

Jameson, Fredric (2005) *Archaeologies of the Future.* London: Verso.

Jarry, Alfred ([1896] 2000) *Ubu Roi.* Paris: Le Livre de poche.

Jousse, Thierry (1994) 'Les insomniaques', *Cahiers du cinéma*, 479–80, pp. 20–3.

Jousse, Thierry and Strauss, Frédéric (1994) 'Entretien avec Claire Denis', *Cahiers du cinéma*, 479–80, pp. 24–30.

Jouve, Valérie, Ors, Sébastian and Tancelin, Philippe (2001) *Bruno Dumont.* Paris: Dis voir.

Kendall, Tina (2012) 'Cinematic Affect and the Ethics of Waste', *New Cinemas: Journal of Contemporary Film*, 10, 1, pp. 43–59.

Korine, Harmony (2008) *The Collected Fanzines.* Chicago: Drag City Incorporated.

Korine, Harmony (2009) '"I am Not Going to Lie and Say that I Don't Like Provoking the Audience", Interview/Feature by Treihaft Lauren'. http://www.indiewire.com/article/harmony_korine_they_were_the_neighborhood_boogeymen_who_worked_at_krispy_k (last accessed 10 June 2014).

Korine, Harmony and Ackermann, Rita (2011) *Shadow Fux.* New York: Agnès B. Endowment Fund and Swiss Institute Contemporary Art.

Koutsourakis, Angelos (2013) *Politics as Form in Lars von Trier: A Post-Brechtian Reading.* London: Bloomsbury.

Krauss, Rosalind (1985) *On The Originality of the Avant-Garde and Other Modernist Myths.* Cambridge, MA: MIT Press.

Krichane, Selim (2011) '*Elephant* ou les jeux vidéo en trompe-l'oeil', *Décadrages*, 19, pp. 70–84.

Kristeva, Julia (2003) *Chroniques du temps sensible.* Paris: Éditions de l'Aube.

Kulezic-Wilson, Danijela (2012) 'Gus Van Sant's Soundwalks and Audio-Visual Musique Concrète', in James Eugene Wierzbicki (ed.), *Music, Sound and Filmmakers: Sonic Style in Cinema.* London: Routledge, pp. 76–88.

Lacan, Jacques ([1964] 1973) *Le Séminaire livre XI: les quatre concepts fondamentaux de la psychanalyse* [*The Four Fundamental Concepts of Psychoanalysis*]. Paris: Seuil.

Laguarda, Alice (2011) '*Elephant*: misère de l'adolescence dans une modernité en crise', *Décadrages*, 19, pp. 21–9.

Laine, Tarja (2006) 'Lars von Trier, *Dogville* and the Hodological Space of Cinema', *Studies in European Cinema*, 3, 2, pp. 129–41.

Laine, Tarja (2011) *Feeling Cinema: Emotional Dynamics in Film Studies*. London: Continuum.

Lakoff, George (2004) *Don't Think of an Elephant*. White River Junction, VT: Chelsea Green.

Lübecker, Nikolaj (2007) 'The Dedramatization of Violence in Claire Denis's *I Can't Sleep*', *Paragraph*, 30, 2, pp. 17–33.

Lübecker, Nikolaj (2009) *Community, Myth and Recognition in Twentieth-Century French Literature and Thought*. London: Continuum.

Lumholdt, Jan (ed.) (2003) *Lars von Trier Interviews*. Jackson: University Press of Mississipi.

Maddock, Trevor and Krisjansen, Ivan (2003) 'Surrealist Poetics and the Cinema of Evil: The Significance of the Expression of Sovereignty in Catherine Breillat's *À ma sœur*', *Studies in French Cinema*, 3, 3, pp. 161–71.

Marks, Laura U. (2000) *The Skin of the Film: Intercultural Cinema, Embodiment and the Senses*. Durham, NC: Duke University Press.

Massumi, Brian (2002) *Parables for the Virtual: Movement, Affect, Sensation*. Durham, NC Duke University Press.

Matheou, Demetrios (2005) 'Fear at Ennui's End: Interview with Bruno Dumont', *Sight and Sound*, 15, 8, pp. 17–18.

Mayne, Judith (2005) *Claire Denis*. Urbana: University of Illinois Press.

McCarthy, Todd (2003) 'Review: *Elephant*', May 18, http://variety.com/2003/film/reviews/elephant-2-1200541588/ (last accessed 10 June, 2014).

Merleau-Ponty, Maurice (2000) *Parcours deux, 1951–61*. Paris: Verdier.

Merleau-Ponty, Maurice (2011) 'Cinéma et psychologie (1945)', in Daniel Banda and José Moure (eds.), *Le Cinéma: l'art d'une civilisation 1920–60*. Paris: Flammarion, pp. 333–7.

Metz, Christian (1982 [1977]) *Psychoanalysis and Cinema: The Imaginary Signifier*. London: Macmillan.

Monaco, James (1979) *Alain Resnais*. New York: Oxford University Press.

Moore, Gerald (2011) *Politics of the Gift: Exchanges in Poststructuralism*. Edinburgh: Edinburgh University Press.

Moore, Sophie (2004) 'Elephant Review', *Film Quarterly*, 58, 2, pp. 45–8.

Murray, Stuart J. (2007) 'Ethics at the Scene of Address: A Conversation with Judith Butler', *Symposium*, 11, 2, pp. 415–45.

Nancy, Jean-Luc (1997) *Hegel – l'inquiétude du négatif*. Paris: Hachette.

Nancy, Jean-Luc (2000) *L'intrus*. Paris: Gallilée.

Ngai, Sianne (2007) *Ugly Feelings*. Cambridge, MA: Harvard University Press.

Nizan, Paul (1938) *La Conspiration*. Paris: Gallimard.

Nobus, Dany (2007) 'The Politics of Gift-Giving and the Provocation of Lars von Trier's *Dogville*', *Film-Philosophy*, 11, 3, pp. 23–37.

Nussbaum, Martha (2010) *Not for Profit: Why Democracy Needs the Humanities*. Princeton: Princeton University Press.

O'Brien, Geoffrey (2003) 'Stop Shooting', *Artforum*, 42, 2, p. 39.

Östlund, Ruben (2011) 'Vänd inte bort blicken! Ruben Östlunds *Play*', *Dagens Nyheter*, 29 November. http://www.dn.se/kultur-noje/kulturdebatt/vand-inte-bort-blicken/ (last accessed 10 June 2014).

Palmer, Tim (2011) *Brutal Intimacy: Analyzing Contemporary French Cinema*. Middletown, CT: Wesleyan University Press.

Peretz, Eyal (2008) *Becoming Visionary: Brian de Palma's Cinematic Education of the Senses*. Stanford: Stanford University Press.

Peucker, Brirgitte (2007) *The Material Image: Art and the Real in Film*. Stanford: Stanford University Press.

Prager, Brad (ed.) (2012) *A Companion to Werner Herzog*. Oxford: Wiley-Blackwell.

Quandt, James (2011 [2004]) 'Flesh and Blood: Sex and Violence in Recent French Cinema', in Tanya Horeck and Tina Kendall (eds.), *The New Extremism in Cinema: From France to Europe*. Edinburgh: Edinburgh University Press, pp. 18–25.

Quinlivan, Davina (2009) 'Material Hauntings: The Kinaesthesia of Sound in *Innocence* (Hadzihalilovic, 2004)', *Studies in French Cinema*, 9, 3, pp. 215–24.

Rancière, Jacques (1987) *Le Maître ignorant* [*The Ignorant Schoolmaster*]. Paris: Fayard.

Rancière, Jacques (2004) *Malaise dans l'esthétique* [*Aesthetics and Its Discontents*]. Paris: Gallilée.

Rancière, Jacques (2008) *Le Spectateur émancipé*. Paris: La Fabrique.

Rancière, Jacques (2009) *The Emancipated Spectator*, trans. Gregory Elliott. London: Verso.

Reisinger, Deborah (2007) *Crime and Media in Contemporary France*. West Lafayette, IN: Purdue University Press.

Rhodes, John David (2006) 'Haneke, the Long Take, Realism', *Framework*, 47, 2, pp. 17–21.

Romney, Jonathan (2005) 'School for Scandal', *Sight & Sound*, 15, 10, p. 34.

Russell, Dominique (2012) *Rape in Art Cinema*. London: Continuum.

Sade, D. A. F., Marquis de (1977) *Justine, ou les malheurs de la vertu*. Paris: Gallimard.

Sartre, Jean-Paul (1972) *La Nausée*. Paris: Gallimard.

Sartre, Jean-Paul (1993) *What Is Literature?*, trans. Bernard Frechtman. London: Routledge.

Schultz, Laura Louise (2005) 'Når den røde lampe lyser er helligånden til stede' [Interview with Lars von Trier], *Ud og Se*, 5, pp. 46–58.

Shaviro, Steven (1993) *The Cinematic Body*. Minneapolis: University of Minnesota Press.

Shaviro, Steven (2009) *Without Criteria: Kant, Whitehead, Deleuze, and Aesthetics*. Cambridge, MA: MIT Press.

Shaviro, Steven (2010) *Post-Cinematic Affect*. Washington, DC: Zero Books.

Sheehan, Paul (2008) 'Against the Image: Herzog and the Troubling Politics of the Screen Animal', *SubStance*, 37, 3, pp. 117–36.

Smith, Murray (2003) 'Lars Von Trier: Sentimental Surrealist', in Mette Hjort and Scott MacKenzie (eds.), *Purity and Provocation: Dogma 95*. London: BFI, pp. 111–21.

Sobchack, Vivian (ed.) (2000) *Meta-Morphing: Visual Transformation and the Culture of Quick-Change*. Minneapolis: University of Minnesota Press.

Sobchack, Vivian (2004) *Carnal Thoughts: Embodiement and Moving Image Culture*. Berkeley: University of California Press.

Sobchack, Vivian (2005) 'Waking Life: Vivian Sobchack on the Experience of Innocence', *Film Comment*, 41, 6, pp. 46–9.

Sontag, Susan (2003) *Regarding the Pain of Others*. London: Penguin.

Staiger, Janet (2000) *Perverse Spectators: The Practices of Film Reception*. New York: New York University Press.

Stigsdotter, Ingrid (2013) '"When to Push Stop or Play": The Swedish Reception of Ruben Östlund's *Play* (2011)', *Journal of Scandinavian Cinema*, 1, 1, pp. 41–8.

Suleiman, Susan (1983) *Authoritarian Fictions*. Princeton: Princeton University Press.

Tarr, Carrie (2006) 'Director's Cuts: The Aesthetics of Self-harming in Marina de Van's *Dans ma peau*', *Nottingham French Studies*, 45, 3, pp. 78–91.

Taubin, Amy (2003) 'Part of the Problem [Interview with Gus Van Sant]', *Film Comment*, 39, 5, pp. 26–33.

Taubin, Amy (2010) '*Trash Humpers*, Review', *Film Comment*, 46, 3, pp. 70–1.

Thorsen, Nils (2010) *Geniet Lars von Trier: Liv, film og fobier*. Copenhagen: Politikens forlag.

Tierno, Michael (2002) *Aristotle's Poetics for Screenwriters*. New York: Hyperion.

Trotsky, Leon (1975) 'Frank Wedekind: Esthetics and Eroticism', trans. David Thorstad, *Boston University Journal*, 23, 2, pp. 40–7.

Verrone, William (2011) 'Transgression and Transcendence in the Films of Werner Herzog', *Film-Philosophy*, 15, 1, pp. 179–203.

Vignon, Gaspard (2011) 'Ludwig Van Beethoven – Gus Van Sant: vers un idéal romantique, musique et silence dans *Elephant*', *Décadrages*, 19, pp. 30–47.

Vincendeau, Ginette (2001) 'Sisters, Sex and Sitcom', *Sight & Sound*, 11, p. 18.

Wedekind, Frank ([1903] 2010) *Mine-Haha, or On the Bodily Education of Young Girls*. London: Hesperus Press.

Weller, Shane (2011) *Nihilism and Modernism*. Basingstoke: Palgrave Macmillan.

Wheatley, Catherine (2009) *Michael Haneke's Cinema: The Ethic of the Image*. Oxford: Berghahn Books.

Wilcox, Jason (2005) '"But It's Good": Finding Value in *Twentynine Palms*', *CineAction*, 66, pp. 50–60.

Williams, Linda (1991) 'Film Bodies: Gender, Genre, and Excess', *Film Quarterly*, 44, 4, pp. 2–12.

Wilson, Emma (2006) *Alain Resnais*. Manchester: Manchester University Press.

Wilson, Emma (2007) 'Miniature Lives, Intrusion and Innocence: Women Filming Children', *French Cultural Studies*, 18, pp. 169–83.

Wray, John (2007) 'Minister of Fear [Feature article on Haneke]', *New York Times Magazine*, September 23. Online: http://www.nytimes.com/2007/09/23/magazine/23haneke-t.html?pagewanted=all (last accessed 10 June 2014).

Filmography

4 Months, 3 Weeks and 2 Days (Christian Mungiu, 2007)
20 September (Kurt Kren, 1967)
300 (Jack Snyder, 2007)
Les 400 coups (*The 400 Blows*) (Francois Truffaut, 1959)
À bout de souffle (*Breathless*) (Jean-Luc Godard, 1960)
À ma sœur (*Fat Girl*) (Catherine Breillat, 2001)
The Act of Seeing with One's Own Eyes (Stan Brakhage 1971)
Antichrist (Lars von Trier, 2009)
Back to the Future (Robert Zemekis, 1985)
The Bad Sleep Well (Akira Kurosawa, 1960)
Basic Instinct (Paul Verhoeven, 1992)
Beau Travail (Claire Denis, 1999)
Bilder der Welt und Inschrift des Krieges (Harun Farocki, 1989)
Blow Out (Brian de Palma, 1981)
Blow-Up (Michelangelo Antonioni, 1966)
The Boss of It All (Lars von Trier, 2006)
La Bouche de Jean-Pierre (Lucille Hadzihalilovic, 1996)
Bowling for Columbine (Michael Moore, 2002)
Breaking the Waves (Lars von Trier, 1996)
Camille Claudel, 1915 (Bruno Dumont, 2013)
Casualties of War (Brian de Palma, 1989)
La Chinoise (Jean-Luc Godard, 1967)
A Clockwork Orange (Stanley Kubrick, 1971)
Code Blue (Urszula Antoniak, 2011)
Code Unknown (Michael Haneke, 2000)
Come and See (Elem Klimov, 1985)
Daisy Diamond (Simon Staho, 2007)
Dancer in the Dark (Lars von Trier, 2000)
Deliverance (John Boorman, 1972)
Doctor Zhivago (David Lean, 1965)
Dogtooth (Yorgos Lanthimos, 2009)
Dogville (Lars von Trier, 2003)
The Element of Crime (Lars von Trier, 1984)
Elephant (Alan Clarke, 1989)
Elephant (Gus Van Sant, 2003)
Epidemic (Lars von Trier, 1987)
Eternal Sunshine of the Spotless Mind (Michel Gondry, 2004)

Even Dwarfs Started Small (Werner Herzog, 1970)

Fata Morgana (Werner Herzog, 1971)

Festen (Thomas Vinterberg, 1998)

The Fine Art of Love (John Irwin, 2005)

The Five Obstructions (Lars von Trier, 2003)

Flanders (Bruno Dumont, 2006)

Funny Games (Michael Haneke, 1997)

Funny Games US (Michael Haneke, 2007)

Gladiator (Ridley Scott, 2000)

Good Boys use Condoms (Lucille Hadzihalilovic, 1998)

Gummo (Harmony Korine, 1997)

Hadewijch (Bruno Dumont, 2009)

Hidden (Michael Haneke, 2005)

High School (Frederick Wiseman, 1968)

Hiroshima mon amour (Alain Resnais, 1959)

Histoire(s) du cinéma (Jean-Luc Godard, 1988–98)

L'humanité (Bruno Dumont, 1999)

The Humiliated (Jesper Jargil, 1999)

I Can't Sleep (Claire Denis, 1994)

I Stand Alone (Gaspar Noé, 1998)

The Idiots (Lars von Trier, 1998)

Befrielsesbilleder (*Images of Liberation*) (Lars von Trier, 1982)

In My Skin (Marina de Van, 2002)

Inception (Christopher Nolan, 2010)

Innocence (Lucille Hadzihalilovic, 2004)

The Intruder (Claire Denis, 2004)

The Involuntary (Ruben Östlund, 2008)

Irreversible (Gaspar Noé, 2002)

Julian Donkey-Boy (Harmony Korine, 1999)

Kindering (Stan Brakhage 1987)

The Kingdom (Lars von Trier, 1984)

Laura (David Hamilton, 1979)

Le Petit Soldat (*The Little Soldier*) (Jean-Luc Godard, 1963)

Lolita (Stanley Kubrick, 1962)

Manderlay (Lars von Trier, 2005)

Medea (Lars von Trier, 1988)

Melancholia (Lars von Trier, 2011)

Memento (Christopher Nolan, 2000)

Meshes of the Afternoon (Maya Deren, 1943)

Miami Vice (Michael Mann, 2006)

Mister Lonely (Harmony Korine, 2007)

Mouchette (Robert Bresson, 1967)

Muriel, or the Time of Return (Alain Resnais, 1963)

Mystic River (Clint Eastwood, 2003)

Nymphomaniac (Lars von Trier, 2013)

Ordet (Carl Th. Dreyer, 1955)

Outside Satan (Bruno Dumont, 2011)

Paranoid Park (Gus Van Sant, 2007)

Peeping Tom (Michael Powell, 1960)
The Perfect Human (Jørgen Leth, 1967)
Persona (Ingmar Bergman, 1966)
The Piano Teacher (Michael Haneke, 2001)
Picnic at Hanging Rock (Peter Weir, 1979)
Play (Ruben Östlund, 2011)
Psycho (Alfred Hitchcock, 1960)
Psycho (Gus Van Sant, 1998)
Punishment Park (Peter Watkins, 1971)
Rebel Without a Cause (Nicholas Ray, 1955)
Redacted (Brian de Palma, 2007)
Romance (Catherine Breillat, 1999)
[Safe] (Todd Haynes, 1995)
Les Salauds (Bastards) (Claire Denis, 2013)
Salò (Pier Paolo Pasolini, 1975)
Sátántángo (Béla Tarr, 1994)
Saving Private Ryan (Steven Spielberg, 1998)
The Seventh Continent (Michael Haneke, 1989)
The Shining (Stanley Kubrick, 1980)
The Spirit of the Beehive (Víctor Erice, 1973)
Spring Breakers (Harmony Korine, 2012)
Star 80 (Bob Fosse, 1983)
Starship Troopers (Paul Verhoeven, 1997)
Stranded in Canton (William Eggleston, 1973, released 2008)
Strange Days (Kathryn Bigelow, 1995)
Straw Dogs (Sam Peckinpah, 1971)
Superstar: The Karen Carpenter Story (Todd Haynes, 1987)
Taxidermia (György Pálfi, 2006)
The Texas Chainsaw Massacre (Tobe Hooper, 1974)
The Thief (Michael Mann, 1981)
Tranceformer, A Portrait of Lars von Trier (Stig Björkman, 1997)
Trash Humpers (Harmony Korine, 2009)
Trouble Every Day (Claire Denis, 2001)
Twentynine Palms (Bruno Dumont, 2003)
Vendredi soir (Friday Night) (Claire Denis, 2002)
La Vie de Jésus [The Life of Jesus] (Bruno Dumont, 1997)
La Vie nouvelle (Philippe Grandrieux, 2002)
The Virgin Suicides (Sophie Coppola, 1999)
Weekend (Jean-Luc Godard, 1967)
White Material (Claire Denis, 2010)
Zabriskie Point (Michelangelo Antonioni, 1970)

Index